Latin American Adventures in Literary Journalism

ILLUMINATIONS: CULTURAL FORMATIONS OF THE AMERICAS SERIES

John Beverley and Sara Castro-Klarén, Editors

Latin American Adventures in Literary Journalism

. . .

PABLO CALVI

. . .

University of Pittsburgh Press

Published by the University of Pittsburgh Press, Pittsburgh, Pa., 15260
Copyright © 2019, University of Pittsburgh Press
All rights reserved
Manufactured in the United States of America
Printed on acid-free paper
10 9 8 7 6 5 4 3 2 1

ISBN 13: 978-0-8229-4565-9
ISBN 10: 0-8229-4565-7

Cataloging-in-Publication data is available from the Library of Congress

Cover design: Joel W. Coggins

TO MONIKA, LILIANA, JORGE, VIOLET, LAYLA, SCARLETT, AND RAMONA.
THIS IS ALSO THEIR BOOK.

CONTENTS

• • •

ACKNOWLEDGMENTS

• • •

IT TAKES A VILLAGE, they say. It is true. Although, to be specific in this case, it took three cities: Buenos Aires, Paris, and New York.

Books are the result of a collective endeavor. This one owes a long-term debt of gratitude to an equally long list of advisers, colleagues, and friends. To Andie Tucher, Todd Gitlin, and Graciela Montaldo for their mentoring. Their insightful observations and constant counseling helped me see both the tree and the forest in the vast jungle of Latin American journalism, and their generosity with time and ideas exceeded what I could have ever hoped for. To Brigitte Nacos, who was always gentle, attentive, and enthusiastic about this project. Our conversations were unfailingly stimulating and fun and helped me keep track of the happy occasions when I was aiming in the right direction.

A fellowship at CELSA (the Graduate School of Information and Communication Sciences), of the Université Paris–Sorbonne (Paris IV), allowed me to complete the final manuscript of a doctoral dissertation in a comfortable Parisian environment. A few years and some revisions later, that dissertation became a book. The fellowship position also granted me the freedom to design and teach my first two graduate seminars on Latin American journalism in my role as a guest lecturer at Sorbonne. To Véronique Richard and Kyle Schneider I wish to express my most sincere gratitude.

For their encouragement throughout the many years it took me to complete this project, and also for their friendship, I am grateful to Helen Benedict, who rekindled in me a love for literary journalism, and to the late David Klatell, who was always ready and available for a pep talk. My colleagues at the Columbia University PhD program in communications were all a constant source of inspiration.

I am also indebted to my dearest friend, Ben Goldman, to his masterful quill and his overwhelming generosity. Many nights in Fort Greene would have been lost without his company. I am deeply grateful to Kelly Sharp, who once flew from New York to Austin and back with the undeserving company of one of my first drafts. Her patience and kindness went beyond what I ever merited.

My friend and colleague Tessa Ditner read chapters 3 and 4 of the manuscript with enthusiasm, dedication, and care and was kind enough to offer me invaluable advice. David Abrahamson, Richard Keeble, Sue Joseph, Bill Reynolds, Todd Schack, and John Hartsock, all colleagues and friends from the International Association for Literary Journalism Studies, were the sounding board for many of the ideas in this book. Their generous and disinterested advice helped me carry on through moments of uncertainty. Michael Serino and Jeff Cohen have been indefatigable allies during this process, and they deserve my gratitude.

At Stony Brook University's School of Journalism I found a home and the encouragement to finish this book. I thank Barbara Selvin, Howard Schneider, Jonathan Sanders, and Laura Lindenfeld for their patience and guidance. As a member of the Latin American and Caribbean Studies advisory board, I enjoyed the mentorship, advice, and generosity of Brooke Larson and Eric Zolov. Their points of view and encouragement have been invaluable. My students Mike Adams, Lei Takanashi, Caroline Parker, and Andrew Goldstein test-drove some of these ideas during a seminar in the spring 2018 semester. I thank them for their insight and lively discussions.

My parents, Jorge and Liliana, and my siblings, all in Buenos Aires, spent hours on the telephone and trekked through the National Library when I needed a long-lost book or an irretrievable newspaper. Their help, love, and constant support always came through when I needed them most.

This book also belongs to Violet, Ramona, Layla, and Scarlett. Our walks in the park and on the beach gave me peace and joy, and they deserve my full gratitude.

To *moja ukojana*, Monika. My love, my partner, my friend, my first reader, my constant editor and soulmate. This is also your book. You deserve it as much as I do.

All the merits of this work need to be shared with these and many other friends and colleagues who helped me during this experience. Any limitations, errors, or mistakes, however, belong to no one but me.

. . .

An earlier, abbreviated version of chapter 1 appeared in *Information & Culture: A Journal of History* in 2016. An earlier version of chapter 3 appeared in *Global Literary Journalism: Exploring the Journalistic Imagination*, edited by Richard Lance Keeble and John Tulloch (2012). A condensed version of chapter 4 appeared in *The Profiling Handbook*, edited by Sue Joseph and Richard Lance Keeble (2015). Parts of chapter 5 appeared as "From Literature to Journalism: Borges, Crítica and the *Universal History of Infamy* as an Experiment in Democratic Dialogue," in the *Australian Journalism Review* (2015). Some of the ideas in chapter 6 appeared in "Latin America's Own 'New Journalism,'" published in *Literary Journalism Studies* (2010).

Latin American Adventures
in Literary Journalism

INTRODUCTION

. . .

DURING A GATHERING OF Argentine immigrants in New York—exile is sometimes voluntary, and these days some of us don't have more in common than place of provenance and one, maybe two, idiosyncrasies—I was discussing with poet Ezequiel Zaidenwerg the nature of the work that ultimately became this book. It was exciting to share with a knowledgeable writer the core of my ideas and the selection of authors I was considering for its pages. At the center of the book was a unique tradition in Latin America, that of literary journalism: a form that had been forged in periodicals, was meant to have political—sometimes pedagogic—impact, presented itself as factual, and frequently resorted to literary devices, like the allegory and the metaphor, as structuring mechanisms.

In what I assumed was a natural sequence, I listed out loud the names of the first four authors: Francisco Bilbao (Chilean), Domingo Sarmiento (Argentine), José Martí (Cuban), and Juan José de Soiza Reilly (Uruguayan). Less surprised than curious, Zaidenwerg told me that it would be interesting to see the connection I had found between such dissimilar authors, such a heterogeneous bunch. What could the romantic Argentine have in common with the modern Cuban?

In a way, he was asking me to reveal how I had set up the series, what the common thread was. But the question took me by surprise.

Until recently, I thought that the connections between Sarmiento and

Martí, and those between Bilbao and the others, were as self-evident as the lines that form when you look at a tree plantation from a certain distance. It soon became clear to me, however, that in order to find these lines in the first place, it is necessary to have a point of view.

Someone once said—it must have been Sartre, who also believed that literature is passed along diagonally, from uncles to nephews—that you can only read from the vantage point of your own library. I have been a reporter for more than twenty years (and worked for newspapers long before I even dreamed of becoming an academic). My library is packed with journalism. That is my point of origin. From that library I have started this series; from that point of view I begin to trace these lines.

• • •

This book spans a century and a bit more, starting as it does in the mid-1840s with the first political act in the establishment of a free, postcolonial press in Chile and later across the entire subcontinent. It ends during the Cold War, after the Cuban Revolution, with the foundation of the first postmodern Latin American literary genre. In its inception, this book was conceived as an attempt to understand the role of journalism—literary journalism in particular—in the historical processes that gave rise to the idea of Latin America and its nations. The book thus sets out to show a series of correlations among eight writers whose work is representative of the changes during the time in which they lived or has contributed to the transformations that took place in their day. The central aim is to trace back, in the form of a cultural history, the high-water marks of literary journalism in the Americas between the 1840s and the 1960s in order to reveal the effectiveness and influence of the genre as an instrument for ideological formation.

Geographically, the path of this book and the authors who are its protagonists can be located in the most important Latin American urban centers of their time. In that sense, this is a book about modernity, mass audiences, and Western ideas, moving back and forth between the Southern Cone, Cuba, and—at exceptional times—Europe and the United States. In its modernity, this book is predominantly male and white, attributes that must not be ignored and in fact should be accounted for as one of the main conditions imposed by the period it describes and attempts to understand.

As a journalist, I have chosen to fold argumentation into the skin of narrative but not to avoid analysis or polemics. The book does lead to discussion, especially when the core of its ideas moves against the grain of the general bibliography on a topic. But in order to follow the path of the narrative journalists it discusses and their tradition—in order to insert itself into that tradition—it attempts to weave substance and form together.

We sometimes think of journalism as one stable, continuous set of practices with a clear goal: to inform the public about the present, about current developments in our locale and our world, and about our daily life and culture. But both as a discipline and as a form of social discourse, journalism is in fact far more complex. Considered as a discursive formation (Foucault 1968), modern journalism encompasses narrative, descriptive, and argumentative textualities in an array of genres produced and delivered through varied platforms and formats. In their inception, these genres were meant not only to *describe* (based on the mimetic premises of positivism) but also to *enlighten* (based on the idealistic ethos of romanticism) and *inform* about certain aspects of reality.[1] As a craft, journalism is a bridge between an audience in a society and the textual universe of the periodical.

Thanks to the classificatory, sometimes even taxonomical, efforts led mainly by Norman Sims and *Literary Journalism Studies* (*LJS*)—the journal of the International Association for Literary Journalism Studies—we now think of literary journalism as an immersive, factual type of narrative, with a penchant for an authorial voice, scenic structuring, and a meticulous—almost obsessive—attention to accuracy (Sims 1984, 2007; Hartsock 2001, 2009; Keeble and Tulloch 2012). It is important to keep in mind that this definition comes from academic work that pivots around the Anglo-American literary and journalistic tradition. Latin America's literary journalism, on the other hand, developed in a publishing world and a public sphere that differed significantly from those in the North, and it therefore requires a singular historical approach. The Anglo-American tradition and its historical developments—with which the reader will likely have some familiarity—can serve, in this context, as a contrasting point, a background for better understanding the Latin American form.

Among the original differences between these two constellations of literary journalism, a central one lies at this book's point of departure: most of Latin America's foundational literatures were, first and foremost, literatures of—and produced for—the periodical press. They were not conceived as books, and yet today they are known as nothing but. By shifting attention to their journalistic materiality, we can notice that some of their crucial themes and constant aspects reveal themselves in a new light. If the materiality of Latin America's original canon is that of the periodical press and the newspapers, any analysis of its original texts and ideas has to be built on the premise that these works were published in installments and shared the page with other (types of) texts.

Following that idea, this book's six chapters attempt to trace the origins of some of the attributes that appear unique to Latin American literary journalism, in particular those that have been passed forward as the indelible marks of an original writing tradition.

Latin America's foundational narratives are fully resignified when viewed from the vantage point of literary journalism as a conflation of genres that allows a certain fluidity between texts, as long as they are produced for periodicals. Obliquely positioned toward the book-centric tradition in which Latin American studies have usually been anchored, a cultural history of literary journalism will offer new alignments and connections, as well as render new ideas and approaches to the modern history of Latin America.

In fact, writers like Francisco Bilbao, Domingo Sarmiento, José Martí, and Jorge Luis Borges had a clear sense of the potential of the periodical format, as well as the limits it would impose on their work. As discussed in chapter 2, for instance, Sarmiento viewed newspapers as the most vital, immediate, and impactful among the scarce publishing alternatives available in the young subcontinent, yet he also understood that the periodical press relied heavily on the support of its public via subscriptions and sales. In a region that was very slowly starting to develop its print capitalism (to use a term coined by Benedict Anderson), the immediate connection to new audiences, literate society and political power brokers, fast response time to civic and societal shifts, and a constant need for renovations and format changes (required to support an organic expansion of the readership) outweighed some of the downsides of the periodicals, such as their reliance on sales and the ephemeral nature of the platform.

If we agree with Roberto González-Echevarría that the three main discursive models for Latin America's foundational narratives were the legal model, during colonial times; the scientific prose of the mid-nineteenth century; and anthropology, in the early twentieth century, it is also clear that the textual manifestation of these discourses was first channeled by the periodical press and not the book. This materiality had a direct impact on not only the text itself but also how it was circulated and how it was read. Yet, with some notable exceptions, few attempts have been made to understand the implications of these specific conditions under which Latin America's foundational narratives were originally accessed by their publics.

Unlike a literature made of books, which can dialogue among themselves, a literature that grounds its materiality in periodicals creates a conversation not only among texts but also—and, in the historical synchrony, more importantly—between the texts and genres that coexist in the pages of a periodical, as well as with the dynamic readerships of those periodicals and their social contexts.

THE STEPPING STONE

Like all genres, the journalistic ones vary—sometimes a lot, sometimes not so much—across borders, societies, and time. From newscasts to breaking news, from open letters to the first modern interviews, from political editorials to video documentaries, news spots, human-interest stories, profiles, local color stories, editorials, opinion columns, forecasts—all these forms have added their own defining features to journalism and have presented variations from place to place and from one historical moment to the next.

Considered as a series of concrete practices, journalism has matured in newsrooms that were part of living cities, small and large, immersed in societies—central or peripheral—within specific sociohistorical circumstances. These work practices were established, perfected, and discussed by journalists—human beings who defined their own methods, deontological codes, and strategies on the job, in bars and cafés, press clubs, letters and lectures, in manuals of style, editorial meetings, and foundational speeches.

The emergence of the penny press in the United States in the 1830s, during what historians have branded the era of Jacksonian democracy—a time of expanding democratic institutions, urban middle classes, and market capitalism—had a direct influence on the consolidation of modern American journalism and its forms and especially on how newspapers were integrated into urban life and how journalists thought of themselves and their work (Schudson 1978, 12–60; Tucher 2006, 132). But as true as it may seem that historical, political, and technological aspects are key to understanding the development of such formats as the inverted pyramid, the interview, and the feature story, as well as the emergence of the American journalistic model of objectivity in the mid- to late nineteenth century, the same factors in a different order, during the same time period, fostered the development of distinct genres such as the French *chronique* on the other side of the Atlantic or the *crónica* in Latin America.

Originating far apart from one another, in a world much less interconnected than the one we live in today, these journalistic traditions do share some common origins, print capitalism and democracy being two of the most salient ones.[2] In a sense, the general notion of market capitalism can still provide a preliminary framework for approaching the evolution of certain journalistic genres and forms in different societies. But it should be clear that market capitalism and democracy did not evolve at the same pace, in the same historical phases, or even in the same direction in the United

States, Europe, and Latin America. And neither did journalism. By studying the unique pace and processes of democratization and the expansion of market and print capitalism in Latin America, we can also begin to understand how and why certain specific journalistic conventions, models, forms, and genres developed and coalesced into their specific configurations—models and genres that, in their own particular way, have been part of the foundation of journalism and have defined the profession as it has existed for the past one hundred years.

LITERARY JOURNALISM AND THE FOUNDATION OF LATIN AMERICA

This book focuses on a group of genres that accompanied the development of modern Latin American journalism, literature, and politics and influenced these three realms.[3] Following Norman Sims, it is possible to group these genres under the umbrella of literary journalism.

Before the reader dives into this study, two categories at its core need to be discussed: the first, Latin America as a political and cultural unit, and the second, literary journalism as a form within the field of journalistic practice and its specific Latin American manifestation.

To assume Latin America's cultural, political, historical, and geographical homogeneity can be problematic (Halperín Donghi 1993; Mignolo 2007; Rojas 2009). But many times, even within the history of each Latin American nation taken separately, we can also observe the same dispersion and variety. Tulio Halperín Donghi has interestingly pointed out that it would be hard to consider even Mexican history, from the "indigenous splendor" to the revolution in the twentieth century, as the unique frame for the constitution of a people. Historically, politically, and culturally, Mexico presents itself as a heterogeneous mix. Geographically, from the plateaus to the deserts and the tropical coastal jungles, it could also be hard to perceive it as a unit if it were not for its forged national identity, which was a product of the nineteenth century. Much the same could be said about the history of most other countries in the region. What is also true, however, is that beyond that multiplicity, there lies a transversal factor that is at the same time political, economic, linguistic, cultural, and historical: in the fifteenth century Latin America was incorporated into the world economy under a colonial pact, and between then and the early nineteenth century, the entire region was ruled by one of the most archaic European nations of its time (Halperín Donghi 1993, 17–18).

Colonial rule and the incorporation of Hispanic tradition into the region in a process that lasted more than three hundred years served as common ground to the Latin American revolutionaries in the early nineteenth century. When journalists, intellectuals, and politicians all over the subcontinent started a dialogue to move past the colonial model and enter modernity, Spain, its legacy, and its language provided a common point of departure, common topics for debate, and the potential for mutual understanding but also the basic political structures to prepare for the revolution, a common historical burden, and a common past that needed to be overcome.

This revolutionary dialogue was, in fact, started in public reunions of the elites and later on consolidated in the revolutionary presses all over the subcontinent. First in Argentina and Venezuela, later in Chile and Mexico, the postcolonial press in the region spread the voices of Esteban Echeverría, Francisco Bilbao, Domingo Sarmiento, Juan Bautista Alberdi, José Enrique Rodó, José Martí, and many other intellectuals, journalists, and politicians who not only fostered and helped consolidate independent and national identities of their own countries but also coalesced in the definition of an overarching entity: Latin America. These journalists, writers, and statesmen read each other, debated in a common language, and recognized a common heritage. The cultural and political unit of Latin America, which came to exist due to a shared colonial past and became a reality in the twentieth century, was made possible by the revolutionary and the postcolonial press during the nineteenth century. Domingo Sarmiento's *Revista de Ambas Américas* and José Martí's "Letters from New York" were key in the promotion of that already widespread notion of pan-Hispanism. Literary journalism was also at the core of the process, a central instrument for the formation of that supranational notion of a Latin American culture and identity. However, as Walter Mignolo has noted, these identities—and the debates that brought them about—were held under the Western, modern erasure of pre-Columbian cultures. Journalism was central to this process as the means through which the fragmented cultural markets in the erstwhile colony decided who their audiences were and what they would become and, consequently, what the acceptable ideas about both "public" and "citizen"—ideas that generally excluded any possible indigenous representation—were. This takes us to the second point.

When we talk about literary journalism in Latin America, we are referring to a genre that was already well established in the nineteenth century. Sarmiento, Rodó, and Bilbao, to mention only a few, considered themselves not only men of the press but also literary figures and politicians. Their identities as intellectuals were defined in the intersection of these three realms; no other site for the formation of their identities was possible. Without nations or markets or a consolidated reading public, the role of these men of letters was to develop the conditions that made possible the existence of their own work. Echeverría, Sarmiento, Rodó, and many others had to create their own markets and their own reading public. They did so by promoting a republican culture yet resorting to the raw materials that remained from a colonial past. The consolidation of nation-states and national literatures, the education of citizens, and the development of a reading public all required the adoption and the propagation of a strong set of core values inherited from the French and the American Revolutions. Literary journalism in Latin America was (and had to be) a heavily moral and deeply political genre.

Of course, as a genre and a practice, literary journalism has had multiple iterations throughout Latin American history. Since its inception, which was contemporaneous with the transitional *caudillismo* period after the independence wars between the 1830s and 1880s, it ran parallel to the consolidation and development of republican systems. Literary journalism was also pivotal for the constitution of national and transnational narrative frameworks during the phase of stabilization and democratic transition of the 1880s and early 1900s. Two of these frameworks, "civilization or barbarism" and "our America and their America," are formative and fundamental conceptual dyads that at one time helped Latin Americans see themselves as part of the world and today are central to understanding Latin America's cultural and political history. Both of these dyads—the first coined by Domingo Sarmiento and the second by José Martí—originated in literary journalism and were first printed in newspapers less than a half century apart.

In essence, literary journalism provided the narrative framework for a full integration of a young Latin America and its nations into the world market, sealing the erasure of the pre-Columbian cultures as part of this process; it also played a central role in the development of open, popular, democratic systems to rise in the region, particularly after the passing of laws protecting secret, universal, and compulsory male suffrage in the mid-1910s. Finally, between the 1930s and 1970s, literary journalism played at first an indifferent—if not supportive—and later a fiercely antagonistic role vis-á-vis the development and consolidation of bureaucratic authoritarian regimes in the subcontinent.[4]

In its many iterations, Latin American literary journalism has been instrumental in the production of social and political narratives, the constitution of national and regional identities, and the rise of national literatures. And in part due to the late—and vertiginous—development of Latin American market capitalism, a process that took place in less than three decades, between the 1900s and the 1930s, the spheres of journalism, politics, and literature never gained full autonomy from each other. It could even be argued that, compared to the situation in the United States, these spheres never became autonomous from one another at all.

Taken as a historical series, certain structural and thematic aspects of the genre could be summarized to create a working definition: Latin American literary journalism comprehends a type of medium-to-long-form referential narrative whose protagonists, characters, and situations have documented existence in the real world, whose focus is usually a current event, and whose intention is social, deeply political, actively militant, and—lastly—aesthetic.[5]

Sarmiento and many of the journalists and writers discussed in this book, did in fact seal with their readers an accuracy contract by emphasizing the referential nature of their work. However, the type of referentiality on which this contract was based differed from the modern American journalistic notion of objectivity that became the dominant covenant in the United States between the 1880s and the 1920s, indelibly marking the profession in the years that followed.[6] In *Facundo*, Sarmiento (2003, 29; my italics) sketches this contract in a passage that reads, "[But] I do state that in the notable events to which I refer, and which serve as *the basis for the explanations I give*, there is *irreproachable accuracy*, to which the existing *public documents* about those events will attest [. . .]. Perhaps there will be a moment when, unburdened by the worries that have precipitated the writing of this little work, I may remold it according to a new plan, stripping it of accidental digression and supporting it with the numerous official documents to which I now make only passing reference."

In the United States, the notion of literary journalism as we know it today was first used by Edwin H. Ford, who taught at the University of Minnesota and in 1937 published *A Bibliography of Literary Journalism in America* (Sims 2007, 8). In Latin America, the use of this notion dates back to the late nineteenth century, and it was the journalist and author Juan José de Soiza Reilly who in 1909 popularized it: "[Today's] journalism is not the barren profession of years past. It is no longer a profession. It is not a craft. It's an art. A delicate and profound one. An art of goldsmiths. Of poets. Of philosophers. An art that has its heroes and victims. I imagine that you don't believe in what I say, but I am talking—with utmost devotion—about *literary journalism*" (qtd. in Cilento 2009, 81; my italics and translation).

In fact, literary journalism had already defined the intellectual work of figures such as Sarmiento, Martí, and Rubén Darío, who used their newspaper articles not only as test benches for their poetry and narrative prose but also as platforms to project their political ideas. Latin American literary journalism accompanied most of the political processes during the nineteenth and twentieth century in the region, and it is central to understanding the constitution of Latin America as a political entity.

SECTIONS

This book describes the development of literary journalism and the media systems in the subcontinent in three parts, each corresponding to three singular historical phases.

Part I, "In-Forming the New Publics," spanning the first three chapters, addresses the period between the 1840s and the early 1900s. It discusses the role of literary journalism in the formation of the nation-states after the independence wars, the coalescing of the new liberal orders with *modernismo*, and the expansion of the urban centers that stimulated the development of the new publics and the editorial boom that ensued. This is a time in Latin America during which a debate around different national identities takes place, and with the consolidation of national identities—and presses—the development of a pan-national, transnational, and interclass entity also becomes possible. Of course, to the extent that journalism was instrumental in developing the cultural identity of Latin America, it was complicit in how narrow and unrepresentative of the population that identity became, privileging first the male voices of the white and wealthy ruling classes and later the middle-class voices, albeit still predominantly white and male, of the new masses.

Chapter 1, "The Trial of Francisco Bilbao and Its Role in the Foundation of Latin American Journalism," sheds light on a little-known event that took place in Chile in 1844 and set the tone for the discussion about freedom of the press in the subcontinent during the next fifty years. The trial of Chilean writer and journalist Francisco Bilbao paved the way for authors such as Domingo Sarmiento and José Martí. Chapter 2, "Domingo Sarmiento, *Facundo*, and the Birth of Latin American Nonfiction in the Hands of a Political Exile," discusses the role of the Argentine writer and politician in the foundation of literary journalism as a genre and as a tradition in the region. Chapter 3, "José Martí and the Chronicles That Built Modern Latin America," analyzes the Cuban writer's use of literary journalism to further his idea of a pan-American union based on language and culture and to oppose US Secretary of State James Gillespie Blaine's attempt to subject the entire American continent to the economic imprint of a free trade agreement.

Part II of this book, "Leveling the Playing Field"—comprising chapters 4 and 5—analyzes the surge in the mass press during the first decades of the twentieth century and the development of publishing strategies targeted at a wide audience in the interwar period. The chapter also shows the new reading contracts established between writers and readers, thanks to the emergence of democracy and mass markets in the subcontinent.

Chapter 4, "Modernity, Markets, and Urban Bohemia: The Southern Cone in the Early Twentieth Century," describes the incorporation of middle-class readers into print capitalism and the new vernaculars as instruments of the mass press channeled through the popular magazines and embodied in the writings of one of the first mass journalists: the Uruguayan writer Juan José de Soiza Reilly. Chapter 5, "The Mass Press," discusses the integration of the Latin American city into a universal context, a direction embodied in Roberto Arlt's and Jorge Luis Borges's periodical interventions, which also show a new type of collaboration with the audience. This chapter reinforces the idea that Latin American foundational literatures were not conceived or produced in the abstract, as a solipsistic game or achievement, but as a journalistic, collective, and collaborative effort between writers and audiences.

Part III, "Bottom-Up Journalism," comprising chapter 6, discusses the crystallization of a long tradition of Latin American journalism in a new hybrid genre, *testimonio*, which becomes formalized in the early years of the Cuban Revolution.

Chapter 6, "Latin American Narrative Journalism and the Cuban Revolution," deals with one of the most critical moments in the region during the twentieth century: the implosion of the model of progress that modernity had emplaced, the fragmentation of the nation-states during the Red Scare, and the crisis of the basic ideas—legality, democratic stability, republicanism—under which journalism had until then operated. The incorporation of testimonial literatures undertaken by Rodolfo Walsh and Gabriel García Márquez and the creation of the Cuban institution Casa de las Américas are a response to the spread of bureaucratic authoritarian military regimes. These dictatorships undermined the laws upon which Latin America's founding narratives were structured and forced journalism to shift to a stronger moral stance to compensate for the de facto legal vacuum.

A hybrid of Latin American studies, comparative literature, literary journalism studies, journalism history, and postcolonial studies, this book is an attempt to enter into a conversation that began in the works of Carlos Alonso, John Beverley, Guillermo Bonfil Batalla, Aníbal González, Roberto González Echevarría, Josefina Ludmer, Walter Mignolo, Sylvia Molloy, Graciela Montaldo, Ricardo Piglia, Ángel Rama, Susana Rotker, Sylvia Saítta, Beatriz Sarlo, Mariano Siskind, and many others that preceded them. It owes the debate around, and the consolidation of, literary journalism as a genre worthy of academic study to Norman Sims, David Abrahamson, John Hartsock, Richard Keeble, John Tulloch, and the International Association for

Literary Journalism Studies, with its publication *Literary Journalism Studies* (*LJS*). Literary journalism is an exceptionally difficult genre to classify, not only because of its historical, geographic, and national variations but also due to the very elusive nature of factuality—a notion with which journalism must always remain tightly associated.

FACTUALITY AND THE PRESS

As Michael Schudson (1978, 70–71) has argued when discussing the professionalization of journalism in the United States in the late nineteenth century, "[Competing] with one another for circulation, newspapers tried to satisfy public standards of truth, public ideas of decency, and public taste in entertainment." Clearly, these public standards, ideas, and taste were not the same in Latin America, since the public was also different. A different public, with different backgrounds, a different exposure to philosophical and political ideas, different social, political and economic realities, and a much different vision of the world can explain in part some of the dissimilarities between Anglo and Latin American journalism that will become apparent in this book.

In that light, among the central questions of this work are how the main principles of factuality and referentiality developed in this Latin American journalistic genre—patterns that have ultimately transcended literary journalism to reach other genres—and why they have differed (and how much, if they have) from the ones contemporarily in vogue in the United States.

As part of that tradition, but also due to its particular social and political context of origin, Latin American literary journalism has always been imbued with a dominant political undertone, a progressive teleology, a sense of journalistic urgency, and a humane disgust for the aberrations committed by authoritarian regimes. These narratives have consistently expressed concerns for the dilemmas rooted in Latin American political instability, while displaying a moral vision aimed at the democratic establishment—sometimes its restoration—in the region. This mostly anti-authoritarian undertone has not only given the genre an ethical imprint but also resulted in a politically motivated stance that has defined the genre beyond its factual or aesthetic preoccupations.

Journalism, like history, produces narratives—accounts of sequentially and causally connected events. As such, literary journalism is a type of discourse that tells a story. But unlike other types of nonfiction, Latin American literary journalism has produced narratives that have systematically operated on at least two semantic levels: allegorical and referential. On the allegorical level, these narratives are produced as accounts of the present through the narration of past events. On the referential level, these stories can either be fully loaded with political undertones or plainly interpreted as a novelized historical record.

This dynamic, discussed in chapters 2 and 3 with regard to the journalistic works of Domingo Sarmiento and José Martí, was not only a consequence of the political context in which these narratives arose but also a response to a writing tradition. Reporting in repressive, politically or economically unstable societies creates a number of hurdles not only in terms of the investigative process that literary nonfiction requires but also and especially in terms of the "authorial stance towards one's material" (Foster 1984, 42–43).

Due to the consolidation of literary journalism as a tradition, even when political restraints were momentarily—or permanently—lifted, these narratives were still produced and read through the lens of their foundational ethos. The common points of the writings of Francisco Bilbao, Domingo Sarmiento, José Martí, Juan José de Soiza Reilly, Roberto Arlt, Jorge Luis Borges, Gabriel García Márquez, and Rodolfo Walsh will be central to substantiating many of these ideas.

PART I

• • •

IN-FORMING THE NEW PUBLICS

CHAPTER 1

• • •

THE TRIAL OF FRANCISCO BILBAO AND ITS ROLE IN THE FOUNDATION OF LATIN AMERICAN JOURNALISM

ON THE AFTERNOON OF June 17, 1844, hundreds gathered in an angry crowd outside the courthouses in Santiago de Chile. Hissing, whistling, booing, and cursing were somewhat typical on such occasions, but the unruliness and high-voltage excitement surrounding the ending of a spectacular trial against an obscure student named Francisco Bilbao were unprecedented in the short history of this young republic.

A little-known journalist and philosophy student, Bilbao had been taken to court and ultimately fined for the publication of an antireligious piece, "Sociabilidad chilena." The trial was one of the most talked about events in the subcontinent in those days. Bilbao's supporters, the liberal Pipiolos, offered a strong public defense of the writer. His detractors, the conservative Pelucones, attacked the journalist in every public forum available at the time and brought him before a conservative court, which did its best to censor the piece and pillory Bilbao as an example of incivility.

It all began in the early days of June. After six uneventful months on the Chilean political scene during the first part of 1844, an explosive debate escalated almost to a civil upheaval in the otherwise calm and isolated capital city. On June 1 *El Crepúsculo*, a liberal and up-and-coming independent monthly, released the second number of its second volume, and it featured "Sociabilidad chilena." The article was a thirty-four-page Saint-Simonian–Rousseauian tirade against Spain's religious monarchy, along with its morals, uses, and the ideas it had infused into Chilean society during colonial times. In his essay Bilbao (1897, 11, 17) claimed, among other things, that Spain represented Latin America's past: "Spain is the Middle Ages," he wrote, and the future of Latin America belonged to France, where a "new era is blossoming."

The essay irritated a group of Catholic government officials, who prosecuted the young journalist for blasphemy, immorality, and sedition. But the disproportionate reaction of the conservatives exasperated Santiago's liberal sectors in turn; they confronted the government of Pres. Manuel Bulnes with a vigorous response and the full force of an emerging liberal press. By galvanizing their demands for openness and democracy, as well as freedom of speech, religion, and thought, the trial helped push the liberal sectors to become not only a government watchdog but also an agent of cultural change in Chile and the subcontinent.

The discussion around the trial and its consequences had a direct impact on how journalism developed in the Americas over the next fifty years. The episode was the first stress test of a new set of laws destined to protect and assure freedom of expression in postcolonial Latin America. In triggering these laws, the trial signaled the emergence of an unprecedented audience—a nascent postcolonial readership in need of its own voice, whose very existence would lead to the invention of a new literary genre.

THE INSTRUMENT OF ENLIGHTENMENT

Until the independence wars, the Spanish Crown had exercised tight control over the printing presses on the subcontinent, and it had for the most part banished local newspapers. The press was controlled directly by the Church or the Crown, and until the end of the seventeenth century, only Mexico City and Lima had any active printing businesses (Anderson 1983, 61; Kanellos 2005, 688). However, with the revolutionary uprisings, local patriots started to circumvent these controls until the newly established republican governments finally abrogated the Spanish regulations.[1] By 1812 many Latin American countries had well-established newspapers. But due to *caudillismo* (a system of regional strongmen, or *caudillos*, who had access to arms and horses on account of their own personal wealth and charisma) and a complicated transition to republicanism, many of these young nations were waylaid on their road to a free press until the late nineteenth century.[2]

Chile's printing business had a late start but a precocious maturity compared to other Latin American countries. Mateo Arnaldo Havel, a Swedish refugee who had been involved in the assassination of Gustav III and later became a naturalized Chilean citizen, imported from New York the first printing press to operate in Chile. In April 1811, at the beginning of the independence war, the equipment arrived in the port of Valparaíso aboard the frigate *Gallervais*, together with three American master printers—Samuel B. Johnston, Guillermo H. Burbidge, and Simon Garrizon—and a tall pile of republican newspapers (Alberdi 1846, 14).

"In our hands is the great and precious instrument of universal enlightenment—the printing press," read a letter addressed to Havel from the Congress (Alberdi 1846, 14). And right they were to hail its arrival, since the machine would soon become the cornerstone of the Imprenta del Supremo Gobierno (the Printing Office of the Supreme Government) in Santiago and a key weapon in the war with Spain.

On Thursday, February 13, 1812, *La Aurora*, the first Chilean periodical, saw the light of day.[3] Beneath the banner was the announcement that the publication was a *periódico ministerial*, an official organ of the new Chilean government. Directed by of Camilo Henríquez, a republican priest who had been commissioned by the first government junta and would receive a salary of 600 pesos, *La Aurora* disseminated the new republican ideas with passion and ardent lyricism. "The printing press is in our hands. . . . The voice of reason and truth will be heard among us after the sad and insufferable silence of three centuries," the priest wrote in one of his first articles for the publication (qtd. in Lipp 1975, 6–7). And yet, the newspaper's epigraph read, "Viva la Unión, la Patria y el Rei" (Long live the union, the motherland, and the king).[4] The references to the motherland and the king foretold the conflicts of interest the Chilean press was about to experience in its first attempts at freedom.

Unlike most of its neighbors, Chile had a relatively smooth transition to republicanism. Its progressive press legislation, a sustained growth in commerce, and the rapid development of the financial and mining sectors in the 1800s turned the young Andean republic into the most fertile ground in Latin America for the establishment of a thriving printing business. By the mid-1840s, only thirty years after the *Gallervais* docked in Valparaíso, Chile had developed the strongest and most vibrant free press system in Latin America (Jaksić 1994, 55).

By 1843, laws affecting the press included provisions to enforce the free circulation of newspapers and to guarantee intellectual property, thus expanding on the original press legislation of 1828. In 1833, the Congress incorporated norms to crack down on censorship, adding a progressive twist to an already liberal body of law. The 1843 press legislation in Chile also included a privacy clause that put newspapers at the same level of inviolability as private correspondence (Alberdi 1846, 21–22).

Although such regulations should have made the environment conducive to a free press, Chile's postcolonial reality would reveal itself to be far more complicated, especially when the liberal periodicals started to confront the remnants of a Catholic-Hispanic colonial culture. This antagonism was one of the main elements that in June 1844 prompted the curious trial against an obscure twenty-one-year-old student, Francisco Bilbao.[5]

THE TEACHING STATE

At the time of Bilbao's trial, Santiago counted a few more than sixty thousand souls. Chile, whose first autonomous government had been formed in 1810, stretched some three thousand miles, from the aridity of the Atacama Desert in the north to the freezing Strait of Magellan at the southernmost tip of the American land mass. Most of the population, however, was concentrated in a modest fertile patch some four hundred miles long and fifty miles wide in the central valley, encased by the unconquerable Andes to the east and a barren, inhospitable lower coastal strip facing the Pacific Ocean to the west. It was a small piece of land soon to become the cradle of the free press in Latin America.[6]

The development of Chile's journalism had been unique. In the few years after the war of independence, the nation had steadily moved toward a vigorous, liberal publishing industry. A constant influx of literate exiles and writers from neighboring countries, most of them under severe dictatorships, pollinated Santiago's newsrooms with liberal ideas imported from England and France. These ideas soon started to spread across the Chilean borders to the rest of Latin America. In that context of a sustained and vibrant liberal expansion, the trial against Francisco Bilbao would dramatically polarize the opposition against conservatives in Chile, while testing the limits, strengths, and weaknesses of the young republic's press legislation.

In those days, social divisions in Chile's central valley were fairly uncomplicated. As David Bushnell and Neill Macaulay (1994, 108–10) point out, "The dominant group was a creole landed aristocracy, whose great estates took in perhaps eighty percent of the good land, for a rate of land concentration matched in few other parts of Latin America." The rural lower classes, mainly mestizo, occupied a dependent position, working either as service tenants (*inquilinos*, as Chileans called them) or as a "floating landless population whose members served as day laborers in harvest or other times of peak labor [. . .] in return for little more than a temporary abundance of food and drink and associated fiesta type entertainment."

Chile's population, including the Araucanian groups that still ruled in the far south, reached about two million in the 1840s. The two main cities were the administrative capital, Santiago, and the more cosmopolitan port of Valparaíso. They had flourished, thanks to the easy transportation and communication provided by the thriving trans-Pacific commercial corridor, and had rapidly become key social and economic poles, where the most established and prosperous mining and tobacco businesses in the region were concentrated.

It was not until April 25, 1844, almost twenty years after the end of the devastating revolutionary war, that the Spanish ruling family finally recognized the former colony as an independent state and the tension between Chile and Queen Isabella started to subside. While conservative circles, led by President Bulnes, were still open to the cultural and moral direction set by the monarchy in Europe and the papacy in Rome, a postwar, anti-Spanish sentiment spread among the Chilean middle classes and liberal intellectuals.

A hero of the decisive Battle of Yungay in 1839 and the son of an army officer, Bulnes was a strong advocate of the press as an instrument for educating an elite cohort. During his tenure between September 1841 and September 1851, a flurry of newspapers came into existence. They were partially supported by their own sales, but the national budget and the new press legislation played a role as well. The government's decision to underwrite newspaper subscriptions was emblematic of the importance it placed on periodicals as a means of economic and social development.[7] The consolidation of the press was in more than one way a by-product of policies Chileans referred to as the *estado docente*, or the "teaching state." Fiercely advocated by conservative pedagogues such as Juan Egaña, Mariano Egaña, and the Venezuelan humanist Andrés Bello—the first rector of the Universidad de Chile—for the enlightenment mainly of the upper classes, this exclusivist application of education and the press was met with vehement opposition by liberal pedagogues such as the Argentine writer, journalist, and politician Domingo Sarmiento, as well as Bilbao himself, who believed that the state had the obligation to promote and support the education of the masses in order for Latin America to leave behind the colonial mentality and fully enter modernity.

A KINK IN THE (PRINTING) MACHINE

Manuel Bulnes understood the importance of a vibrant press. Following a decree of 1825, his administration guaranteed a government subscription of two hundred issues for every newspaper published in the country. The law had been easily put into effect in the mid-1820s, as there were no more than twenty or thirty newspapers in circulation in Chile at the time. But with the unprecedented expansion of the periodical press in the 1840s, the norms started to be applied discretionarily, favoring only publications that, "due to their enlightened principles[,] contained useful ideas" and "deserved to be communicated to the people" (Alberdi 1846, 57–58).[8]

In the 1840s the press was at the heart of a heated discussion between liberals and conservatives about Latin American traditions and the development of a postcolonial identity. To North American observers such as Lt. James Melville Gilliss, who had already seen the emergence of the penny press in the United States, the political nature of the Chilean press—which, in fact, set an early editorial direction for the Latin American press at large—was not only noticeable but also worth mentioning. Leader of the US Naval Astronomical Expedition to the Southern Hemisphere between the 1840s and the 1850s, Gilliss wrote in his travelogue that "the taste for the reading of current events is not very general; and one may perhaps justly infer that there is a like indifference to more serious literature" (qtd. in Jaksić 1994, 41). Even in exile, the overwhelming reason for Latin Americans to bear the costs of printing and distribution of their newspapers and books was to influence politics in their homelands (Kanellos 2005, 687–92).[9]

The periodical *El Crepúsculo* was certainly representative of this political direction in the Chilean press. In 1844 it counted little more than 200 subscribers, a small following compared to those of more established ones but large enough to make it self-sustaining, given that 450 readers was the benchmark for many Chilean weeklies at that time (Lastarria 1885, 200–201; Prieto 1994, 259–71). Like most publications in Chile, the periodical enjoyed some level of government support, in the form of subscriptions destined for public institutions, libraries, and colleges.

El Crepúsculo had started as the brainchild of a group of Chilean liberal intellectuals, the Sociedad Literaria, formed in Santiago in 1842 in the context of a traditional rivalry between Chilean and Argentine intellectuals. The Sociedad Literaria was, primarily, a response to the arrival in Chile of a vigorous Argentine liberal intelligentsia fleeing the clout of Buenos Aires's dictator, Juan Manuel de Rosas.

"[Our] distinguished youth, which not too long ago was reduced to the small circle of the creatures of the dominant oligarchy and their offspring [. . .] received a substantial boost [. . .] from an enlightened and boisterous Argentine immigration," wrote José Victoriano Lastarria, a prominent Chilean intellectual, in his memoir. Lastarria was also a member of the Bulnes administration at the time, as well as one of the founders of the Sociedad Literaria and *El Crepúsculo*. "In that exchange of honest and cordial relations," he wrote, "the notable enlightenment and erudition of the sons of el Plata [the

Argentines] was always a highlight, and inspired not a few pangs of jealousy, while making the narrowness of our literary knowledge all too apparent. [. . .] That jealousy spurred the author of this memory to encourage his colleagues and disciples [. . .] to form a literary society" (Lastarria 1885, 85).[10]

Intent on regaining the lead in the battle for public opinion, the Sociedad Literaria launched *El Crepúsculo*.[11] Expectations ran high for the new monthly, especially among the liberal elites. But after a year of existence the publication had not garnered the attention of the broader reading publics of Santiago. And had it not been for Bilbao's piece and the reaction of a few overzealous Catholics, *El Crepúsculo* would have easily remained under the government's radar.

In fact, "Sociabilidad chilena" went largely unnoticed until Bilbao was unexpectedly indicted by a government official. It was only then that the acerbic anti-Catholic, anti-Spanish piece began to gain notoriety around town, crystallizing a new power struggle among the Chilean elites.[12]

Almost twenty-two years after the Francisco Bilbao trial, Manuel Bilbao (1866, 24–26) described how Chilean society in Santiago had reacted to his brother's article: "Those who have found themselves in the middle of a volcanic cataclysm; those who have witnessed the sudden collapse of a population; those who have felt a lightning bolt striking at their feet, only those could have an idea of the effect that 'Sociabilidad chilena' produced in Chile's capital."[13]

The reactions to the article took Lastarria, one of the top editors at *El Crepúsculo*, by surprise. He believed the government had exaggerated the potential influence that the essay would have on Chilean society (Lastarria 1885, 282–83). In the eyes of some of Bilbao's contemporaries, the ideas in "Sociabilidad chilena" were not particularly fresh or remotely revolutionary. And to most urban readers, the piece was of little concern.

Even before publication, the essay's originality had been questioned by the editors of *El Crepúsculo*. Some of the notions that Bilbao was introducing as his own were clichéd, Lastarria claimed in his memoir. The piece was anchored in an eighteenth-century ideological mind-set, which could easily be shown "in the criticism to which [. . .] Bilbao subjected our Catholic and feudal past, our revolution, the governments that understood or opposed it, the Pelucón [conservative] party that reacted against the revolution and aimed at re-establishing and strengthening our Spanish and colonial past." For Lastarria, Bilbao's article did not even present "with enough clarity the criticism that had been cast in various forms against Catholicism throughout the past century" (Lastarria 1885, 282–83). Some of this was also mentioned by Bilbao himself years later, when he conceded that "'Sociabilidad chilena' [was] an extrapolation of 18th century ideas regurgitated by a young soul" (qtd. in Lastarria 1885, 281).

What Lastarria and other intellectuals missed in their reading of Bilbao's piece was the broader range of his critique: not merely a takedown of the old regime, the essay was a direct indictment of the current one, whose mentality had been inherited from its colonial predecessors almost wholesale by the Chilean conservatives. In perceiving Bilbao's ideas as outdated, Lastarria mistook the young journalist's discussion of the Spanish monarchy and his praise of French republicanism as a revisionist attack on an old caste system when the text was in fact an attempt to question Chile's contemporary class system and social structure. Bilbao proposed that the monarchic mentality was being perpetuated in Chile at the core of the new ruling parties and that it was vibrant among both conservative and liberal elites. In order to fully rid Chile of Spanish oppression, Bilbao thought it necessary for Chilean society to oust not just the monarchy but the monarchic mentality reproduced through both religion and land ownership. He proposed instead a radical shift on a class level, suggesting that Chile move in the direction of public education and the democratization of knowledge and resources equivalent to the ones put in place in modern France:

> Catholicism is a symbolic religion and its practices create a hierarchy and therefore a class that controls science, an authoritarian religion that believes in the infallible authority of the church. [. . .] The men who led the thought revolution, finding themselves unable to organize a belief system logically connected to political freedom, reverted to religion as the politics of the people. Thus, we see in many nations constitutional despotism and the promotion of ancient beliefs. [. . .] See the enemy camp, look at the rich and privileged men favored by the establishment; see those lawyers of the Spanish code interested in the perpetuation of the old laws; watch as the clergymen meet in the dark of night to protect this cause. [. . .] Finally, see that multitude of old men and Spaniards who flood the camp, and tell me if you do not see the pulse of ancient Spain come back to life. (Bilbao 1844, 60, 73–74, 80–81; my translation)

Bilbao was aware, on some level, of the undercurrent that Walter Mignolo (2007, 33), citing Aníbal Quijano, calls "coloniality": a logical structure of colonial rule, or the manufactured mentality that secured the colonial powers' influence over the Americas' economy and politics. This is why he aimed his writing with such lethal, perhaps intuitive, precision at the very institutions that had made journalism possible in Chile. His perspective is especially extraordinary considering how fully immersed in modernity Bilbao was and how difficult it must have been for him to reconcile the contradictions of being a modern journalist (arguably, journalism is among the most powerful ideological arms of colonialism) while advocating against the grain of coloniality. He was tentative at including African Americans and indigenous Americans in the collective he called "the people," yet Bilbao was writing from a mentality of inclusivity that was so beyond the comprehension of Lastarria (who was a liberal but could only read "Sociabilidad chilena" through the lens of the creole elites) as to be completely missed by him and the editors at *El Crepúsculo*.

In this sense, and contrary to Lastarria's arguments, the government was perhaps justified in the intensity of its reaction to the piece. It had read the deeper implications of Bilbao's attack and understood its dangerously far-reaching potential.

Just two days after the article was published, ultra-Catholic government prosecutor Máximo Mujica indicted Bilbao, accusing him of blasphemy, immorality, and sedition in the third degree, the three highest possible violations of the Chilean press code (Alberdi 1846, 34–38). Sedition in the third degree was punishable with up to four years of exile or imprisonment. A sentence of sedition in the first or second degree was easily commuted for a fine of 200 or 400 pesos, respectively, the equivalent of one-sixth or one-third of the yearly salary of a highly skilled press worker such as a typist, editor, or star writer.[14] The charges of sedition, however, were dropped as soon as the trial began.

The severity of the accusations took Bilbao's circle by surprise. At first most of his colleagues offered him support. Even Lastarria, who was at the time attached to the Ministry of the Interior, and intellectuals like Francisco P. de Matta, who edited *El Crepúsculo* with Lastarria, voiced their opposition to Bilbao's indictment in several editorials.

But soon Matta, who was also publisher of *El Siglo*, started to distance himself from Bilbao in an attempt to protect his own interests. In the weeks that followed, Matta described "Sociabilidad chilena" as an individual expression of the young man's ideas and not views necessarily shared by his colleagues at *El Crepúsculo*. Later on he even wrote that the article was "the expression of intellectual anarchy in our society" (Lastarria 1885, 285).

Bilbao still had some friends in the government. Ramón Luis Irarrázaval, who was by then the interior minister and would become interim vice president of the republic in October 1844, made unsuccessful efforts to have the prosecutor withdraw the charges. This failure led Lastarria, a key mediator between Bilbao and the political power structure, to hand in his resignation at the ministry in protest over the whole affair.

A student at the time, Bilbao was enrolled in the Instituto Nacional, the oldest and most prestigious high school in Chile. Founded in 1813, the Instituto Nacional was one of the instruments devised by the new government to create an opportunity for elite education in Chile and to produce, as the newspaper *El Monitor Araucano* reported, "opinion, public spirit [and] the men to build the state" (qtd. in Yeager 1991, 73).[15] But when conservatives led by Mariano Egaña, dean of the law school at the Universidad de Chile, primary author of the Chilean constitution of 1833, and editor of the conservative weekly *La Abeja Chilena* (the Chilean bee), noticed Irarrázaval's attempt to downplay the implications of the "Sociabilidad chilena" affair, they started crying for blood.

The case became an ideological crusade for Egaña, and, as a result of his pressure, Bilbao was expelled from the Instituto Nacional. The young journalist never had fit the mold of the postcolonial ruling elites. Following his expulsion, a strong grassroots movement and crowds of conservatives organized to repudiate Chile's most liberal institutions—its newspapers—and poured through the streets to protest against Bilbao and his supporters.

Backed by the conservative press, the Catholic factions in power, and large parts of the public, prosecutor Mujica demanded the complete destruction of the issue of *El Crepúsculo* containing Bilbao's article in an overwrought demonstration of defiance and political bravado. There were no provisions for such action in the Chilean press legislation, so Mujica was forced to appeal to the Supreme Court. And based on an obscure Spanish law of 1609, the court finally authorized the burning of the newspaper by an executioner in a public ceremony—an unprecedented and unusually spectacular display of the political backwardness of Chilean conservative power.[16] Criticized for his eighteenth-century ideas, Bilbao was being punished under the dictates of a seventeenth-century law.

The decision caused consternation among most liberals who stirred up the debate, making it clear that it was not just Bilbao's reputation that was at stake; the entire future of Chile's freedom of the press was in jeopardy. However, the liberal reaction further escalated the conservative backlash.

Francisco's brother, Manuel, remembered the agitation that ensued:

> Churches opened their doors, and from the pulpits, and in the public plazas, and on the streets, propaganda was hurled against the "heretic, the atheist, the corrupt, the immoral, the one who burns in the depths of hell and against whom society needs to raise its arms of extermination as an offering to God." It was the main topic of sermons. Fathers forbade their children to see Bilbao; thus he suffered abandonment by a good number of his friends. Liberals in politics thought their cause would be ruined if they opened their ranks to any-

one who was attacking dogmas: they denied him, they declared him a calamity. Conservatives were wise to excommunicate him from the mother country. [Public] spirit had reached such a fever pitch of derangement and dementia that people who passed in front of Bilbao's windows would make the sign of the cross, and move to the other side of the street. (M. Bilbao 1866, xxiv–xxvi)

Naturally, the accusation fueled a sudden interest in both Bilbao's piece and his trial, capturing the attention and imagination of the general public. This reaction in turn opened an avalanche of small fractures within the ruling party, forcing some of the most liberal members of the government to resign. It could even be argued that it was the fuss the government made about "Sociabilidad chilena" that drew the attention of a broad swath of the population and even audiences far beyond Chile. The piece had, in the vernacular of today, "gone viral"—the first instance of such mainstream reach in the history of Chile's press.

Defiant, while at the same time trying to capitalize on the sudden public interest in the article, *El Crepúsculo* produced a second edition of the issue in question after the first one quickly sold out. The piece was also published separately as a small pamphlet, which raised Bilbao's status to that of a new star in the firmament of Latin American public opinion.

The article catalyzed a latent political dispute floating in the undercurrents of postcolonial Chilean society. The intellectual ferment, of which the article was the clearest sign, had its origins in the social and economic changes led by an ascendant urban bourgeoisie that was reformist, liberal, and Francophilic. Imbued with British parliamentary ideals, the Pipiolos, who favored a federalist type of government, found themselves in direct opposition to the traditional Chilean, pro-Spanish, centralizing upper classes—the Pelucones, or bigwigs—directly associated with the decaying colonial ranks.

Bilbao, of course, was not alone in his attacks on the Church and what he perceived as the backward nature of Chile's colonial heritage. Lastarria and many others at *El Crepúsculo* and *El Siglo* had already voiced their criticism of the conservative elites and the Catholic Church, denouncing religion as an instrument of despotism rather than the basis of freedom, civilization, and a guarantee of the rights of men (Lipp 1975, 13). Many liberals became concerned about the censorship role that conservatives wanted to play amid the strong journalistic, literary, and ideological revolution that was taking place in Chile during those years. But it was Bilbao's piece, as well as his quixotic approach to the indictment and the controversy that ensued, that turned the young man into the main target for conservative anger and indignation. Bilbao—a liberal romantic interested in the works of Rousseau,

Hugues-Félicité-Robert de Lamennais, Edgar Quinet, and Jules Michelet, and, later in life, a fervent reader of Mikhail Bakunin and Karl Marx—was the perfect scapegoat in the eyes of the Pelucones and the Catholic Church.

THE TRIAL

The trial was short and intense.[17] Bilbao, who was "a beautiful man of Spartan aspect and words," undertook his own defense, and one by one he addressed the charges with eloquence and sometimes even a little arrogance (Quinet 1897, 2).[18]

Solomon Lipp has suggested that Bilbao's profound knowledge of the Bible and his reading of works by the French philosophical and political writer Lamennais—in particular, *Le livre du peuple*—molded the young man's oratorical style, shaping its declamatory, aphoristic, and argumentative liveliness. "Bilbao spoke like a man possessed," Lipp writes (1975, 20). "He revealed startling flashes of imagery which compensated for the inconsistencies of content." His vehemence is central to this short exchange between the judge, the prosecutor, and the young writer. The back-and-forth offers a clear example of how unapologetic, sarcastic, and tenacious his self-defense was:

DEFENDANT. Mr. Prosecutor, all you have done is condemn innovation. For look you at my crime.

Now, Mr. Prosecutor, who are you, to make yourself the echo of the society I have analyzed; you who oppose innovation, hiding behind Spanish laws. What crime are you committing?

JUDGE. Sir, you are not here to accuse the Prosecutor.

DEFENDANT. I do not accuse, Your Honor; I merely classify. Philosophy, too, has its code of laws, and that code is eternal. Philosophy has assigned to you the name "reactionary." Well then, innovator—that is what I am; reactionary—that is what you are.

JUDGE. Come to order. Do not be insulting. [. . .]

DEFENDANT. I do not insult, Your Honor. Let the Prosecutor say what he is. Mr. Prosecutor, do you consider yourself insulted by virtue of my having told you the truth?

PROSECUTOR (smiling). You are just a ridiculous creature; you are not capable of insulting.

DEFENDANT. Ignorance always clothes its replies with the sarcasm of impotence. (Lipp 1975, 6–22)

THE REACTION TO THE SENTENCE

On the afternoon of June 17, 1844, after sedition charges had been dropped, the tribunal sentenced Bilbao to six months in prison with the option of paying a fine of 1,200 pesos.[19] The sentence could have meant an immediate victory for the conservative Pelucones. But in fact, during the ten days of the judicial process, "Sociabilidad chilena" had spread like wildfire all over Chile and neighboring countries, turning Bilbao into a celebrity, a modern romantic martyr and hero, and the first victim of political censorship in postcolonial Chile. The trial had also put the young Chilean republic on the brink of an explosive liberal backlash, due to what was starting to be perceived by the Pipiolos as a recalcitrant, inflexible, and retrograde government. In Santiago and Valparaíso everyone had at least heard of "Sociabilidad chilena," and opinions in favor of and against the Catholic Church, the conservative government, and its laws were the order of the day. Bilbao was the talk of the town, and the oratorical displays at the courthouses of Santiago mobilized large crowds of supporters for each side, who gathered in public to root either for the impetuous prosecutor Mujica or for the brave, heroic, and romantic Bilbao. Lastarria argues, though, that few people had clearly understood the young writer's piece. But that did not prevent anybody from taking sides.

As if the situation had not backfired enough on the conservatives, right after the sentence was pronounced a group of Bilbao's followers collected enough money to pay his fine, surrendered the amount to the government, and amid joyful celebration demanded that the prisoner be liberated and that the judges be handed over to the people (Lipp 1975, 18–19).

Feeling cornered by the liberals, the Bulnes administration soon introduced more restrictions in the press law, adding two notorious articles to the code of 1846: Article 5, which stated that "he who attacks or ridicules the official religion of the state, or any of its dogmas," would be subject to a maximum penalty of four years in prison and a fine of 1,000 pesos, and Article 16, which prohibited the public raising of funds to pay for fines imposed as a result of the judicial process (Jaksić 1994, 39).

The disruptions and protest against the government, which escalated in subsequent years after a notable expansion of the liberal press, became another topic of concern for the administration. In 1845, a few months after Bilbao's trial, the government sued Pedro Godoy's *El Diario de Santiago* for libel but lost. And the celebrations of Godoy's supporters turned into a series of violent clashes with the police. The fight lasted for a few hours until a heavy rain finally dispersed the crowds.

In practice, Bilbao's trial gave the Pelucón government a perfect excuse to pass new press legislation in 1846. The new law would afford the administration tighter control over public opinion and give it the power to limit expressions of dissent. While the 1833 constitution had banned prior censorship and had limited the government's power to determine who had "abused" freedom of expression, the new press law, a direct consequence of Bilbao's trial, allowed the administration to censor information considered insulting, immoral, or seditious, while increasing penalties for printers to include imprisonment and even exile.[20]

. . .

After the trial, young Bilbao, exhausted and disappointed in the Chilean political system, retired to Valparaíso, a city he considered more tolerable than the backward Santiago. Then, still unhappy in Chile, he undertook a long, self-imposed exile that led him to France, in the early stages of the 1848 revolution, and then to Prague, Munich, Vienna, and Rome.

In Paris, he studied philosophy at the Collège de France, where Lamennais, Michelet, and Quinet were his mentors. He finally returned to Chile in 1850 to found the Sociedad de la Igualdad (Society for Equality) with his friend and traveling companion, wealthy businessman Santiago Arcos.[21] Soon after his return, however, it was apparent that Chile would not welcome him back with open arms. His books and publications were systematically suppressed and attacked by the conservatives, and after finally being excommunicated from the Catholic Church, Bilbao fled, first to Peru and later to Buenos Aires, where he died in January 1865. He was only forty-two years old.

THE LEGACY

The trial of "Sociabilidad chilena" became a watershed moment in the history of the press in Latin America. It polarized the opposition against the conservative government of Manuel Bulnes, opening the way for the liberal sector, which would expand its demands for democracy and freedom of speech, religion, thought, and the press. The trial also cleared space for a more active and vibrant journalism, which would become not only the government watchdog but also an agent of education and ideological dissemination in the new republics of the subcontinent.

In the years to come, the press in Chile would undergo an extraordinary expansion. Between 1828—the year when the first comprehensive press legislation was passed—and 1851, at least 152 newspapers that lasted more than one issue were published in the young republic, the largest number of them during the 1840s, under the Bulnes administrations (Jaksić 1994, 35). These newspapers were conceived, produced, and nurtured not only by the local intelligentsia but also and most especially by a large group of literate immigrants arriving from different corners of the continent, eager to enjoy the freedom of expression and thought they lacked in their respective countries. Paradoxically, many of these immigrants had learned about Chilean freedom of expression from the Bilbao affair.

Years after Francisco's death, his brother Manuel published a letter that Rafael Bilbao, their father, had sent to the young student during those difficult months of 1844. An old-time democrat, member of Congress, and one of the most fervent advocates of religious and press freedom in Chile, Rafael Bilbao set the tone in his letter for what the liberal press movement would accomplish in the country in the years to come. "It matters not that you may be condemned," Bilbao wrote to his son. "You are not going to appear as a criminal, but as a man . . . who favors oppressed humanity. . . . If I could only sit by your side. . . . I repeat, calmness and courage. It is the first time that you perform a public act, one of great importance for your father. Head up, for you have not committed any crime" (qtd. in Lipp 1975, 17).

Bilbao's defense and the reaction to his trial were the first public acts in support of a liberal Latin American press, the first moves toward the affirmation of freedom of speech, and a firm step toward the consolidation of democracy and a free market society in the region. As public acts, they also had a tremendous impact on the direction, scope, and nature of the region's literature and journalism: they activated, in turn, an emerging postcolonial readership and, in so doing, opened up a public arena for the press. It is precisely this unexpected trial of an obscure journalist that galvanized an entirely new audience and fertilized the ground for the most innovative phase of Latin American literary journalism yet to come.

CHAPTER 2

• • •

DOMINGO SARMIENTO, *FACUNDO*, AND THE BIRTH OF LATIN AMERICAN NONFICTION IN THE HANDS OF A POLITICAL EXILE

ONE EVENING IN 1835, Maj. José de los Santos Mardones, a veteran of the Argentine war of independence, invited a very unusual guest for dinner. Social life was scarce in the Chilean town of Copiapó, where Mardones had been managing a mining operation since the end of the war. The former soldier and his wife grew accustomed to entertaining, almost every evening, a conspicuous group of expatriates, mostly Argentine miners under Mardones's supervision. After work, the boisterous bunch, sometimes three, sometimes five, oftentimes more, would gather at the Mardoneses' home and hang out by the stove, discussing politics and the future of the fatherland for hours on end.

Some eight hundred kilometers north of thriving Santiago, Copiapó was the capital of the Atacama region. The town, connected to the capital by the river of the same name, was an unlikely oasis of civilization consisting of no more than a few thousand settlers, mostly tired miners and avid entrepreneurs, in the rainless heart of the Atacama Desert. Mardones and his wife had a tidy, comfortable house in the town of Placilla, not far from the center of Copiapó, and that night, aside from the regulars, their special guest from Santiago made an appearance at dinner.

The visitor, Bernardino Codecido, was a sybaritic city type from Lima, and a talkative gentleman. It was therefore no surprise that, after a few drinks, he was deeply engaged in conversation with the locals, monopolizing the gathering with his unending complaints about the inconveniences and hard work in the mine. In the kitchen he shared news from Santiago with excitement and exchanged thoughts and jokes with all the other guests—except for a hulking man with a colossal head who sat alone in the corner. A regular at these gatherings, the fellow sported the standard attire of a miner: slippers with woolen outer socks, blue pants and a striped work shirt, a red cap crowning the head, and a ribbed leather belt—the kind that Argentine gauchos were keen on wearing—tied around the waist and from which hung a large bag, like a pendulant marsupial pouch.

The conversation veered from local and Argentine politics to European current events, history, and finally geography, while Codecido, a full-fledged urbanite, did his best to ignore the silent man's presence in the room. But at a certain point, when disagreement arose around a few names and facts, the miners turned their heads to the giant, clearly expecting him to set matters straight. Moving toward the center of the kitchen, the colossal head began to dispense a detailed lecture on the topics at hand: "I set them straight, but in such dogmatic terms and with such a wealth of details that Codecido's jaw dropped lower and lower as page after page of information poured forth from the lips of one whom he had taken for a simple miner. [. . .] The reason for his mistake was explained to him, in the midst of general laughter, and from then on I remained in his good graces" (Sarmiento 2005, 163–64).[1]

In fact, it was not a mistake but perhaps something more like a practical joke played on Codecido. The big man in the corner was no miner at all but Domingo Faustino Sarmiento, a twenty-four-year-old foreman, autodidact, and teacher who actually had extravagant taste in clothing and enjoyed playing mind games with strangers. Fleeing the Argentine government's wrath, Sarmiento had crossed the Andes in March 1831, settling first in the port of Valparaíso and then in Copiapó, where he would stay until his return to San Juan in 1836.

At the time, the young Argentine was, in the words of historian Tulio Halperín Donghi (1994b, 20), "obscure among the obscure." Destined to become the most prominent figure in Latin American literature up to the first decade of the twentieth century and one of the most influential Argentine politicians of all time, Sarmiento had been denied a formal education due to both the loss of his family's economic position in postcolonial San Juan and the rise to power of the federalist caudillo Facundo Quiroga.[2] Homeschooled by his uncle, the priest José de Oro, Sarmiento grew eager to fight the caudillos, whom he blamed for the backwardness of Argentina and the hardships he personally had to endure. He was only sixteen years old when in 1828 he joined the Unitarianist ranks under the command of Manuel

Gregorio Quiroga, governor of San Juan, at whose orders he fought in the Battles of Niviquil and Pilar. But a Unitarianist defeat led to his house arrest for five months. Soon thereafter, he went into his first exile in republican Chile—in Valparaíso first, and later in the town of Copiapó, where he went to work in the silver mines.

That momentary defeat was only the beginning of Sarmiento's story. His journalism and literature would flourish under Chile's blooming democracy. And a combination of passion, determination, talent, and shameless self-promotion would soon catapult the young man into a stellar career in multiple fields. It was a cáreer that, thanks to Sarmiento's genius, would revolutionize Latin America's postcolonial culture, uniting journalism, politics, and literature on one common path.

THE POLITICAL ROLE OF CAUDILLOS IN POSTCOLONIAL LATIN AMERICA

Sarmiento, who had been born in 1811, just one year after Argentina formed its first national government, had witnessed the rise to power of regional leaders during the independence war and had developed a personal animosity toward many of them, particularly Facundo Quiroga, the leading caudillo in the provinces of the Northwest, and Juan Manuel de Rosas, the most powerful rancher in Buenos Aires. This animosity had led to Sarmiento's exile in Chile because of his role in the Unitarianist rebellion. It is also the animosity that fed his inspiration for Latin America's foundational work of literature.

In order to understand Sarmiento's resentment toward these provincial strongmen, as well as the real influence of caudillos in postcolonial Latin America, it is necessary to briefly go back to the end of Spanish rule and review the process through which Latin American nations gained their independence.

Since the early years of the colony, all commercial and social activities in the Spanish viceroyalties were dependent on urban networks formed along the routes to the mining centers of Upper Peru and Mexico. These economic networks generated much of the social infrastructure upon which Latin American cities were later established.

With independence wars starting in Venezuela in 1809 and Argentina and Mexico in 1810, the colonial centers and their cities became separate entities. Mining ceased to be the main economic activity, and the whole political and bureaucratic structure inherited from the motherland soon began to obsolesce and implode (Cortés Conde 1994, 115–17).

Amid a prolonged campaign against Spain, and without the backing of silver wealth, Latin American central governments began to lose control over large stretches of former colonial territories and had to resort to a system of regional strongmen, the caudillos, in order to fight back. These caudillos had access to arms and horses on account of their own personal wealth and charisma, and by functioning as regional commanders, they sealed the Spanish defeat.

But the war had so drastically depleted the resources of central administrations that the young republican governments found their authority reduced to a nominal shadow, with little or no power to collect taxes or pass laws, much less enforce them. At the same time, it became clear that the caudillos still held the real military power in the provinces, and they were proving reluctant to lay down their arms and leave the authority they felt they had earned in battle in the hands of small groups of urban intellectuals.

Organizing politically, many of these caudillos aimed to maintain their provincial autonomy under the guise of an allegedly federative political system (Losada 1983, 131–40). In the Río de la Plata, antagonism between the provincial caudillos and an urban central government soon led to a bloody civil war that lasted more than thirty years.

The two political factions disputing the national government in the Southern Cone were the Unitarianists, a Francophile group to which most intellectual, urban types adhered, and the Federalist caudillos, described by many historians as bands of gauchos united in their disdain for urban centers and European culture and letters (González Echevarría 2003), although the lines between the two were blurrier than many authors suggest.

By 1835, four years into his exile in Chile, Sarmiento had fallen seriously ill with typhoid fever. Still in Copiapó, he managed to obtain special permission, issued by Federalist strongman Nazario Benavídez, to return to his homeland. Benavídez, *el caudillo manso* (the serene caudillo), had always tried to maintain a reputation for fairness and benevolence in his province. And, although Sarmiento was an old political enemy, the caudillo saw no harm in consenting to his return to Argentina for what was expected to be a long convalescence.

Sarmiento was back home by 1836. He worked as a schoolteacher and remained in the shadows for months, increasing his political activities only at the slow pace of his physical recovery. On July 9, 1839, his health and his public visibility almost totally restored, he inaugurated the Santa Rosa School for Girls. And on July 20, with his friend and political ally Manuel Quiroga Rosas (no relation to either caudillo Facundo Quiroga or Juan Manuel de Rosas), he cofounded *El Zonda*, the first weekly newspaper in San Juan, starting a ferocious campaign against the local government and the national Federalist caudillos (Garrels 2005).

Both Sarmiento and Quiroga Rosas had pledged allegiance to the Unitarianists and had also adhered to the May Association, a clandestine group founded by lawyer and constitutionalist Juan Bautista Alberdi to spread republican ideas in South America. Using their newspaper, *El Zonda*, Sarmiento and Quiroga Rosas set in motion a vigorous ideological crusade against not only the regional Federalist government but also the powerful central administration of Buenos Aires strongman Juan Manuel de Rosas.

Rosas was a wealthy rancher and business leader who had started his career as the owner of a meat-salting plant on the outskirts of Buenos Aires. After the war with Spain he had garnered enough political and military power to become the governor of his province, and on March 7, 1835, he was granted the *suma del poder público* (sum of all public powers). By virtue of this title, Rosas controlled the three branches of the Argentine government and the foreign relations of the Confederation, functioning in practice as a head of state for life, virtually a postcolonial dictator, until he was deposed on February 3, 1852 (Katra 1996, 144–234).

The press played a central role in the activities of the May Association against Rosas's profoundly anti-intellectual regime. While directing its efforts toward the organization of an armed resistance to depose the caudillo, Alberdi and his followers found it necessary to reach out to the public in order to disseminate republican ideas. To this end they wrote for newspapers wherever they went. And, as William Katra (1996, 68) has noted, "this was not only their preferred means of earning a living, it was also a most effective weapon for carrying their struggle."

The activities of the May Association, Katra notes, involved not only the publication of republican editorials but also the translation and publication in the popular press of the most important writings by European theorists of social romanticism: Henri de Saint-Simon, Pierre Leroux, and Hugues-Félicité-Robert de Lamennais. Some of the association members founded more than one publication, but they all cultivated an active presence in the press:

> [José] Mármol, [Luis] Domínguez, and [José] Rivera Indarte [three of the
> youngest members of the group] were the principal names associated with several short-lived newspapers. [. . .] Three of these newspapers—*El grito arjentino*
> (The Argentine shout), ¡*Muera Rosas!* (Death to Rosas!), and *El puñal* (The dagger)—had the specific goal of disseminating a highly politicized, negative image
> of Rosas. Later *El talismán* (The talisman) and *El tiroteo* (Gunshot), directed
> by [Juan María] Gutiérrez and Rivera Indarte; *La nueva era* (The new era),
> under the direction of Andrés Lamas and Alberdi's *El corsario* (The privateer),

would join the list of progressive publications. After the demise of most of these publications, Florencio Varela's *El comercio del Plata* (Commerce of the River Plate), founded in 1845, would become the region's most praised organ for disseminating democratic thought. [. . .] In the provinces the impact of the young militants' journalistic activities was also substantial. In San Juan, Quiroga Rosas and Sarmiento published several issues of *El zonda* (Zonda) during 1839. (Katra 1996, 68–69)

Although short-lived—*El Zonda* lasted only six issues, until August 25, 1839—the newspaper was instrumental in Sarmiento's ideological battle against the caudillos. But, as expected, the Federalist governor of San Juan soon shuttered the periodical and in 1840 imprisoned Sarmiento under the charge of conspiracy. By November, barely surviving an attempted lynching by a Federalist mob, the writer fled to his second and ultimately most productive exile in Chile, where together with Quiroga Rosas he continued to battle against the powerful governor of Buenos Aires from the pages of *El Mercurio* and *La Revista de Valparaíso*.[3]

Sarmiento was not alone as an exile in Chile. During Rosas's tenure in Argentina, which was contemporaneous with the ruling of other powerful caudillos in Central and South America, a large number of dissident republican intellectuals found themselves heading over the Andes to become part of the openness of Chile's young democracy and to spread their ideas through the vehicle provided by its free press.

Regrouping in Chile, writers like Sarmiento, Vicente Fidel López, and Juan Bautista Alberdi from Argentina, Juan García del Río from Colombia, and Andrés Bello from Venezuela (the latter had accompanied Alexander von Humboldt during part of his expedition and was considered at the time to be the best-educated man in Latin America) continued to project their influence across the Andes, stimulating the development of a lively public sphere in Santiago and Valparaíso that would soon spread to the rest of the subcontinent.

In the 1845 introduction to *Facundo*, in a passage that would reappear in the fourth edition of the book in 1872, Sarmiento eloquently praised the Chilean press for having offered a home to so many republican exiles and for providing them with a fundamental perspective from which to understand the state of affairs of their own countries:

From Chile, there is nothing we can give *to those who persevere* in the struggle. [. . .] Nothing, except for ideas, except for consolation, except for encouragement; no weapon is ours to bring to those combatants beyond the one that the *free press* of Chile provides to all free men. The press! The press! Behold, tyrant, the enemy you suffocated among us. Behold the golden fleeces we try to win. Behold how the presses of France, England, Brazil, Montevideo, Chile, and Corrientes will disturb your slumber, amid your victims' sepulchral silence; behold how you have been compelled to steal the gift of language in order to excuse your evil, a gift given only to promote good. Behold how you stoop to justify yourself, and how you go among all the peoples of Europe and America begging for a venal, fratricidal pen to defend, through the press, the one who put it in chains! Why don't you permit in your homeland the discussion you maintain with all other peoples? For what were so many thousands of victims sacrificed by the dagger? What were so many battles for if, in the end, you had to decide on a peaceful discussion in the press? (Sarmiento 2003, 36–37)

SARMIENTO'S USE OF JOURNALISM IN HIS SECOND EXILE IN CHILE

Once he was back in Chile in 1840, Sarmiento found himself completely devoted to his journalism, taking decisive yet diplomatically astute steps that would prove key for his trajectory. More specifically, this second period of exile saw the foundation of a daily newspaper, which gave Sarmiento experience as a journalist, provided him with a laboratory for his growth as a writer and pedagogue, and served as a tool for engaging in the political warfare he would need to consolidate his influence in the region and beyond.

The first article he published, on February 11, 1841, was an anonymous first-person piece written in the voice of a fictitious man, an aging veteran of the Battle of Chacabuco. Entitled "12 de Febrero de 1817"—one day into the future—it was published by what was then Chile's only daily newspaper, *El Mercurio de Valparaíso*, four days before Sarmiento's thirtieth birthday (Garrels 2005, lvi). In *Recollections of a Provincial Past*, Sarmiento described the emotionally groundbreaking experience:

Those who have received a systematic education, attended classes, taken examinations, felt empowered by the acquisition of diplomas, are incapable of appreciating the emotions of novelty, of terror, of hope, and of fear that assailed me when I launched my first article in the Chilean press. If I had asked myself at the time whether I knew anything about politics, economics, or criticism, I would have answered frankly, "No," and like the lone traveler approaching a big city who sees only the domes, roofs, and towers of the lofty buildings, I did not see a public before me, but only names, like Bello, Oro, Olañeta, and schools, chambers, courts, and other such centers of knowledge and opinion. (Sarmiento 2005, 186–87)

The article caused quite a commotion in Santiago. Before Sarmiento became a staff writer at *El Mercurio*, the newspaper had usually reproduced pieces on science, literature, art, history, and politics taken from American and European newspapers and would only sporadically publish political columns by young Chilean authors. But Sarmiento's piece changed the editorial line so drastically that historian José Peláez y Tapia (1927, 88) compared it to a "long, vibrant trumpet call to battle, aggressive and rumbling like a cannon."

In a mid-twentieth-century study of the Chilean press, one scholar noted that "whether or not the *Mercurio de Valparaíso* was edited by Argentine quills or rocking along in pleasant apathy, one thing was certain [. . .] Sarmiento brought new life and vitality to the paper, and impetus to the nascent national literature" (Campbell 1962, 551).

In fact, Sarmiento's writing talent and literary genius were extremely well received in Santiago. The public, accustomed to the sober style that Venezuelan writer Andrés Bello had popularized in Chile, applauded Sarmiento and welcomed his journalism like a breath of fresh air. So swift was his rise to popularity that he was immediately offered a staff position at *El Mercurio*. Not long after, Sarmiento was also approached both by the liberal Pipiolos, to work for the presidential campaign of their candidate, and by their political enemies, the Pelucones, to support the candidacy of Manuel Bulnes.

Curiously, Sarmiento, who openly identified with the liberal opposition to Rosas in Argentina, turned down the offer from the Chilean liberals and began to collaborate with the Pelucones, editing together with Miguel de la Barra the conservative *Tribuna Nacional*. This publication ran only nine issues, until July 7, 1841, but facilitated Manuel Bulnes's rise to the presidency. In those days, Sarmiento worked closely with the head of the conservative party, future Chilean president Manuel Montt, who became his longtime friend and ally and helped Sarmiento stay in Chile despite Rosas's several requests for his extradition.

Very few people in nineteenth-century Latin America were more aware than Sarmiento of the power of the press as a medium for social, cultural, and political change (Kirkpatrick and Masiello 1994, 11). Working as an editor, the Argentine always undertook responsibility for building a readership that could fully support his publications. That is why at *El Mercurio* he devoted so much time and attention to understanding the mechanisms through which a publication could become popular, while at the same time still realizing the pedagogical and political roles that were its missions in the context of a young republic.

Sarmiento and his colleagues at the May Association—most of them also living in exile—all believed in a press whose main social function was to promote freedom and public education, a press that was responsible for calling for political changes geared toward an open society. But Sarmiento was not naïve. He was aware that, especially in young republics, the press needed its limits in order to not become a politically destabilizing force. In many of his articles at *El Mercurio* he discussed the role of the government when confronted with particularly belligerent newspapers such as *La Guerra a la Tiranía*, which routinely engaged in slanderous attacks on political leaders of opposing views (Jaksić 1994, 43).[4]

On September 10, 1842, having garnered considerable experience as an editor at *El Mercurio*, Sarmiento founded Santiago's first daily newspaper, *El Progreso*, which would publish nine hundred editions during its three years. The periodical, owned by the powerful Vial family, soon became a laboratory for Sarmiento's ideas and a platform for his best works of nonfiction. As a *redactor*, or principal staff writer, the Argentine exile enjoyed enough freedom to begin experimenting with supplements, new sections, and columns while he focused on expanding the newspaper's readership and its political clout. But Sarmiento also used *El Progreso* to consolidate his public persona, as both the brilliant writer and the extraordinary politician he was.

Newspaper subscriptions were particularly weak in Chile. Until 1842, *El Mercurio*—published in Valparaíso—was the sole national daily, with only eighteen subscribers in Santiago, a city of sixty thousand. Sarmiento knew these numbers made any publication in Chile basically unsustainable. And, in an article in *El Progreso* on November 26, 1842, while comparing Santiago to other Latin American cities, he argued that in order to cover printing costs alone a newspaper in Chile needed at least two hundred subscribers. In this same article Sarmiento also complained about the lack of support Chileans offered to their own press. Sarmiento wrote, "There are in Buenos Aires, and there have been for the past twenty years, two to three thousand subscribers to the different papers. In Montevideo the figure stands above a thousand for the Spanish, French, English, and Italian papers; even in Lima, *El Comercio* has more than eight hundred; and in Santiago we cannot secure enough subscribers to support a fledgling publication whose length, interest and importance always stand in relationship to the number of subscribers" (qtd. in Prieto 1994, 270).

After five months of work, however, Sarmiento's efforts were modestly rewarded. By February 1843 the newspaper had garnered more than one hundred subscribers. We know this thanks to a curious editorial note in which the publishers at *El Progreso* apologized to their readers for the distribution problems of the previous evening. The piece stated that "more than one hundred subscribers, that is to say, nearly all of them, [had] failed to receive their papers" because two of the distributors decided to kill some time in a tavern, neglecting their obligations after one drink too many. The article proceeded to argue half-jokingly that there was no way to keep those in charge of distribution from "killing time where time is exchanged for liquor" (*El Progreso*, April 10, 1843, qtd. in Prieto 1994, 265, 270).

But subscriptions to *El Progreso* continued to stall. Although by 1843 the readership was still not generating enough revenue to fully cover printing costs and it had also become apparent that the newspaper would never reach the self-sustainability for which its publishers had aimed, vital government support through the printing of official announcements infused new life into the project, while the connections with the government proved vital for Sarmiento's personal agenda.

During his years at *El Progreso*, Sarmiento became extremely knowledgeable about the journalistic, pedagogical, and political issues that became the foundation for his literature at large.

First, thanks to his role in the printing business, he had developed extensive experience as a newspaper writer, editor, and publisher. He knew that the press could not survive without subscribers, and Chileans—or Latin Americans in general, for that matter—would not buy their newspapers as a pure act of patriotism. Therefore, Sarmiento began experimenting with different forms of entertainment, publishing feuilletons, articles on theater, fashion, and gossip, and humorous columns. As Iván Jaksić (1994, 44) has noted, the *folletines* were Sarmiento's most legitimate vehicles for capturing public interest in a context where, due to the lack of resources—few libraries and no bookstores —the reading public resorted to the press as its main source of information and education.

Second, due to his frequent contact with the government, Sarmiento was able to test-drive in Chile some of his ideas on cultural and pedagogic policy. In 1842, for instance, he invested major effort into a linguistic reform of the Castilian language, parts of which were eventually adopted by the Chilean Academy of Language (Academia Chilena de la Lengua) and some newspapers in Chile, Peru, and Argentina. Success in this crusade, however, came at the high cost of exposing himself to slanderous attacks from opposing intellectuals and politicians.

Third, in those years, thanks to his close ties to Manuel Montt, Sarmiento could also pursue his ideological attrition warfare against Rosas in Argentina without risking the possibility of being extradited. Despite the ongoing diplomatic requests from Rosas's delegates in Chile, the Chilean authorities systematically declined to extradite Sarmiento, thus straining trans-Andean relations.[5]

Sarmiento would later say in his memoirs that in America, great personalities built not only their own destinies but also, and more importantly, the theater for their actions. And in a way, his battles for public education and against the tyranny of caudillos were certainly building the theater and the audiences for his own work (Altamirano and Sarlo 1994, 164).

As the extraordinary writer he was—undoubtedly the best and most prolific of his generation—Sarmiento used his years at *El Progreso* to develop his own literary persona, consolidating all of the aspects of his political, journalistic, and pedagogical aspirations in one single node. On May 2, 1845, at a time when he was already considered one of the most influential intellectuals, pedagogues, and writers in Latin America, the Argentine started publishing his masterpiece *Facundo* in a series of installments in the *folletín* section of *El Progreso*.[6] A work of the most unorthodox nonfiction, *Facundo* is the first major piece in the convoluted puzzle of Latin American literature, and it has been plausibly described as "the most important book written by a Latin American in any discipline or genre" (González Echevarría 2003, 1).

HYPERBOLE AND THE DEVELOPMENT OF A POLITICAL AGENDA

Since his early days as a teacher in San Juan, Sarmiento was a fierce advocate of public schools, which he considered the only path to modernity. Sarmiento was convinced that education for the masses was possible even in the poorest of nations, but it could only be achieved within the context of a firmly established republican system. He therefore aimed most of his political, journalistic, and literary efforts toward that end, writing extensively and brilliantly about the evils of totalitarianism and personalism. In pursuit of public education, Sarmiento not only fought the caudillos in Argentina but also turned his own life into a mythical-literary example, as well as the living proof that success was possible, if the path was that of perseverance, self-sacrifice, and abnegation.

In his 1850 memoir, definitely hyperbolic, Sarmiento showed on the one hand the trials and tribulations of a young intellectual struggling to overcome adversity. But on a deeper level the book was a powerful instrument devised by a brilliant writer and pamphleteer to place a success story before the public eye, in anticipation of his 1868 presidential run. *Recollections of a Provincial Past* shows how Sarmiento as a writer and a politician masterfully used literature and journalism to achieve his electoral goals and his political objectives in the longer run. But the book also serves as a perfect introduction to some of the rhetorical devices Sarmiento had created in order to integrate facts and literature—devices that would soon become a trademark of Latin American literary journalism as a genre.

Sarmiento never wrote a single line, not literary, not in a news article, nor even in a letter, without a political purpose. That understanding colors the reading of some passages of *Recollections* in which he describes how he taught himself French and English: "I got the idea of learning it with a Frenchman, a soldier of Napoleon, who did not know Spanish or understand the grammar of his own language. But my greed had been aroused by the sight of a French library belonging to Don José Ignacio de la Rosa, and with a borrowed dictionary and grammar, after one month and eleven days of having begun my solitary study, I had translated twelve volumes, among them the *Mémoires* of Josephine" (Sarmiento 2005, 162). By narrating how during those five months of house arrest after the Battle of Pilar, under the candlelight, with only the company of a French dictionary and a borrowed grammar, he devoted his hours to the higher goal of learning the language of Rousseau, Sarmiento was creating one of the most enduring myths of self-accomplishment in the history of Latin American literature, while crafting at the same time an extremely powerful ideological instrument, one that would become central to his entire political career.

Just as in the anecdote on the mines of Copiapó, here Sarmiento has clearly manipulated the scene in order to show his readers how, through extreme self-sacrifice and education, a final reward can be achieved. In Copiapó, education and the articulate, well-timed expression of knowledge helped Sarmiento make the transition from the peripheral kitchen corner to the center of the scene, from being the object of cold indifference to becoming the center of respectful consideration from a complete stranger (Altamirano and Sarlo 1994, 167).[7] The rewards of his solitary study would soon multiply, together with the increasing satisfactions offered by knowledge:

In 1833 I was a clerk in a firm in Valparaíso at a salary of one *onza* per month, and of this I spent half on my English teacher Richard and two *reales* a week on the night watchman of the *barrio* to wake me at two in the morning to study my English. On Saturdays, I stayed up all night to make of them a single piece with Sunday, and after a month and a half of lessons, Richard told me that all I had left to learn was pronunciation, which to this day I still have not been able to master. I went to Copiapó, and as an unworthy foreman of *La Colorada*, which hid so much silver bullion from my eyes, I translated the whole sixty novels by Walter Scott at a rate of one volume a day, and many other works that I owed to the solicitousness of Mr. Edward Abbott. Many people in Copiapó will remember the miner who was always reading. (Sarmiento 2005, 162–63)

In Chile, where he spent a substantial part of his life, Sarmiento was nicknamed "Señor YO" (Mr. Me). And in Argentina he soon became famous for his megalomaniacal outbursts and tendencies. A caricature of Sarmiento walking on telegraph wires over the Argentine Constitution was published on October 12, 1873, during the final years of his presidency, in *El Mosquito* magazine (Reggini 1996, 123). The massive figure of the statesman balancing on the wires while holding a rolled-up Argentine Constitution in one hand gives an idea of how Sarmiento was perceived by the public in those years. The epigraph read, "Imbeciles! As if the President couldn't be everywhere! [. . .] / The Constitution! Without the President, without *I*, what is it? / And I, the President, what do I need it for?" (my translation).

With that information in hand, it is hard to believe that the readers of *Recollections of a Provincial Past*—which had been published only twenty-three years before this caricature—would not have thought of Sarmiento's anecdote of language acquisition as an overblown story, a myth, and of his linguistic learning curve as a little bit too steep to be believed.

These anecdotes, however, do show a very frequent *topos* in Sarmiento's narrative: the transition from poverty to riches, from civilization to barbarism, thanks to the painstaking efforts invested in education, mostly pursued during the dark hours. This persistence pays off, on the one hand, in the joyful success of accessing culture: after learning English, Sarmiento was able to read *sixty novels* in English. But his effort also leads to the satisfaction of opening to others that access door to culture, by translating at a rate of *one volume a day*—a clearly hyperbolic figure—these same works. As a symbolic plus, Sarmiento also gains the recognition of Copiapó's settlers, who praise and recall the miner who spent his days reading.

It is the effort and its rewards that Sarmiento wants to feature through these two anecdotes. The movement from darkness to light owed to painstaking dedication, and the passage from barbarism to civilization, are central structuring elements in Sarmiento's nonfiction. These transitions are also presented as the result of personal and collective investment, aimed at self-improvement and self-development. Sarmiento usually describes the passage from one state to the other with overblown exaggeration, as if he meant to contrast in sharp tones the differences between a *before* and an *after*.

Altamirano and Sarlo have suggested that the mythological aspect of these success stories is confirmed by the fact that, in reality, "Sarmiento does not speak English [and] he probably speaks French with serious difficulty. And yet he writes about learning these languages as if he achieved his goal" (Altamirano and Sarlo 1994, 162). They have also proposed that these stories are part of Sarmiento's myth of literary self-creation. However, due to the resonance they had among the public at large, it is difficult to consider such powerful structuring narratives as purely rhetorical devices.

In fact, these anecdotes and their underlying structuring myths go far beyond their immediate narrative function. They do more than create Sarmiento's literary persona and present to the public his aggrandized sense of self-worth. More often than not, these exaggerations delineate the political direction pursued by Sarmiento as a statesman. Like most Latin American intellectuals of his time, Sarmiento believed that progress—upward social mobility, but also and especially a radical, positive, and desirable social transformation—could be achieved only through public education and democracy. This direction, akin to Sarmiento's most profound philosophical ideas and his notions of civilization and progress, was deeply imbued in his literary journalism. But since, in his view, ideas and action were inseparable, and because as a good romantic he was also a man of action, Sarmiento intently aimed each one of his literary and journalistic efforts toward the realization of his political cause. In that vein, his articles and literary journalism can be read as a theoretical cornerstone, as a means for the author to achieve his political objectives, and as the definitive road map for his political career.

Considered in this context, the mechanisms of hyperbole and exaggeration in Sarmiento's factual narratives—either literary or journalistic—could be interpreted not as the violation of a factuality agreement between journalist and readers, but as the realization of a contract of a different magnitude. Personal, social, political, and cultural development—in that order—were Sarmiento's programmatic goals and the underlying motivations for both his journalism and literature. And, in that sense, truth was secondary to the realization of a long list of political goals.

None of the contemporary critiques of *Recollections of a Provincial Past* or *Facundo* questioned Sarmiento's factuality, objectivity, or accuracy, thus suggesting that his audience was probably attuned to—and comfortable with—Sarmiento's reading contract. Truthfulness, in this relationship, was of secondary importance, and the lack thereof did not necessarily undermine the straightforward expression of certain political messages in the press or invalidate their intent. If sacrifice led to knowledge and knowledge to personal and social progress (as one of Sarmiento's most frequently visited narratives seems to suggest), the effort it took to produce *Facundo* was probably worth making. And Sarmiento, who had already walked the walk, was someone worth following, despite all of his self-promotional stunts.

Exaggeration and hyperbole, therefore, should be understood not only as purely narrative devices but also, and more importantly, as mechanisms that connect Sarmiento's nonfiction with his extraliterary goals. A seasoned publicist, Sarmiento knew that aspiration drives behavior. His hyperbolic statements primed the audience to accept his political program, guiding the transition between written ideas and concrete action. Sarmiento was probably the first Latin American intellectual to clearly understand how nonfiction narratives and literary journalism could be combined to inject a young public sphere with unprecedented political drive.

BOOKS AND ENLIGHTENMENT IN THE LAND OF THE RANCHERS

To say that for Sarmiento a book could make a man's fortune is not only figurative. It is, in fact, an accurate description of how Sarmiento came to view publishing, based on what he saw happening in literary markets in Europe and the United States (Altamirano and Sarlo 1994, 163).

In *Ambas Américas* (Both Americas), a magazine that he published for four numbers in 1867 while posted in Washington as a plenipotentiary minister of the Argentine government in the United States, Sarmiento expressed his conviction that culture and writing could yield handsome rewards, even of the monetary kind. "We do not know, in fact, if there are men in the Argentine Republic who have garnered the fat of the land, fortune, glory, status, and power without having opened a book in their lives, or without even being able to read. We do know that Walter Scott paid his debts with his novels, that Victor Hugo is rich thanks to his own, and that Dumas would be a millionaire, had he not been so profligate" (Sarmiento 1867, 96).[8] However, it is important to understand how slim Sarmiento's chances of making a fortune off his book actually were. Instead of selling newspapers to an existing reading public, he had to first create an audience.

Sarmiento had only anecdotal knowledge of the extent to which the powerful ranchers in the Argentine countryside were detached from the European Enlightenment, its literature, philosophy, customs, and morals. But today we have a much clearer sense of how disconnected the rural upper classes in young Latin America were from European modernity, at least until the late 1870s. This gap was accurately described in Juan Carlos Garavaglia's study of more than eight hundred ranch inventories.

In the study, which spans the period between 1750 and 1850, Garavaglia found, with rare exceptions, the near total absence of books in rural homes. Only a few of the inventories listed any books, and most of those were religious in nature (Garavaglia 2007, 144–45). If this dearth was the norm among ranchers, who constituted one of the more educated echelons of rural Latin America, one can only imagine how little exposure to modernity the lower social strata had.

Most European ideas reaching the countryside in the early days of the Latin American republics were spread by readings at bars and *pulperías*. These small stores were the center of rural social life and the place where most provisions, including alcohol, were sold. Locals from the middle and lower classes would hang out in the pulperías to learn about current events, have a drink, talk politics, play cards, dominoes, or craps, play guitar, bet on cockfights, and sometimes engage in riskier activities, such as dueling. By the mid-1800s, Buenos Aires and its periphery counted more than four hundred pulperías, while the illiteracy rate in both Argentina and Chile remained high (Garavaglia 2007, 132).[9]

As a newcomer to Chile, Sarmiento stayed away from the heated debate around "Sociabilidad chilena" in 1844, and he assumed a neutral position vis-à-vis Bilbao's article. However, by the time he published *Facundo* in 1845, and later in his writings from the United States, it became clear that the Argentine had agreed with the young Chilean all along. The political and cultural systems of the former colonies and their anachronistic governments were, Sarmiento believed, deeply rooted in the customs that Latin American societies had acquired during Spanish rule, undoubtedly influenced by religion. By removing the mediation between ideas and people (i.e., by removing the Catholic Church from the path between ideas and people), Sarmiento was sure to gain a new reading public.

Years later, Sarmiento expressed these notions in the first issue of *Ambas Américas*: "With the books currently in circulation in South America that are written in Castilian [Spanish], no nation can be civilized; those books were left to us from Spain's past and were the result of a spiritual development in a direction contrary to the one we are taking in current times, and nothing in those books except the formative aspects of our language could be of use to us today" (Sarmiento 1867, 63; my translation).

Books and newspapers were powerful ideological tools, and Sarmiento knew how to use them. *Facundo* had been conceived primarily as a means to challenge the government of Rosas in Buenos Aires, and it certainly did that.

However, *Facundo* also positioned Sarmiento among the most respected writers of literary works in Hispanic America. While delivering the author's ideas about progress and modernity, it also presented to the reading public a clear political platform that would soon put Sarmiento on his way to the presidency of Argentina, connecting him with the most relevant intellectual and political figures in Chile, Europe, and the United States.

Facundo was the realization of Sarmiento's literary, political, and editorial dreams all at once. As a feuilleton, the book was widely read and extensively reviewed, and it had a tremendous impact on *El Progreso*'s sales, prestige, and political clout. It was thanks to Sarmiento that *El Progreso* started to incorporate serialized novels into its pages, and in the words of the French critic Paul Verdevoye (1963, 268), it was the Argentine who "inoculated" the Chilean—we could very well say the Latin American—press with the "virus of the 'feuilleton.'" In fact, the melodramatic style of *Facundo* probably derives from Sarmiento's readings of Eugène Sue's *Les Mystères de Paris* and his desire to introduce the aesthetics of romanticism in Chile and Latin America. As Elizabeth Garrels has noted, however, Sarmiento considerably altered the rules of the feuilleton, sometimes translating and publishing in that format texts that had not been conceived as serialized novels but as complete books (Garrels 1988, 425, 436).

Facundo gave birth to a purely Latin American literature, with a writing style anchored in reality—evocative, allegorical, and militantly political all at once. This description of the city of Córdoba shows some aspects of Sarmiento's new approach:

> Córdoba was—I shall not say the most coquettish of American cities, because that would offend its Spanish gravity, but certainly one of the prettiest cities of the continent. Situated in a hollow formed by an elevated terrain called Los Altos, it has been forced to fold back over itself, to crowd and push together its symmetrical buildings. The sky is very pure, the winter, dry and tonic, the summer, hot and stormy. On the eastern side, it has a beautiful promenade of capricious shapes, suddenly magical to the eye. It consists of a pool of water squared in by a broad walkway, shaded by colossal, ancient willows. Each side is a block long, enclosed by wrought-iron grating with enormous doors in the centers of the four sides, so that the promenade is an enchanted prison within which one circles, always around a gorgeous pavilion with Greek architecture. In the main plaza is the magnificent Gothic cathedral, with its enormous cupola carved into arabesques, the only example I know of in South America of medieval architecture. [. . .] This learned city to this day has not had a public theater, has known no opera, still has no daily newspapers, and the printing industry has not been able to establish itself there. The spirit of Córdoba, up to 1829, was monastic and scholastic; drawing-room conversations always revolved around processions, saints' days celebrations, about university examinations, nuns' professions, the receiving of a doctor's tassel. (Sarmiento 2003, 118–19)

The passage illustrates one of the main tensions undergirding Sarmiento's book: a glorious medieval past, symbolized by the "monastic and scholastic" spirit of Córdoba, versus a still unattained modernity in which daily newspapers, public theaters, and a thriving printing industry become the missing emblems of progress.

Facundo was without a doubt the first major accomplishment in Latin American literature and in many ways it still remains at the center of Hispanic American literature today. Equally important is the fact that the book became for its author a powerful ideological weapon to use against the remnants of colonial traditions in the region. The conflation of fiction and history and of ideas and stories that Sarmiento brilliantly wove into his masterpiece enhanced the author's status as not only a savvy newspaper editor and publisher and extraordinary writer but also an intellectual who had succeeded at developing a completely new literary genre and a writer skillful enough to push his political program to the top of the public agenda. Its unifying impact on an as-yet-undefined public served to eliminate the Catholic Church as intermediary between people and ideas and insert in its place the possibility of new myths based on new national identities.

In the words of Gwen Kirkpatrick and Francine Masiello (1994, 9), "[Using] the literary metaphor to represent projects of state, [Sarmiento] also saw in literature the potential for one's rise to power." In that sense, literature and political action were, for Sarmiento, one and the same thing.

FACUNDO, THE PARROT CANNON AS PASSPORT INTO THE WORLD

The need to separate Latin America from its Spanish heritage became even more urgent for Sarmiento following his first trip to Europe and the United States, particularly after he witnessed the vitality and scope of the American publishing industry in 1847. *Facundo* would prove useful in these early explorations, providing a Latin American writer access to European and American elites on unprecedented levels.

After the publication of *Facundo*, it became clear that Sarmiento's presence in Chile and his ever-increasing journalistic activities against Rosas were putting a heavy strain on relations between Santiago and Buenos Aires. In an attempt to tone down the intensity of his attacks and reestablish relations with Argentina, Manuel Montt, Sarmiento's longtime friend and a minister in Bulnes's government, proposed that Sarmiento travel under the auspices of the Ministry of Education to study pedagogic systems in Europe and the United States.

Sarmiento embraced the idea enthusiastically, and by October 1845 he was on his way from Valparaíso to Paris. As a delegate of the Chilean government, he stayed in Europe until July 1847, when, disappointed in the French Revolution and the extreme poverty he witnessed in France, he set sail for the United States with only $600 in his pocket. The money would barely have been enough to make a return trip to Chile around Cape Horn, and it was certainly not enough to permit him to enjoy even the shortest stay in the United States had he not casually encountered in New York a wealthy Chilean business leader, Santiago Arcos, who was Francisco Bilbao's dearest friend. Arcos, who became Sarmiento's traveling companion during the two months the Argentine spent in North America, also helped fund his return to Chile (Rockland 1970, 16–18).

From the day he published it, Sarmiento relied on *Facundo* as his passport to access the highest echelons of the civilized world. Therefore, he always carried a few copies of the book on his trips. In Paris, Sarmiento had *Facundo* translated and published, and after glowing reviews from French critic Charles de Mazade in the prestigious *Revue des Deux Mondes*, the Argentine also put a few French copies of the book in his luggage as he prepared to travel to the United States.

Years later, in 1867, having already been appointed as Argentina's ambassador in Washington, Sarmiento again made sure to bring several copies of *Facundo* in French. The book was proof of his cultural accomplishment and had the symbolic power to position him not only as an internationally acclaimed writer but also as a serious political analyst, competent and knowledgeable in the realities of Latin America and Europe. "This book serves me as a means of introduction," he wrote to his friend, lover, and confidant Aurelia Vélez in a letter dated October 15, 1865. "Being Minister isn't everything, and being an educator is not so distinguishing in a nation of professors and teachers. But I still have my *Facundo*, my Parrot cannon. No one resists it" (Sarmiento 1962, 221).

THE POLITICAL POWER OF BOOKS

Facundo is a difficult book to pigeonhole for many reasons in addition to its literary unclassifiability. Indeed, it is the book's very fluidity that could explain its legacy—a range of influence and longevity that has as much to do with *Facundo's* instrumental nature as it does with its artistic achievement. Constant iteration, urgency, scene construction, flexibility of facts, dialectical narrative, conclusion-evocation, the metaphoric-allegorical axis, and the use of symbols—many of these mechanisms drawn directly from journalism—when combined with existing literary and rhetorical forms became the basis for Latin America's first literary genre. In fact, *Facundo* laid the groundwork for genres still to come (such as *crónica*, *testimonio*, and magic realism).

Serving ever-changing political functions, *Facundo* had always been a text subject to constant mutations, suppressions, and additions. Ancillary to Sarmiento's political agenda, the book operated on a number of different, sometimes contradictory levels: it was first a feuilleton aimed at increasing the readership of *El Progreso*; it was also an irate pamphlet against the tyranny of Rosas in Buenos Aires; then, after Rosas's fall, *Facundo* rapidly became a generational road map to building the new Argentina on the "deserted grounds" of the Pampas; and finally, the book was, from the get-go, Sarmiento's letter of presentation, a key that opened for its author the doors to social, academic, and political circles in Europe and the United States.

In part due to the instability of Sarmiento's political alliances and his often-changing ideas, sympathies, needs, and aspirations but mostly because the book was perceived by Sarmiento as an instrument and not as an end in itself, *Facundo* became a malleable text, subject to frequent alterations and internal contradictions.

Clear indications of these changes were, in fact, revisions to *Facundo*'s title throughout its successive editions. When it was first published in 1845 in Santiago, the book was called *Civilización y barbarie: Vida de Juan Facundo Quiroga y aspecto físico, costumbres y hábitos de la República Argentina* (Civilization and barbarism: Life of Juan Facundo Quiroga and the physical aspect, customs, and habits of the Argentine Republic). In its second edition, in 1851, Sarmiento dropped the controversial *Civilización y barbarie* pairing, calling the book instead *Vida de Facundo Quiroga y aspecto físico, costumbres y hábitos de la República Argentina, seguida de apuntes biográficos sobre el general Fray Félix Aldao* (Life of Facundo Quiroga and the physical aspect, customs, and habits of the Argentine Republic, followed by biographical sketches of the general Friar Félix Aldao).

There were several editions of the book released during Sarmiento's lifetime, one printed in English in New York in 1868, and another in French, printed in Paris in 1874 (González Echevarría 1994, 224–25). And it is clear that all the substantial changes introduced between impressions—not changes in vocabulary or printing errors—can be attributed to political reasons. A fascinating example of these variations would be the suppressions in the 1851 edition of chapter XIV, "Unitarianist Government," and chapter XV, "Present and Future," the two final chapters of the original *Facundo*.

Following suggestions by Valentín Alsina, the powerful leader of the Partido Autonomista Porteño (Autonomist Party of Buenos Aires), Sarmiento omitted those two chapters from the 1851 edition, and the book thus ended with the death of Facundo Quiroga. By suppressing the final part of *Facundo*, Sarmiento cut out of his book the most explicit connections between Facundo Quiroga and Rosas in chapter XIV, as well as some of his own ideas about the consolidation of the Argentine state, laid down in chapter XV. With these changes, Alsina believed, the animosities between the political factions that had supported Rosas and those that had opposed the federalist caudillo would heal, and both groups would become more likely to back the government of Justo José de Urquiza, who had deposed Rosas in the Battle of Caseros. In 1852 Alsina was elected governor of Buenos Aires, but he resigned soon thereafter due to disagreements with Urquiza and joined forces against him with Sarmiento and the powerful newspaper publisher Bartolomé Mitre. After the fall of Urquiza in 1861, Alsina turned into a close political ally of Sarmiento and became his vice president when they won the elections of 1868.

Sarmiento never hesitated to change *Facundo* whenever he had a political reason to do so, making addenda, suppressions, or corrections if the occasion so required. Literary and political ambitions were always intertwined for the Argentine, but it is clear that his political goals were a constant priority. This becomes apparent in an 1851 letter Sarmiento sent to Alsina thanking his friend for the notes to *Facundo*, a letter Sarmiento included in that year's edition of the book: "I have literary ambitions, my dear friend, and dedicate many long nights, extensive research, and careful study toward satisfying them. Facundo died in body at Barranca-Yaco, but his name in History was able to escape and survive for some years, without the exemplary punishment it deserved. The judgment of History has now fallen on him, and the repose of his grave is maintained through the suppression of his name and the scorn of the people" (Sarmiento 2003, 40–41).[10]

Of course, Sarmiento believed that he, indirectly, and *Facundo* had operated as historical agents delivering a punishment that Quiroga rightfully deserved. Like any good romantic writer, he portrayed Quiroga as a Hegelian hero, assuming in his writing an equivalent historical role himself.

In 1868, when Sarmiento ran for president, with Alsina on the ticket for vice president, *Facundo* was edited once again. But this time the author dropped a section in which he had proposed the transformation of the city of Buenos Aires into the capital of Argentina while federalizing its port. Argentine critic Noé Jitrik (1993, 19–20) has suggested that Sarmiento was politically motivated to edit out this section of the book because the Autonomists, Sarmiento's party, opposed the federalization of Buenos Aires's port and would not have supported his candidacy otherwise.[11]

It is clear so far that, to a certain degree, the connection between literature and history in Sarmiento's work is anchored in his romantic background, although as a writer the Argentine always put his political goals before his literary ambitions. There were, however, other forces that motivated Sarmiento to write his masterpiece. Letters, articles, and passages of his later work make clear that his first impulses in writing *Facundo* had more to do with his training as a journalist than with his literary aspirations.

The narrative core of *Facundo*, its feuilleton structure, the scenic constructions that kick-start the tradition of narrative journalism in Latin America, show that Sarmiento intended the book to be read not only by an elite but by a general public—an audience that would be more attuned to the concrete aspects of a story in opposition to the abstract reasonings and argumentative nature of the essay. In that sense, Sarmiento may have learned from Bilbao's "Sociabilidad chilena" and its trial: Do not write to the elites who oppose your views. Write to the masses who will support you.

On May 1, 1845, an article signed by Sarmiento in the *folletín* section of *El Progreso* announced the publication of *Facundo*: "A momentary interest of mine, pressing and urgent in my judgment, makes me rapidly trace the lines of a picture I thought I would be able to present some day, as complete as I believed possible. I have thought it necessary to crowd onto the paper my ideas as they appear before me, sacrificing all literary pretenses to the need of preventing an evil that could be transcendental for us" (qtd. in Jitrik 1993, 3).

Both the urgency of the task and the "momentary interest," fueled by the celerity with which Sarmiento is set to accomplish his objective, speak to the author's journalistic frame of mind and training. In fact, the idea of political urgency as the central motivation for a book would soon thereafter become one of the most frequent topoi in Latin American literary journalism. More than a century later, it still resonates in the works of authors such as Rodolfo Walsh and Gabriel García Márquez.

In a sense, *Facundo*'s opening lines also bear testimony to the journalistic nature of Sarmiento's enterprise. In the "Advertencia del autor" (Author's note), which was suppressed by Sarmiento in the second, third, and fourth editions but reincorporated in the book when it was issued again in volume 7 of his *Obras completas*, Sarmiento's first phrases define *Facundo* as a work that, even before publication, had already undergone several corrections. These amendments that Sarmiento has garnered "from different friends" amount to "several facts" and were the result of "a work done quickly, far from the scene of the events, and on a topic about which nothing had been written" until then (Sarmiento 2003, 29).

The emphasis on the factual nature of *Facundo* is carried along to the following paragraphs, where Sarmiento describes the difficulty of a writing process that involved "bringing together incidents that took place in different and distant provinces and at diverse times, consulting an eyewitness on some point, searching through rapidly written manuscripts, or invoking personal recollections" in what feels like a fairly journalistic reporting process (Sarmiento 2003, 29).

At the end of this forewarning, Sarmiento seals what reads like an accuracy pact with his readers: "[But] I do state that in the notable events to which I refer, and which serve as *the basis for the explanations I give*, there is irreproachable accuracy, to which the existing public documents about those events will attest. [. . .] Perhaps there will be a moment when, unburdened by the worries that have precipitated the writing of this little work, I may remold it according to a new plan, stripping it of accidental digression and supporting it with the numerous official documents to which I now make only passing reference" (Sarmiento 2003, 29; my italics).

Although this pact may resemble the reading contract that gained relevance with the emergence of the penny press in the United States, it is worth recalling here that, for Sarmiento, facts were just the groundwork for his political goals. In the author's own words, facts were the basis for explanations. In that sense, objectivity and reporting were, by definition, always subordinated to political ideas and aspirations, which was the bottom line of *Facundo*.

Facundo's style floats between that of the novel, the confession, the epic, the scientific treatise, the political pamphlet, and the travelogue (González Echevarría 2003, 2), but, as most critics have noticed, the book is extremely hard to classify under any of the traditional genres that arose and became popular in Europe during modernity.

A journalistic biography of the caudillo Facundo Quiroga, a taxonomic description of the pampas and its social types, and a comparison between Quiroga's rule in La Rioja and Juan Manuel de Rosas's tyranny over the Argentine Confederation, *Facundo* is structured around a series of anecdotes, colorful descriptions, and vignettes, generally followed by Sarmiento's attempts to make sense of them through some philosophical concepts derived from French romanticism, and then some pseudosociological analyses.

It could be argued that the book evolves dialectically, from the "general aspects" of the Argentine republic and its types to the particular events of the 1810 revolution and the life of Facundo Quiroga in La Rioja until his assassination in Barranca Yaco, then back to the generalities of a hypothetical future of the Argentine nation under the tyranny of Rosas and its potential for development under a democratic regime.[12]

On the chapter level, the narrative structure follows a conclusion-evocation pattern typical of the journalism that preceded the Associated Press's development of the inverted pyramid in the mid-1800s.[13] The structure is succinctly presented by Sarmiento in the introduction: "It has occurred to me to explain the Argentine Revolution with the biography of Juan Facundo Quiroga because I believe he sufficiently explains one of the tendencies, one of the two different aspects that struggle in the bosom of that singular society." Of course, Sarmiento is talking about Quiroga's tendency toward barbarism (Sarmiento 2003, 37).

There are innumerable examples of this technique throughout the book, but one, in which Sarmiento refers to the nature of the Argentines, is worth quoting here:

> The result is that the Argentine people are poets by character, by nature. How could they not be, when, in the middle of a serene, pleasant afternoon, a grim, black cloud appears from who knows where, stretches itself across the sky before two words can be said, and suddenly a stampede of thunder announces a storm that leaves the traveler cold and holding his breath, for fear of attracting one of the thousands of lightning bolts coming down and around him? Darkness is followed by light; death is everywhere; a terrible, incomparable power in one moment has made him go inside himself and feel his nothingness in the midst of that disturbed nature, to feel God, to put it plainly, in the terrifying magnificence of His works. Is this color enough for the palette of fantasy? Masses of darkness that cloud the day, masses of trembling, livid light that illuminate the darkness for an instant and show the infinite distance of the Pampas, lightning flashing across them, the final symbol of power. These images are meant to stay deeply ingrained. Thus, when the storm passes, the gaucho is left sad, pensive, serious, and the succession of light and darkness continues in his imagination, in the same way that the disk of the sun stays on the retina for a long time when we stare at it.
>
> Ask the gaucho whom the lightning bolts prefer to kill, and he will introduce you to a world of moral and religious idealization, mixed with badly understood facts of nature and superstitious, crude traditions. Add to this, if it is true that electric fluid is part of the economy of human life and is the same as what they call nervous fluid, which when excited, arouses passions and sparks enthusiasm, [then] a people inhabiting an atmosphere charged with electricity to the point where clothing, if rubbed, gives sparks like a cat's fur stroked the wrong way, must be quite disposed to the workings of the imagination.
>
> How could he who witnesses these impressive scenes not be a poet? (Sarmiento 2003, 61–62)

Both structures—the dialectical operating on a macro level and the conclusion-evocation, on the micro level—show that *Facundo* was conceived neither as a biography, nor as a confession, nor as an epic or a novel: Sarmiento wrote it as another journalistic piece, following some of the standards of mid-nineteenth-century European news writing.[14] However, due to the Argentine's enormous talent as a storyteller, as well as a series of innovative narrative resources he employed, the book produced its own deviations from the norms of the European factual-referential genres, delivering a very particular rendition of both, with its special style, flavor, and idiosyncrasy.

Facundo was not only published in a newspaper as a feuilleton. Sarmiento also presented it as being journalistic when he wrote his "Author's Note," and this is probably one of the reasons why the author treated his book as an adaptable, mutable, and contingent piece. The book followed the precepts of French romanticism, with overwhelming descriptions of the natural and biological forces at stake in the Pampas, and larger-than-life heroic characters and types. Just a hint of this appears in the grand introduction: "Terrible specter of Facundo, I will evoke you, so that you may rise, shaking off the bloody dust covering your ashes, and explain the hidden life and the inner convulsions that tear at the bowels of a noble people!" (Sarmiento 2003, 31).

But Sarmiento also added to the mix a few of his favorite personal enhancements that underscored the book's militant nature. I have already described the political use of hyperbole in Sarmiento's narrative. He certainly used this rhetorical mechanism in *Facundo*. But on a deeper level his masterpiece was also structured as an allegory: by talking about the caudillo Facundo Quiroga, Sarmiento was really referring to the authoritarian threat of Juan Manuel de Rosas, the contemporary strongman from Buenos Aires. The author anchored the metaphorical reference to Rosas in the following statement, also included in the forewarning: "Writing the life of Rosas would be an affront to History, and to remind our homeland, after its rehabilitation, of the degradation it went through would be humiliating" (Sarmiento 2003, 40–41). Yet, writing about the caudillo is exactly what Sarmiento does, and he is indirectly slandering the rancher by attacking Quiroga. Putting some distance between himself and Rosas, Sarmiento was, in fact, anchoring the metaphorical reference to the Buenos Aires rancher, while preparing the reader for a relentless attack on his political enemy.

Of course everybody—the public, Rosas, and the Chilean government included—understood this mechanism and read the book more as an attack on the powerful governor of Buenos Aires than as a reflection on the life of Facundo Quiroga, murdered ten years before *Facundo* was even published. In a famous quote that Adolfo Saldías (1973, 193) transcribed in his *Historia de la Confederación Argentina*, Rosas praises *Facundo* by acknowledging it as a masterful political strike: "The book by that crazy Sarmiento is by far the best that has been written against me. That's how you attack someone, yes sir: you will see, sir, that nobody defends me so well."[15]

Distancing himself from Rosas while writing about his homologous Quiroga, Sarmiento developed another durable literary-political strategy in

Latin American nonfiction: an allegorical referentiality through which the main topics of a narrative are centrifugally displaced toward a metaphoric-allegorical axis that still dominates the core of the plot. Sarmiento thus inaugurated Latin American literary journalism as a political-allegorical genre that obliquely refers to the present by narrating past events; this is a genre that could be interpreted both as an indirect account of current events or as a purely novelized historical record.

An example of this technique, which became standard for Latin American writers in the twentieth century, can be found in a passage of Sarmiento's *Recollections of a Provincial Past*.[16] In this fragment, Sarmiento writes about the enormous yet idle wealth of his family during colonial times. By so doing, he correlates a feudal past with the dismal poverty of the provinces under Federalist rule. And by showing the backwardness of both colonial and present times, he finally notes that, in the United States, enormous sources of wealth have become available as a result of industry, education, and democracy, laying down a third element in the comparison, which opens a political question about the future: What type of nation do Argentines want for their children?

> In the house, once or twice a year, a strange activity would take place. The heavy doors to the street, studded with enormous copper nails, would be closed shut, and both patios would be sealed off from each other, in order to keep the children and the servants out; then, my mother tells me, the black woman Rosa, cunning and curious like a monkey, would whisper the news to her: "There's a *sunning* today!" Cautiously placing a small ladder under a window that faced the patio, the crafty slave lifted up my mother, still but a slight child, taking care that very little of her head showed, in order that she might spy on what was going on in the big patio. My mother, who is truth incarnate, tells me that, large as it was, the patio was covered with hides upon which they had laid out in the sun a thick layer of blackened pieces of eight [silver coins or Spanish dollars] so as to rid them of their mold; and two old Negroes who were the custodians of the treasure moved from hide to hide carefully turning the sonorous grain. Patriarchal customs of those bygone times, in which slavery did not corrupt the good qualities of the loyal Negro! I have known Uncle Agustín, and another black, Antonio, a master mason, who belonged to the estate of Don Pedro del Carril, the last man of enormous wealth and power in San Juan, who together, until 1840, held two bars of gold and several bags of coins in safekeeping for their master's family. It was the mania of the colonials to hoard peso upon peso, and to take pride in doing so. In San Juan people still talk of caches of silver buried by the old-timers, a popular tradition that recalls the past opulence, and

not even three years ago the storehouse and patios of Rufino's vineyard were excavated in search of the thousands that he was said to have left and that at his death could not be found. What could have happened, oh you colonials, to the fortunes of your grandfathers? And you, federal governors, military scourges of the people, could you amass, by squeezing dry, by torturing an entire city, the sum of pesos that only sixty years ago was enclosed in a single patio belonging to Doña Antonia Irarrázabal?

I have been astounded in the United States to see one or two banks in every town of a thousand souls, and to know that there are millionaire property owners everywhere. In San Juan not a single fortune remains after twenty years of confederation: the Carrils, Rosas, Rojos, Oros, Rufinos, Jofrés, Limas, and many other powerful families lie prostrated in poverty, and descend day by day into the mass of the destitute. The Spanish colonies had their way of life, and they got along well under the king's indulgent tutelage; but you people, convinced that the least qualified is the one who governs best, have invented kings with long roweled spurs who just dismounted from the colts they were taming on the *estancias*. The wealth of modern nations is the exclusive issue of cultivated intelligence. It is fomented by the railroads, steamships, machinery, the fruits of science; they give life, liberty for all, free movement, the postal service, the telegraph, newspapers, debate, in short, liberty. Barbarians! You are committing suicide; in ten years' time your sons will be beggars or highwaymen. Consider England, France, and the United States, where there is no *Restaurador de las Leyes* [Restorer of the Laws], nor stupid *Héroe del Desierto* [Hero of the Desert], armed with a whip, a dagger, and a gang of wretches to shout and put into effect the slogan of "Death to the *savage* unitarianists," that is to say, those who no longer exist, and among whom there were so many distinguished Argentineans!

Have you heard, re-echoing throughout the world, any names other than those of Cobden, the wise English reformer; Lamartine, the poet; or those of Thiers and Guizot, the historians; and always everywhere, on the rostrums, in congresses, the government, savants and not peasants or rude herdsmen, like the ones you, at your own peril, have endowed with absolute power? (Sarmiento 2005, 44–45)

The passage, which perfectly synthesizes Sarmiento's rhetorical battery, not only follows the conclusion-evocation structure. It also anticipates some of the techniques that would be used in Latin American literature throughout the twentieth century in a style that blends marvelous, exceptional elements into a realistic situation, delivering an effect of magic realism.

Sarmiento truly believed in the power of books. But an anecdote recounted by Mary Peabody Mann, who was the first to translate *Facundo* into English and also the wife of the pedagogue Horace Mann, Sarmiento's lifelong friend, may show to what extent the Argentine believed in the power of symbols. Mann wrote this as part of Sarmiento's biographical sketch, published in 1868, in the introduction to the first English-language edition of *Facundo*:

> Thus prepared, and matured by study, experience, travels in foreign lands, and years of beneficent action in a true cosmopolitan spirit, he left Chili [sic] in 1851 with the present President, Colonel Mitre, and the present General Paunero, to incorporate himself in the army of General Urquiza, who was about to open the campaign against Rosas. The battle of Caseros, which disposed of Rosas, took place on the third of February, 1852, and Señor, now *Colonel Sarmiento, had the pleasure of writing a description of it upon the tyrant's own table with the tyrant's own pen.* Six days after, he left Urquiza's army, for he saw that that old servant of Rosas meant no good to the country, but purposed to make himself a tyrant in Rosas' place. Derqui had been made President, who fell in with Urquiza's plans. The event proved that his prophecy was right, though Urquiza was not wholly successful. (Mann 1868, 359; my italics)

Sarmiento's ultimate means of overpowering Rosas was to take the caudillo's place in front of his desk and, with Rosas's own pen, write the chronicle of the battle in which the rancher was finally defeated. In a way, Sarmiento took that same approach to reigning over what he considered the more barbaric aspects of Latin America. Through words, through his newspaper articles and his literary journalism, he strived to tame what he saw as barbarism, paving the way for progress. His presidency in Argentina, between 1874 and 1879, opened a thirty-year period of sustained Westernization, democratization, and economic expansion in the region. But this only happened at the expense of silencing the groups that, in Sarmiento's view, resisted the modernizing push.

THE PENNY PRESS AND SARMIENTO'S FIRST JOURNEY TO THE UNITED STATES

Sarmiento's experience in the United States had a transformative impact on his vision for mass media in Latin America, expanding his ideas about the potential of the press and the type and scale of audience it could foster. In the United States he found the avant-garde of a journalistic, political, and pedagogical movement that, he concluded, would lead the way toward a freer and more democratic society. And although he headed back to Chile some six months before the formation of the Associated Press (AP) and did not experience the unprecedented cultural impact that the newspaper syndicate led by the *New York Sun*'s cautious editor, Moses Yale Beach, had on American journalism, in New England the Argentine did in fact witness some of the early incarnations of the neutral reportorial style that was soon to become the AP's standard.

Sarmiento arrived in the United States for the first time on September 15, 1847. He had already been deeply disappointed by Europe's social conditions. As a passenger on the *Montezuma*, "a large sailing packet which did eleven miles per hour with the slightest breeze," he had shared the trip with 480 Irish emigrants who had just escaped starvation and the complete lack of prospects in the Old World. And this was probably the final impression that Europe made on the writer:

> I have just come from going about Europe, from admiring her monuments, prostrating myself in front of her science, and I am still astonished by the wonders of her arts. But I have seen her millions of peasants, proletarians, and mean workmen, and I have seen how degraded and unworthy of being counted as men they are. The rust of filth which covers their bodies and the rags and tatters in which they are dressed do not sufficiently reveal the darkness of their spirits; and with regard to politics and social organization that darkness is enough to obscure the minds of the wise men, of the bankers, and of the nobles. (Sarmiento 1970, 14)

This experience stood in high contrast to what he was about to witness in the United States. Comparing his observations on both sides of the Atlantic, he would soon write in his *Travels*, "The only country in the world where the ability to read is universal, where writing is practiced by all in their daily lives, where 2,000 periodicals satisfy public curiosity, and where education, like welfare, is everywhere available to all those who want it is the United States" (Sarmiento 1970, 152).

Sarmiento bought newspapers in the United States and read them as efficiently as his poor English permitted. He praised them for their power to spread and encourage the adoption of new technologies and ideas:

> There are no unconquerable habits that retard for centuries the adoption of an obvious improvement, and, on the other hand, there is a predisposition to try anything. An advertisement in one newspaper for a new kind of plow, for example, is carried in every paper in the Union next day. The day after that they are talking about it on every plantation, and the blacksmiths and manufacturers in two hundred places are at the same time considering putting out the new model. Soon the new machines are put on sale, and a year later they are in use all over the Union. You would have to wait a century for something like this to happen in Spain, or in France, or in our part of America. (Sarmiento 1970, 132–33)

Sarmiento saw newspapers as the beachhead of postcolonial moderniza-tion. In his *Travels*, the Argentine paid special attention to what he defined as the "civilizing and catalytic influence of the periodical press" in the United States (Sarmiento 1970, 192). He also understood the enormous impact that the connections between newspapers and the new communication technol-ogies had on urban life in the United States. Thanks to telegraph lines, the news could be carried even "200 leagues through the thickest forests." And when a new settlement emerged around a "coal or an iron mine," the new settler "draws up a city plan, gives the city a name, and returns to the set-tlements to announce by means of the thousand echoes of journalism the discovery he has made of the site of a famous city of the future, the crossing point of one hundred commercial routes." When the public reads the an-nouncement in the newspaper, another "Babel raises up in the middle of the forest. [. . .] Communications are inaugurated. The newspaper of the place keeps everyone informed of society's progress. Agriculture gets underway. Temples, hotels, docks and banks rise up" (Sarmiento 1970, 159–67).

Sarmiento did not seem to notice any differences, however, between these popular new US newspapers and the more elitist political press that, although dwindling in the United States, was still the dominant type in Latin America.[17] Because he was not fully competent in English, or because the penny papers were still actively political, or simply because he was reluc-tant to embrace the mercantile model of the penny press, Sarmiento por-trayed US newspapers as still "expressing the interests, passions, and ideas of various groups" rather than as the popular entertainment and escapist fare they were actually becoming. The entertainment model was, in fact, the dominant paradigm at the time when Sarmiento returned to the United States in 1865, after he had been appointed plenipotentiary minister to the United States, a position he held until elected president of Argentina in 1868 (Sarmiento 1970, 175–76).[18]

For Sarmiento, the American literary sphere of "20 million men who know quite a bit, who daily read what is necessary to exercise their reason and public and political passions," was in fact a product of popular educa-tion and democracy (Sarmiento 1970, 176). And democracy was in turn a di-rect consequence of the American system: "When there is a school in town, a press in the city, a ship on the sea, and an asylum for the sick, democracy and equality begin to exist. The result of all this is that the power of the mass is immense" (Sarmiento 1970, 267).

The tremendous literary market in the United States had allowed for a separation between the spheres of literature and journalism, spheres that in Latin America remained largely overlapping until at least the mid-twentieth century. Sarmiento understood that the American literary sphere was still deeply connected to England's, and in part that was the reason why it could afford this division of literary labor. But the Argentine also foresaw the tremendous potential of American literary production, and he anticipated in *Travels* that the US book market would soon outpace that of Britain: "It is enough to say that, in the twelve years from 1830 to 1842, 106 original works of biography were published; 118 books on American history and geography; 91 in the same fields on other countries; 10 on philosophy; 103 books of poetry; and 115 novels. In almost the same period of time 382 original American works have been reprinted in England and accepted by that same public which twenty years before asked through the medium of a magazine: 'Who reads American books?'" (Sarmiento 1970, 283).

In the 1840s, the Industrial Revolution was entering a time of fast-paced expansion on both sides of the Atlantic. Steamboats and locomotives enhanced commerce between the former colonies and London, and an expanding industrial working class, highly concentrated in the urban centers, launched a demand for new and different forms of entertainment.[19]

In the United States, Sarmiento witnessed the establishment of an industrial and commercial bourgeoisie and the unprecedented growth of a literate working class. The increase in leisure time was fostering an expansion of popular genres like the novel, and many authors had begun catering to these new audiences while introducing original styles and topics. The consolidation of the publishing industry in New York and other American big cities, helped by technological innovations like typesetting machines, faster printing presses, and the development of wood-pulp paper, made books cheaper and easier to manufacture.

Three decades later, in the post–Civil War period in the United States, the growth of this incipient literary market made room for a categorical separation between journalists and writers, manifest not only in different professional circles but also in different social castes (Tucher 2006).

Novels were mainly aimed at female readers, while newspapers targeted males. William Dean Howells used to say of prewar Bostonians that only women read books, while men read nothing but newspapers. "The man of letters must make up his mind that in the United States the fate of a book is in the hands of the women," the author noted in his "Man of Letters" (qtd. in Robertson 1997, 30). In fact, a majority of the writers and readers of novels in the United States of the post–Civil War era were women, whereas journalism was a mainly masculine craft and pastime (Robertson 1997, 30–37).

As Michael Schudson, Andie Tucher, and Michael Robertson have noted, after the Civil War most metropolitan newspapers had expanded from four or eight pages to sixteen pages. This expansion intensified the demand for reporters, while increasing the professionalization of journalism and the separation between two different occupational groups: fiction writers and journalists.[20]

Sarmiento was perfectly aware that, contrary to what was happening in the United States in the mid-1800s, Latin America was far from developing an independent literary market. Latin American audiences, their roots going back to a Catholic monarchy, had a much slower start than their British-colony neighbors in terms of literacy. The metropolitan centers in Spain were still deeply tied to a retrograde rural economy. The Iberian Peninsula was undergoing a series of staggering financial and political difficulties that would slowly evolve into a long and painful civil war, and the publishing industry both in Spain and in its former colonies was stalling.[21]

Illiteracy rates in Spain were high, and, where a literary market did exist, it was dependent on obsolete forms, patronage, and government subsidies. The literary and poetic renovation of the Spanish language would have to await the advent of *modernismo* and the generation of 1898. But this renovation would, for the most part, originate in newspapers, in the vibrant metropolitan centers of Latin America and in Spanish-speaking communities of Cuban exiles in the United States.

In the former colonies and those territories in Central America and the Caribbean still ruled by the Spanish Crown, illiteracy rates were even higher than in the metropolis. A local bourgeoisie, mainly agrarian, was developing, but the urban centers had not yet reached a size sufficient to allow for the development of a newspaper-reading public, let alone a dynamic public sphere. Sarmiento was very aware of these limitations. That is why he devoted most of his efforts to stimulating migratory inflows from Europe. The eradication of indigenous persons, the inmigration of Europeans and white Americans, education, and the press were the unquestioned pillars of a modern postcolonial "civilization."

Sarmiento explored many of these ideas in a number of treaties, papers, journalistic articles, and long nonfiction pieces but especially in his *Facundo*. And after his first visit to the United States, the Argentine focused much of his energy on importing into the southern nations the pedagogical innovations he had observed in Massachusetts. Developed by his friend Horace Mann, the secular educational model would serve Sarmiento as both a case study and a roadmap to modernity: Latin America needed its own teachers, its own literature, its own mores, and its own culture. Toward that end, the development of a literary sphere, a free press, and a solid, nonclerical school system was of utmost urgency.

"In England and the United States more books are published every year than all the ones, old, modern, foreign and in translation, that are kept in the Library of the [American] Senate," Sarmiento would concede in the first issue of his *Revista de Ambas Américas* in 1867. "When we examine the publication dates of the books [in Spanish] that we're having to deal with, it becomes apparent that Spain's culture was more active in the 16th and 17th centuries than today; and it was also more solicitous in translating and acquiring books from other nations in the 18th century than today" (Sarmiento 1867, 67).

It was clear that improvements were past due. And Sarmiento, a politically interested observer of some of the journalistic and pedagogical advances in the United States, continued raising his authoritative voice, both as a journalist and a scholar, to argue against totalitarianism and in favor of public education, making his case in the daily columns of newspapers like *El Mercurio*, *La Crónica*, and *La Tribuna* in Chile and a few years later in *El Nacional*, *La Tribuna*, and *La Nación* in Argentina. But most of his ideas had already been introduced in his literary journalism, particularly *Facundo* and *Recollections of a Provincial Past*.

Secular education would soon become the cornerstone of most Latin American national projects. And undoubtedly, newspapers, the main "tribunes of doctrine" (to quote the banner of *La Nación* of Buenos Aires) in the region, would supply a still weak literary market and a growing public sphere with vibrant daily and weekly columns about actuality, education, literature, and politics. The role of the press in Latin America was to weave the first ideological fibers in the fabric of nations. The Latin American daily press and its literary journalism would soon showcase the development of the region's ideas about civilization, education, and its literary, political, and public spheres.[22]

It was not therefore by chance that Sarmiento, basing his continental position on the presidency of the Argentine Republic between October 1868 and October 1874, led the region into a movement toward the American model of progress he so admired. Undoubtedly Eurocentric, Sarmiento's presidential term was marked by a number of quandaries: a ruinous war against Paraguay, a yellow fever epidemic that decimated the population of Buenos Aires, and a blind devotion to European immigration that all but paved the way for the violent extermination of the native populations of South America, which took place in the decades to come. These setbacks, added to the many complaints about Sarmiento's personalism and caudillo-like style, turned him into an extremely controversial political figure.

His talents as a writer and ideologue brought Sarmiento to power. And as the best Latin American author of his generation, the Argentine devoted his skills as a literary journalist to catapulting his political agenda over the barbarism of the caudillos and laying the groundwork for modernity in the region. But when Sarmiento reached the pinnacle of political power, writing became secondary and less important to him. Quoting Manuel Gálvez, the Argentine author Ricardo Piglia points out that, after winning the presidential race, Sarmiento, the most brilliant, prolific, and eloquent writer and orator in the Americas, could not produce an acceptable inauguration speech. Despite many attempts, Sarmiento's drafts were systematically rejected by his ministers until a final version was composed by the minister of justice and education, Nicolás Avellaneda, a journalist himself. The time for writing was now in Sarmiento's past.

It is unquestionable that as a newspaper editor and publisher, an author, and a politician, Sarmiento had put Latin America on a path to democratic government that, with a few exceptions, would last for more than three decades uninterrupted. Clearly enough, this political accomplishment should not be separated from Sarmiento's literary and journalistic achievements. However, it is also evident that Sarmiento was fully immersed in a postcolonial idea of modernity that rejected traditions native to the Americas and had its eyes set on Europe and its cultures.

It is in this context that *Facundo* becomes relevant as a primordial link in the tradition of Latin American literary journalism. The book stands at the crossroads of Sarmiento's political, literary, and journalistic activities and delivers a perfect synthesis of the three. In its structure, quality, scope, and contradictions, *Facundo* also had a tremendous stylistic impact on the Latin American literature that followed. But perhaps most importantly, in its journalistic nature, Sarmiento's masterpiece became a lethally efficient political instrument, marking the direction of a young Latin American literary journalism, permanently binding it to the sphere of politics.

As powerful and influential as it has been, Sarmiento's legacy would come to be deeply tarnished by his consistent degradation of the indigenous peoples of the Americas and the racist undercurrent in his work that has left a somber cloud over his name. During his lifetime, however, Sarmiento would define a new postcolonial audience, consolidating his influence not just as a writer but as a statesman. Whereas Bilbao revealed the existence of such an audience, it was Sarmiento who claimed and forged it, tailoring his readership to his own vision of the future.

CHAPTER 3

• • •

JOSÉ MARTÍ AND THE CHRONICLES
THAT BUILT MODERN LATIN AMERICA

SOAKED IN THE COLD, gray rain of a late September morning in 1889, the US Coast Guard cutter *Manhattan* crossed New York Harbor. It carried a diplomatic mission comprising a representative of the US government, Charles R. Flint; two delegates of the business world in New York, William H. T. Hughes and F. G. Pierra; a member of the Chamber of Commerce, Henry Hertz; envoys of the Argentine and Uruguayan governments in the United States; and a thin, pale journalist dressed all in black and wearing a silver ring engraved with the word *Cuba* as his only adornment.

Not long after 6:00 a.m. the cutter approached its destination: the *City of Paris*, a 560-foot mooring steamer with double black chimneys and three masts towering above the lapping waves. Inside, a group of high-ranking visitors had just arrived in New York after a long journey from South America. Using a hand ladder, the envoys on the *Manhattan* climbed aboard the steamer and, after fetching umbrellas and raincoats, waited on deck for a few minutes until an officer invited everyone inside. In the ship's library, two Argentine politicians, Manuel Quintana and his assistant, Roque Sáenz Peña, awaited them.[1]

Quintana, a white-bearded fifty-three-year-old statesman, and Sáenz Peña, fifteen years his junior, were the last diplomats to arrive in the United States for the first Pan-American Conference. The event, they knew, could change the course of history for the American hemisphere. The Argentines would soon join the representatives of sixteen other Latin American countries, all invited to the United States by Pres. Benjamin Harrison and his high-profile secretary of state, James Gillespie Blaine (Karras 1974, 77–99).

The Pan-American meeting was scheduled to begin on October 2, 1889, in Washington, DC, and last until early 1890. It was the first official attempt by the United States to establish its hemispheric dominance, arguing for the formation of a customs union spanning both continents, the implementation of an inter-American arbitration system, and the development of a pan-American common currency.[2] On October 5, the guests were to take part in a six-thousand-mile excursion by train, complete with a dining car serving French cuisine, to some of the most inspiring destinations in the United States—a not-so-discreet attempt to dazzle them with scenes of American industry and unparalleled prosperity (Karras 1974, 86–87). The trip, however, never took place. Although the meeting did start on schedule, the conference completed its agenda only in April 1891, a year after the planned end date, with the dissolution of the Inter-American Monetary Commission. The conference, Blaine's brainchild, also became his worst political misstep.

Although some Latin American countries could afford a permanent diplomatic mission in the North and had kept their delegates busy with briefings, letters, and memos, most other statesmen in the hemisphere had remained updated on the preliminaries of the summit through the daily press. It was no surprise, then, that many of the envoys were familiar with the slightly built Cuban journalist with the black mustache, who was now shaking hands with the Argentines. In a curious case of performing multiple roles at the same time, José Julián Martí had already written a series of articles from New York for *La Nación* newspaper in Buenos Aires, as well as diplomatic letters to the Uruguayan and Argentine chancellors, determined to plant in the press—and in the minds of the conference participants—an inauspicious seed that would set the hostile tone for the encounter ahead.

For months after the invitations to the conference were announced, Martí had been consumed with anxiety about this first meeting with the Argentines. Now, with the steamer approaching the docks, he was starting to feel a sense of relief.

Although this was their first personal encounter with the Cuban, Quintana and Sáenz Peña had long been acquainted with Martí's work for *La Nación*. And at least one of the members of the Argentine mission, Miguel Tedín—in New York since early 1888—had already met him in person. Tedín confessed years later that more than anyone else in the United States, it was Martí he wanted to meet: "One of my first projects was to look for Martí, whose correspondence for *La Nación* had impressed me vividly" (qtd. in

Martí 1911, 9). Between 1882 and 1889 the Cuban had dispatched from New York more than two hundred chronicles for the Argentine newspaper in the style of the best literary journalism of that time. His pieces appeared every two weeks on the front page of the daily and added to an impressive body of literary work, one that would be central in the renovation of the Spanish language as fostered by *modernismo*.

In his role as delegate to the Inter-American Monetary Commission of 1890 and 1891, for Uruguay first, and later for Argentina and Paraguay, Martí was also able to operate politically at a continental level, taking an active part in the discussions opposing the creation of a common hemispheric currency. But long before that, his stories in the press were key to initiating a Hispanic American understanding based on culture, interests, and shared political goals, which deepened the regional reluctance to follow Blaine's agenda (Karras 1974, 77–99). Martí's literary journalism helped debunk Blaine's proposals while establishing the groundwork for a postcolonial Latin American covenant.

The chronicles of this gifted thirty-six-year-old writer, poet, journalist, and Cuban revolutionary not only marked one of the highest points in the young literature of the region; they also realized the potential of Latin American literary journalism as a political, artistic, and journalistic genre. Martí's dispatches, especially those written between 1889 and 1891 in the militant tradition inaugurated by Domingo Sarmiento, show to what extent, to borrow the words of Chilean Nobel laureate poet Gabriela Mistral, the Cuban writer "divided himself like a pomegranate into two uneven halves—the literary and the civic" (qtd. in Mañach 1950, xv).

Thanks to his writings for the daily press, Martí became one of the most respected political voices in the Americas, and the impact of his ideas on the delegates would play a central role in the final outcome of this first Pan-American Conference encounter. In a way, Martí's premonition about the Argentines was correct: following his ideas on the front pages of Argentine daily *La Nación*, Argentina would rapidly become a polarizing Latin American force during the historic meeting.

ECONOMIC AND SOCIETAL CHANGES DURING LATIN AMERICA'S EXPANSION, 1880–1900

In those final years of the nineteenth century, Martí witnessed unprecedented economic, political, and cultural changes in Latin America. But it was the confluence of literacy development and state formation that made it possible for him to have a position of influence rarely if ever enjoyed by any other journalist until then.

Trailing behind the United States both politically and economically, the subcontinent was by the 1880s becoming a relevant force in the world of international commerce. Fully functioning modern states had started to provide a stable framework for political treaties and private commercial agreements with a Europe increasingly in need of primary goods to access the second phase of its industrial revolution. These new republican structures ended seventy years of caudillism in the region.[3] With a substantial improvement in transatlantic communications and the consolidation of an international division of labor, the Americas were poised to become Europe's main supplier of primary goods, while entering what historian Tulio Halperín Donghi (1969, chap. 3) has called the "age of economics."

"Order and progress," Brazil's national motto—inspired by a phrase from Auguste Comte—and "peace and administration," coined by Argentine president general Julio Argentino Roca, crystallized the political and ideological aspects of this shift toward modernization.[4] Roca, whose campaigns in the Pampas during the late 1870s had decimated the native population of the Southern Cone, became the ninth constitutional president of Argentina in 1880, and was famous for another catchphrase, one that many other leaders in the region would probably have agreed with: "Revolutions—that is[,] political uprisings—are not quoted on the Stock Exchange in London" (Rouquié 1982, 61).

Between the 1850s and the 1880s, the goal of state-building was progressively achieved in South America and Mexico, while many of the countries in Central America, such as Nicaragua and the Dominican Republic, would be continually torn by political convulsions until well into the twentieth century. Consequently, especially between the early 1880s and World War I, most of Latin America experienced a rapid economic expansion that was accompanied by significant social changes.

In Mexico, the Porfirio Díaz administration opened the economy to a large inflow of foreign capital to facilitate mineral production. After its victory in the War of the Pacific against Bolivia and Peru, Chile achieved a monopoly on nitrates. Cuba, even before its independence, multiplied tenfold its economic integration with the United States through an unprecedented expansion of its sugar production. In Brazil, the spread of coffee plantations over the São Paulo highlands and a sustained arrival of European immigrants separately contributed to the collapse of the slave economy. And in Argentina, the largest economy in Latin America, a massive wave of European immigration was also accompanied by a large influx of European capital (Furtado 1970, 50–51).

A closer look at the three largest nation-states in the region—Mexico,

Brazil, and Argentina—reveals in further detail the depth and speed of these changes.

In Mexico, between 1877 and 1910 the population increased from 9.4 million to 15.2 million, while the GDP per capita grew at 3.1 percent annually, just one percentage point below the US rate during the Gilded Age (US Census Bureau 1901). Oil and mineral production skyrocketed at a rate of 7.2 percent annually, twice as fast as the manufacturing sector and three times as fast as agriculture.

In Brazil, the population grew from 10.1 million in 1872 to 17.3 million in 1900, and more than 600,000 European immigrants moved into the country. In the three decades after 1880, the total trackage of railways in Brazil increased from 2,100 to 13,200 miles—still less than one-tenth of the US total by 1900 (US Census Bureau 1901). Coffee exports, which had averaged 240 million kilograms during the 1890s, reached 600 million in 1900, and cacao and rubber exports increased seven times over in those years, to reach 40,000 tons in 1900.

But the most rapid changes took place in Argentina. Between 1890 and 1904 the population doubled, from 3.6 million to 7.2 million. Railroad networks, thanks to Sarmiento's modernizing impulse, expanded from a total of 8,000 miles to 20,000—exactly one-tenth of the mileage in the United States; cereal exports rose from 1.0 million tons to 5.29 million tons, while frozen meat exports grew from 0.027 million tons to 0.376 million tons (Furtado 1970, 51–53).

The astounding scale and the extremely swift pace of this economic development, paired with the rapid increase in population in metropolitan areas, triggered a series of radical social and political changes. Middle and working classes slowly started to take part in the electoral process, while Latin American presidential democracies began to decentralize (Negretto and Aguilar-Rivera 2000). But unlike in Europe or the United States, where the Reformation had triggered an increase in literacy levels, leading in turn to the development of a public sphere and the subsequent democratic revolutions of the late eighteenth century, in Latin America the independence processes took place before any large-scale increase in literacy levels. Therefore, literacy, key to entering modernity, had to be pursued as a state policy.

In the late 1800s, the highest literacy rates in the region—close to 60 percent—belonged to Argentina and Uruguay. A distant second tier of nations included Chile, Colombia, Trinidad and Tobago, Jamaica, Guyana, and Cuba, with rates averaging 30 to 45 percent, followed by a third echelon that included Brazil and Mexico, with rates between 14 and 30 percent (Núñez 2005, 127).

While these percentages were low compared to those of Europe and the United States, with literacy averages reaching 80 percent, Latin American levels had grown so fast that in some cases the reading public had tripled, quadrupled, and even multiplied tenfold in only a few decades (G. Rama 1978, 111; Núñez 2005). Countries such as Argentina and Uruguay had made literacy mandatory by law, and although primary school dropout rates were usually high—between 90 and 97 percent in the first two years of instruction—the new reading public grew stronger by the day, increasing the demand for literature, journalism, and other forms of entertainment for the educated (Rotker 1999).

Consequently, a publishing boom, especially in journalism, accompanied the expansion of the reading public. In 1877, Argentina had 2,347,000 inhabitants and 148 newspapers—one newspaper for every 15,700 people—becoming the number-four country in the world for its newspaper-habitant ratio. It would advance to third place in 1882. The United States, with a substantially longer print tradition, had barely double that ratio (Rotker 1992b, 29; 2000, 38).

The print tradition consolidated at the pace of democracy, while Latin America's integration into world commerce increased. A national self-awareness, anchored in the expansion of the public sphere, the press, and the development of national literatures, stimulated an interest in European and North American events. Thus, foreign correspondents like Martí soon became essential. The confluence of two major historical processes in Latin America—literacy development and state formation—found Martí in a singular position, affording him the platform to sway public opinion and to influence the region's foreign policy. Up until then, few—if any—journalists had ever reached this level of power on a global scale.

THE REPORTER AND THE FOREIGN CORRESPONDENT

Martí was not strictly a reporter but rather a foreign correspondent; in fact, he was the first Latin American to play that role (Rotker 1992b, 107). Contrary to the trend of journalist-witness that had started in American journalism during the Civil War, Martí was rarely a direct witness of the events he wrote about (A. González 1993, 91; Tucher 2006, 145). With a few notable exceptions, his chronicles from New York were summaries of weekly events gathered from local newspapers, magazines, and other news sources. Content, in fact, was not nearly as important to Martí as the meaning and the potential impact that a story could have for the development of a politically aware audience. In more than one way, Martí was using the news.

It is therefore relevant to note that, as Kessel Schwartz (1973, 335) has documented following Martí's coverage of the assassination of Pres. James Garfield, in his compositions "Martí relied heavily on and rephrased, paraphrased, and plagiarized from his favorite newspaper, the *New York Herald*."

A paragraph from the *Herald* coverage of Garfield's assassination quoted by Schwartz stands out as proof of this mechanism. By an unknown *Herald* writer, it reads,

> No verdict of yours can recall him. He sleeps the sleep that knows no waking on the banks of Lake Erie whose limpid waters wash the boundaries of his native state, overlooking the city he loved so well, and beneath the sod of that State whose people had crowned his life with the highest honors. It is too late to call that husband back to the bereaved wife and fatherless children. For that waiting little mother whose face will never fade from the nation's memory there will be no relief in this world. The fatal deed is done, and its horrors and griefs must remain. (Schwartz 1973, 337)

Without attribution, Martí translated the above for his article in *La Nación* as follows:

> Ningún veredicto vuestro, decía a los jurados, puede ya llamarlo: duerme el ilustre Garfield el sueño que no conoce despertar, sobre la pacífica ribera del lago Erie, cuyas límpidas aguas bañan los límites de su nativo Estado; duerme en aquella ciudad que él amó tanto, y bajo el suelo del Estado aquel que coronó su vida con os más altos honores. Es demasiado tarde para volver aquel esposo a la doliente esposa, a los desheredados hijos: que en cuanto aquella vigilante madrecita, cuyo rostro no se borrará jamás de la memoria de la Nación, no hay ya en la tierra alivio para ella. Cierto es el fatal caso, y vivos quedan para siempre sus horrores y penas. (Schwartz 1973, 337)

In other cases, also without attribution, the Cuban used the New York newspaper as factual reference, or as direct inspiration for style and structure, adding to his translations a touch of invention, metaphorical intensification, narrative condensation, and drama. Martí often bolstered the narrative and evocative impact of his stories by avoiding long digressions, dialogue fragments, or even descriptions (Schwartz 1973, 340). He also amplified and embellished the source material. An example of this is his article about the 1886 Charleston earthquake, which relies on *The Sun*, the *New York Times*, the *Baltimore Sun*, and *The Tribune* coverage of September 2, 3, and 4, 1886, but adds Martí's moral imprint to the report: "The fifty thousand inhabitants of Charleston, caught by surprise in the early hours of the night by the earthquake that shook their homes like straw nests, are still living in the streets and plazas, on coaches, under tents, under shacks made of their own clothes. Eight million pesos rolled into dust in twenty-five seconds. Sixty have died: some crushed by falling walls, others of horror. And in the same dreadful hour, many children were brought to life" (Martí 1991, 11:66; my translation).

Although he was never present in Charleston to experience the temblor or its aftermath, Martí offered no indication of that in his article. The piece also contained extraordinary images such as "statues [that] have descended from their pedestals" or "men [flapping] about like half-winged birds" that are nowhere to be found in the originals (Martí 1991, 11:67–70; my translation). These amplifications enhanced the story both visually and rhythmically, also providing a narrative frame: life and death, capital and gain are negligible forces compared to the power of nature. They offer an evocative-mythical tint that was not present in the original reportage (Rotker 2000, 99).

To many purists, Martí's direct translations have become a sore point. In this context, however, the use of embellishment, enhancement, condensation, and appropriation prove essential for an author who seemed to have cared less about the literary luster and referential content of his journalism and more about its social and political impact. Similar to Sarmiento's relationship with factuality, Martí's value of authenticity was neither precious nor rigid, and he seemed to subordinate it to his need for effectiveness and efficiency of message.

POLITICS AND THE PRESS

At the time of the 1889 Pan-American Conference, Martí had already organized revolutionary groups in exile and had lectured and fundraised for Cuban revolutionaries during the Little War (an insurgent movement that, between 1879 and 1880, was led in Cuba by Gen. Calixto García). He had also published magazines and plays and created a newspaper, *Patria*, which was edited by an expatriate Puerto Rican, Sotero Figueroa, at New York's Imprenta América and would become the organ of the Cuban Revolutionary Party (Kanellos 2005, 689). Martí's journalistic career, however, had started much earlier in his life—a life seemingly destined, from very early on, to inspire a form of political-journalistic writing that could be read in many ways as a defense of the supranational integration of Latin America.

Born in Cuba in 1853 of Spanish parents, Martí became an early advocate of Cuban independence. By 1870, accused of "anti-Spanish activities," he was sentenced to six years of hard labor, a punishment that, due to his poor health, was ultimately commuted to exile.[5] Thus, at under seventeen years of age, Martí was sent to Spain, where he enrolled in college and earned a law degree, a degree in letters, and another in philosophy. In those formative times, he also became an active contributor to political newspapers and magazines and started to see journalism as a way to advance the revolutionary movement in Cuba. During his exile he also traveled to France, the Netherlands, and Italy, only to return to America in 1875 eager to start working for the Cuban revolutionary movement. His comeback was, in fact, something of an odyssey, with a journey that included two visits to Mexico, a professorial position in Guatemala, two stays in Cuba under a false identity, a second trip to Spain, a professorial position in Venezuela, and two stays in the United States, the second one between 1881 and 1895, the year of his death.

Martí saw journalism as a means to promote the ideals of the modern revolutions in Latin America. Trained in classical Greek, Roman literature, and philosophy, he was also an avid multilingual reader. In Europe he was exposed to the French Enlightenment in the works of Voltaire, Montesquieu, Rousseau, and Montaigne. He became familiar with John Locke's contractualism and European romanticism through Mary Shelley, Victor Hugo, Thomas Carlyle, and Oscar Wilde. He read Ralph Waldo Emerson, Walt Whitman, Henry James, and other notable American writers of his generation, and he devoured some of the finest contemporary literature available in French and Spanish. Before it was translated, Martí reviewed in Spanish Gustave Flaubert's last, incomplete novel, *Bouvard et Pécuchet*.[6] And, despite some controversy around this issue, he was most likely familiar with Karl Marx and Mikhail Bakunin.[7]

Back from Europe, Martí soon discovered Latin American authors such as Diego Barros Arana, whose *Historia de la Guerra del Pacífico* he came across while working as a teacher in Venezuela (Ward 2007, 108). Well versed in Latin American history and political theory, he had also read Sarmiento, who became a model for his own journalism. Unlike Sarmiento, however, Martí advocated against the "whitening" of Latin America through the eradication of native cultures and the intensification of European immigration. In "Our America," for instance, the Cuban would stand against Latin America's acculturation, insisting on the incorporation of subaltern subjects into the discussion on national identity, the study of native languages and cultures in universities, and the inclusion of their political and philosophical ideas as active elements in the development of the state bureaucracy (Gomariz 2007, 187–90).

Martí wrote his first journalistic articles as a teenager. In 1869 he published an editorial piece in *El Diablo Cojuelo* (The lame devil), a newspaper created by Fermín Valdez Domínguez in support of Cuban independence during the Ten Years' War. In the course of his Spanish exile, he contributed to *Revista Universal* under the pen name Orestes. But his journalistic activities really took off after 1874, when he earned a baccalaureate in letters and philosophy at the University of Zaragoza and became a civil and canon lawyer. The constant travels back to Cuba and around the Americas after that year would have a lifelong impact on his journalism. As Mariano Siskind (2014, 103–83) points out, Martí was the first *modernista* to articulate the idea of a world literature within which Latin America's own literature, with its unique identity, would be integrated.

Professionally, however, Martí began to be able to live on his journalism only in 1881, during a short stay in Venezuela. After participating in the founding of the *Revista Venezolana* (Venezuelan review), whose democratic tone raised the wrath of that country's dictator, Antonio Guzmán Blanco, Martí became a correspondent for *La Pluma* (The quill) of Bogotá, Colombia. Having attracted the attention of the industrialist Fausto Teodoro de Aldrey, he also started contributing to *La Opinión Nacional de Caracas*, a large and prestigious Venezuelan daily belonging to the tycoon.

La Opinión was an extremely influential publication in the Americas. Progressive in tone, interested in modernization, science, education, and international politics, it reproduced articles from *The Times* of London, *The Hour* in New York, and the *Paris Herald*. It also included literary translations and articles about prominent cultural figures in France, the United States, Germany, and Spain. Susana Rotker points out that the author whose works most often appeared in translation in the newspaper was Victor Hugo, followed by Goethe (Rotker 2000, 34–35). *La Opinión* was also regularly distributed in Paris, London, and New York. But in order for his newspaper to survive in Venezuela, Aldrey had to play a balancing act with Guzmán Blanco. As a form of concession, the tycoon published the dictator's editorials in *La Opinión* and also appeased his bouts of rage by giving him constant praise, calling him "the illustrious," "the civilizer," "the creator of the glorious septennial," and the hero of "forty years of combat between radical democratic ideas and conservative oligarchic principles, both pernicious extremes." Martí disagreed with all these epithets, something Guzmán Blanco was aware of. Thus Aldrey asked the Cuban to sign his articles with a pseudonym, "M. de Z."

Until the summer of 1882 Martí contributed to *La Opinión*. He even had his own section, "Sección Constante" (Constant section), where he wrote about diverse topics in different genres, always with striking literary flair. The "Sección Constante" pieces used a mix of styles. In them, Martí polished his approach and started to push the boundaries of factuality. An example of this is a fragment of an article about a series of scientific experiments with flies: "It is well known that the microphone is an instrument that allows one to hear, with perfect clarity, sounds so weak that their existence could be rightfully denied. Thanks to the microphone, an English chemist has come to demonstrate that those miserable flies, for which we have no compassion and which so often perish at the hands of children, suffer as vividly as the most sensitive of mortals, and express their pain in prolonged and anguished moans, which the microphone distinctly transmits to the ear, and which sound like the neighing of a horse" (Martí 1991, 9:214; my translation).

The meticulous use of description had the effect of projecting Martí's pieces into a different category of writing, one much more sophisticated and experimental than the type of news coverage that was the norm at the time. The effect of juxtaposing layers of comparison and colorful similes with what was strictly news content expanded Martí's production into a different, unexplored territory, intermediate between the journalistic and the literary, at a time when the boundaries between fact and fiction writing were still blurred (Rotker 2000, 36).

Another example of Martí's writing for *La Opinión* was "El rostro rehecho" (The remade face), a piece about one of the first plastic surgeries ever performed. Martí did not attribute the information to any sources, but the emphasis on style and description overrides its informative side:

> They made an incision in the index finger of her right hand that went from the first joint to the thumb; they put the right hand on the left arm, and after sewing the piece of skin on the incision in the finger with silver wire, they attached the arm and the hand with strong bandages. After a week, the piece of skin had grown on to the hand, although it was fed mostly by the arm. To change the flow of nutrition, they gradually cut the skin from the arm, and when it was about to separate, the skin was receiving its nutrients from the finger, and not from the arm from which it had been taken. This separated it definitively from the arm. The hand, with the piece of hanging skin it was supporting, was taken to the patient's face. They lifted the scarred skin that covered her right cheek and injected the skin under it. With new bandages, they left the hand attached to the cheek. . . . Today she walks around, lovely. (qtd. in Rotker 2000, 35–36)

Martí's contributions to *La Opinión* lasted about a year. The political tension between him and Guzmán Blanco, exacerbated by the Cuban's friendship with government critic Cecilio Acosta, ended up forcing him to leave the country to avoid the dictator's rage.

On July 27, 1881, before sailing to New York from the port of La Guaira, Martí wrote a farewell letter to Aldrey in which he explained with sadness the suddenness of his decision: "In such haste have I decided upon this trip that I do not have time, before going, to shake the friendly hands this city has extended to me" (qtd. in Mañach 1950, 206).

Aldrey, however, did not intend to lose through distance the value of Martí's contributions, and he asked the Cuban to continue corresponding with *La Opinión* from New York. But the agreement lasted only until the summer of 1882, when Aldrey revealed to his readers that "M. de Z." was in fact José Martí (Mañach 1950, 215–16; Rotker 2000, 35). It has been suggested that, after revealing M. de Z.'s identity, Aldrey was forced by Guzmán Blanco to stop publishing Martí's pieces. Instead of explaining this to Martí, the editor tried to introduce a series of changes to the "Sección Constante," probably aware that the Cuban would be unlikely to accept them. In order to continue his arrangement with Aldrey's newspaper, Martí would be required to change his topics ("readers in this country want political news and anecdotes and the least literature possible") and his style ("shorter paragraphs"), and he would finally have to come to terms with the fact that the "Sección Constante," if continued, would become less prominent in the newspaper.[8] Martí rightfully interpreted these changes as a veiled dismissal, and he stopped contributing to the daily altogether (Mañach 1950, 215–16). Years later, in a letter he sent to his friend Gonzalo de Quesada, the Cuban revealed that he had abandoned *La Opinión Nacional* "because the condition for writing in it was to praise in its pages the abominations of Guzmán Blanco" (qtd. in Scarano 2003, 21).

Nevertheless, it was thanks to his contributions to the Venezuelan daily that Martí's fame spread like a wildfire across the Americas. He was continually invited to collaborate with new publications and soon blipped on the radar of New York publisher Charles Anderson Dana. Martí met Dana—who was known as a friend of Cuban revolutionaries—through a shared acquaintance, artist Guillermo Collazo, and the publisher immediately realized that Martí would be an excellent addition to his staff. Dana invited Martí to contribute to *The Hour* and not long after that to his famous newspaper *The Sun*. Soon the two men developed a cordial friendship. Years later, after learning that Martí had been killed by Spanish bullets in Dos Ríos, Dana wrote a tribute to the Cuban in the obituary section of *The Sun*. On May 23, 1895, the piece read as follows:

> We learn with poignant sorrow of the death in battle of José Martí, the well-known leader of the Cuban revolutionista. We knew him long and well and esteemed him profoundly. For a protracted period, beginning twenty-odd years ago, he was employed as a contributor to the *Sun*, writing on subjects and

questions of the fine arts. In these things his learning was solid and extensive, and his ideas and conclusions were original and brilliant. He was a man of genius, of imagination, of hope and of courage, one of those descendants of the Spanish race whose American birth and instincts seem to have added to the revolutionary tincture which all modern Spaniards inherit. His heart was warm and affectionate, his opinions ardent and aspiring, and he died as such a man would wish to die, battling for liberty and democracy. Of such heroes there are not too many in the world, and his warlike grave testifies that even in a positive and material age there are spirits that can give all for their principles without thinking of any selfish return for themselves.

"Honor to the memory of José Martí, and peace to his manly and generous soul!" (Wilson 1907, 498–99)

It was *The Hour,* however, a literary magazine dedicated to "social interests" and to "making New York resemble Victorian London as much as possible," that published Martí's first three features in English (Mañach 1950, 183). Under the title "Impressions of America (by a very fresh Spaniard)," the Cuban took a foreigner's view of New York and showed his admiration but also some of his growing apprehensions about certain aspects of American culture. Martí openly praised the city's work ethic and the freedom people enjoyed in New York to go about their own business. "I am, at last, in a country where everyone looks like his own master," he wrote in his first article for the magazine. His critical observations focused on materialism, racism, the apolitical nature of American citizens, and a marked tendency in the United States toward some forms of plutocracy. "The United States was really the hope of the world, but did it possess all the spiritual factors necessary to serve as a solid home for truth, liberty and human dignity?" he asked (qtd. in Mañach 1950, 188).[9]

In his formative years, Martí's condition of perpetual exile exposed him to diverse societies, norms, and ideas and gave him the perspective to compare them astutely. Writing in, about, and from different countries contributed to the development of Martí's character and his writing style and forged the tenacity that prepared him to confront the biggest political power of all, as well as speak to it. In a sense, Martí is the physical incarnation of modernismo: cosmopolitanism was Martí's training ground, the place from which, as Mariano Siskind (2014) proposes, he could initiate the symbolic exchange between Latin America and the Western world. But unlike other modernistas at the turn of the century, for whom cosmopolitanism was a luxury born of privilege, Martí's was a necessary condition. His journalism and his writing forced him into exile. And in New York, the metropolis of his time,

Martí experienced firsthand the erasure of the subaltern—a secondary exile, one imposed on him by language and origin.

While most of the modernistas who followed him considered themselves white and Western, Martí would not; like his skin and his origin, his language would not pretend to be anything but that of the *other*. It is in this particular way that Martí follows Sarmiento—putting himself out of reach of (Spain's) totalitarianism, while using literature and journalism to find a place on the inside. Martí stays at the margins of modernity. At the same time, he is writing for Cuba and its right to be a nation, and for Latin America to coalesce as a powerful entity. He advocates for the equality of the races through the equalizing possibilities of journalism, using an array of genres considered minor at the time, with short-form narrative, in particular, at the core of his production. Closer to the postmodernity of Borges than to modernistas such as Enrique Gómez Carrillo or Manuel Gutiérrez, Martí's work articulates a connection between the inside and the outside.

Collaborating with *The Sun* and *The Hour*, Martí saw his popularity grow at an astounding pace. And, while his letters to *La Opinión* were being put into book form in the summer of 1882, the Cuban received a momentous invitation to contribute to the largest, most prestigious, and most modern newspaper in Latin America: *La Nación*, of Argentina. From that Buenos Aires daily, Martí would cast his fiercest attacks against his most dreaded and powerful political enemy: the Republican secretary of state of the United States, James Gillespie Blaine.

MARTÍ AND BLAINE

Martí had started to form his opinion about Blaine soon after moving to New York. Covering the presidential campaign of 1884, which Blaine lost to the Democratic candidate, Grover Cleveland, the Cuban scrutinized in his articles every move and declaration of the Pennsylvania-born politician. The critic Bill Karras has noted that no other names, apart from God, were more frequently mentioned by Martí in his work than those of Blaine and Pres. Grover Cleveland. And although he never dedicated an entire profile to either of them, as he had done with Buffalo Bill, Jesse James, and some twenty-five other American personalities, he certainly wrote a great many paragraphs about them in his chronicles.[10]

Martí professed a special admiration for Cleveland. He praised his "ingenuity and audacity [and his being] of the people." He would also say that, "[though] young, he's one of those first Americans with an iron hand and eagle eye, who hasn't taken his boots off yet" (qtd. in Karras 1974, 79). And, at least until 1883, his esteem for Blaine had been equally high. In several earlier essays, Martí had applauded Blaine's "healthy politics" and his "friendship with Southern America" (Ward 2007, 106). But after 1883, he started to focus on the more questionable aspects of Blaine's history and character: "[Blaine] did not think it shameful to use force when one had it [and] thought that now was the time to nail the world, as far as the arm could reach, to the growing edifice of what was once called the home of liberty" (qtd. in Karras 1974, 79). By 1884, Blaine already represented for Martí the most negative aspects of American culture, politics, and foreign policy.

The Cuban understood that, aimed in the wrong direction, the tremendous military and economic power of the United States could lead to the subjugation of the whole hemisphere under the false pretense of freedom and capitalism. Therefore, he started to portray the Republican presidential candidate as a dangerous enemy of Latin American independence: "If [Blaine] had his country in his hands, [he] would give it a navy for spurs, an army for a horse, and with a slap send it to conquer the world. [It would be a day of mourning for *our* America], whose knees are still weak, [. . .] if this sharp, rash and unleashed man seized the presidency of the United States" (qtd. in Karras 1974, 82).

Blaine lost the presidential race to Cleveland in 1884, but by the time the Pan-American Conference began in 1889, Benjamin Harrison, a Republican, had succeeded Cleveland, the anti-imperialist Democrat from New Jersey. To Martí's deep dismay, Blaine easily ascended to the position of secretary of state and was suspected by many to be the power in the shadows of Harrison's administration. The president himself had given Blaine free rein to plan the first hemispheric encounter at full force.

In fact, Harrison had been Blaine's mentee for almost ten years, and during the 1884 campaign the future president ranked Blaine as a statesman comparable in ability to Europe's most sagacious diplomats. Much later, in a letter offering the post of secretary of state to Blaine, Harrison explained his choice: "We have already a pretty full understanding of each other's views as to the general policy which should characterize our foreign relations. I am especially interested in the improvement of our relations with the Central and South American states." Blaine responded in the same cozy tone: "I am glad to find myself in the heartiest accord with the principles and policies which you briefly outline for your administration, and I am especially pleased with what you say in regard to Foreign Affairs" (qtd. in Crapol 2000, 112).

Blaine's intention to control the Pan-American Conference became clear after he was named its president despite not being one of the ten official US delegates to the meeting. The conference presidency offered him enough leverage to promote his economic and political agenda. And he would have largely succeeded had it not been for Martí, who, with his poignant articles for *La Nación* and a series of speeches, editorials, and diplomatic maneuvers, effectively counterbalanced Blaine's influence over the Latin American envoys.

· · ·

In those days of 1889 Martí was corresponding with a long list of newspapers in Latin America and the United States. He lived with Carmen, the mother of his only son, in a rented, newly built luxury cottage in Brooklyn. In addition to his pay from *La Nación*, he received income for translations of French and English manuals he prepared for Appleton's Latin America handbooks. His friend Enrique Estrázulas, the Uruguayan consul to whom Martí had dedicated his poetry book *Ismaelillo* in 1882, had finally succeeded in having the Cuban appointed as Uruguay's vice-consul, and the writer's economic situation in New York seemed finally to be stabilizing.

Martí worked on the fourth floor of 120 Front Street, just below Wall Street, in a somber old brick building with iron steps and shallow halls facing the waterfront. His office, although small, was filled with light. It was furnished modestly: a desk always crowded with papers, as well as a writing chair, a gift from the Argentine delegation to the Pan-American Conference, which had also presented the writer with a fur skin to warm his feet during New York's winters. Against the walls, a few bookshelves of white pine, some of which Martí had crafted himself, held the Cuban's favorite volumes of Latin American literature, the magazines and literary reviews he published and edited in New York, and a large collection of his favorite American fiction. A portrait of his father, Mariano, and a few portraits that still generate controversy today hung from the walls: one of Victor Hugo, one of Karl Marx, one of Charles Darwin, and one of Simón Bolívar (Kirk 1980, 139; Mañach 1950, 248; Aparicio 1969). Also on the wall hung the only adornment that Martí had brought from Cuba: an iron ring, a gift from his mother made of the chain the writer had worn in prison in his teens. The ring represented "a magic talisman in his pilgrimage for his country's liberty" (Karras 1974, 88).

The office was well known to Hispanic Americans in the city. There, the Cuban would take care of diplomatic affairs and sometimes meet independentist leaders to plot upheavals and plan the next revolution in Cuba. In the evenings Martí used his commute on the ferry to read his favorite newspapers, especially the *Herald*, and to write his "literature under pressure" (Rotker 2000, 43). His schedule required him to "leave home on cold, early mornings and to return wrapped in the dark of night," rarely giving him enough time to sit down and write in the office or at home (Mañach 1950, 219).

In New York, Latin Americans of all origins knew that the doors at 120 Front Street were always open to them. And on one fall morning in 1889, a compact group of envoys to the Pan-American Conference visited Martí to ask for advice. After a warm welcome and a brief discussion about Henry James's most recent novel, Martí admonished the envoys to follow in detail "the opinions on the Conference of the [New York] *Tribune, El Avisador* [Hispanoamericano], the [New York] *Post*, the [New York] *Herald*, and the [New York] *Times*," to see and feel for themselves the state of American public opinion and to understand to what extent freedom in their countries was dependent on their performance at the momentous meeting (Mañach 1950, 248; Karras 1974, 89).

MARTÍ SEIZING THE OPPORTUNITY OF *LA NACIÓN*

Martí was first contacted by *La Nación* in 1882 through Carlos Carranza. The Argentine general consul in New York, who was one of the many devoted followers and friends of Martí in the city, tried to persuade him to publish in South America after he stopped his contributions to *La Opinión*. Carranza kept in close contact with the former Argentine president, writer, and journalist Domingo Sarmiento and also the historian and journalist Bartolomé Mitre, so it did not take him long to acquaint Martí with these two brilliant Argentine public figures. Mitre and his son, the journalist Bartolomé Nicolás Mitre y Vedia, had founded *La Nación* of Buenos Aires in 1870, and by 1882 the broadsheet was already considered by far the most serious, prestigious, and modern newspaper in Latin America. The region, undergoing a tremendous economic and social expansion, was ravenous for information and culture from all over the world. Up to the challenge, the daily soon became one of the main modernizing forces in Argentina and the subcontinent, delivering in its articles up-to-date snippets of European and American literature, politics, culture, sciences, arts, and ideas. This timely convergence of *La Nación's* innovative approach and Martí's charismatic persona would have a transformative impact on the future of Latin America.

By 1882 *La Nación* had also become the mouthpiece for Argentina's liberal political party. It ran a telegraph machine in its newsroom and so was able to incorporate cable dispatches into its articles. It also had at least five foreign correspondents on staff: John Roe in Africa, Brocha Gorda writing about the War of the Pacific (the war that, between 1879 and 1883, pitted Chile against Bolivia and Peru), Ernesto García Ladevese in France, Aníbal Latino in Italy, G.Z. in England, and collaborators in Chile and Uruguay. The breadth of its international coverage turned the newspaper into one of the most lucrative in the region, selling an average of thirty-five thousand copies a day between 1887 and 1890 (Rotker 2000, 33; Quesada 1883).

Between 1880 and 1895, *La Nación*'s layout remained essentially the same. Everything on page one had an identical design. Except for the editorial, which appeared in the first column on the left, news, essays, and even short stories were, from a design point of view, undifferentiated. Sometimes informative pieces were preceded by a brief summary, but even when illustrations started to be included in the newspaper—photography was still unexplored in Latin American dailies—they generally appeared in the advertising and the commercial sections. At the bottom of the front page, separated from the rest of the text, there was the regular segment of a serial novel, normally translated from the English, French, or German, rarely from a Spanish author, and almost never from a Latin American. The design of the news elements remained consistent with the rest of page one, which for the readers facilitated the transition—sometimes confusion—between facts, opinion, and even fiction (Rotker 1992b, 86–87).

This lack of differentiation between genres and styles was critical in the development of some early modern forms of Latin American nonfiction like the *crónica* (chronicle), a type of brief article meant to be both entertaining *and* informative—and more often than not, extremely political (A. González 1993, 83–100; Rotker 2000). A very clear example of the dual nature of this genre appears in the editor's introduction to a piece written by Martí about the US presidential race of 1888, which presents the factual coverage as if it were purely fictional. The piece is titled "Fantastic Narration": "Martí has wanted to give us a sample of the creative power of his privileged imagination, delivering a fantasy that, due to the inventiveness of its topic and the animated and picturesque scene development, becomes of interest to the reader. [It takes] an always new and original writer [like Martí] to paint a town, in the modern days we are living, with such complete dedication to the ridiculous minutiae of electoral tasks" (qtd. in Rotker 1992b, 87; my translation).

After Carranza introduced Martí to the editors of *La Nación*, it did not take long for them to become interested in him. Mitre and Sarmiento were both seasoned newspaper figures and ideologues and for decades had been fascinated with the scientific, pedagogic, and political developments happening in United States, a nation that represented the triumph of civilization in the Western Hemisphere. When Carranza sent them examples of Martí's journalism, they did not hesitate to add the New York–based Cuban writer to their staff.

Martí received Mitre's letter in July 1882 and was less pleased by the honor itself than by the opportunity that writing for *La Nación* would afford him to further the political cause of Cuban independence in the Americas. In a personal letter to the editor, the Cuban started delineating a plan for his future contributions: "I will send you in my news-letter, which I will make varied, deep and animated, whatever occurrences that, due to their general character or to the particular interest for your country, happened here. The picturesque will lighten up any seriousness, and its literariness will liven up its more political aspects" (qtd. in Vargas 2003, 62; my translation). Right after accepting the invitation, Martí contacted Enrique Trujillo, director of the New York–based Cuban revolutionary newspaper *El Porvenir*, who also saw Martí's hiring as a fantastic opportunity to further the Cuban cause. That very same night, Trujillo invited Martí and revolutionary leader Flor Crombet, a handsome mestizo with French ancestry, to discuss the timing and potential for a new uprising on the island (Mañach 1950, 216).

By September 13, 1882, *La Nación* had already published Martí's first article, on the trial and hanging of Charles J. Guiteau, who had assassinated US president James Garfield. Mitre y Vedia reported to Martí that the piece had been read "in this country and adjacent ones, with marked interest and it deserves to be widely reprinted," and he also expressed satisfaction at having—as he wrote in English—"the right man in the right place" (qtd. in Mañach 1950, 217).[11] However, in the same letter, he gave Martí a few admonitions concerning future articles. In his first piece, the Cuban had displayed some harsh criticism of a few aspects of American culture, but Mitre y Vedia decided to edit those parts out "so as not to create a wrong impression that he was opening a campaign of denunciation of the United States" (Mañach 1950, 217). Mitre father and son had a clearly commercial vision of what *La Nación* was meant to become as a daily. The newspaper, Mitre y Vedia said in his letter, apologizing for "the brutality of the word used for the sake of accuracy," was a "commodity that looks for its proper placement in the market." And in the Argentine market, the United States was then in very great favor (qtd. in Mañach 1950, 217).

Throughout the years, Martí collaborated with many other newspapers and magazines: *El Partido Liberal* of Mexico, *La República* of Honduras, and *El Economista Americano* in New York. In his chronicles, the Latin American perspective was always one of the main features. As he had editorialized in New York's newspaper *La América*, he conceived his articles as a means to "define, advise, alert, and reveal the secrets of the seemingly—and only seemingly—marvelous success of [the United States]" (Martí 2002, 140).

His Latin American fervor was such that even Sarmiento became at times irritated by it: "I wish that Martí would offer us less of Martí, less of the Latino and of the Spanish race, and less of the South American, to give us a little more of the Yankee," he once wrote to his friend Mitre (qtd. in Rotker 2000, 101). Sarmiento, nevertheless, was also well aware of Martí's talent. In a letter to Paul Groussac, then director of the Biblioteca National (the national library of Argentina), Sarmiento urged the Frenchman to translate into French an article Martí had written on the Statue of Liberty since "[in] Spanish there is nothing else like the clarion calls of Martí, and in France herself, there has been nothing like this tocsin-tone of resonance since Victor Hugo" (qtd. in Mañach 1950, 217).

MARTÍ'S WARNINGS ABOUT EMPIRE IN "ESCENAS NORTEAMERICANAS"

Back in New York after his forced departure from Venezuela in 1881, it became clear to Martí—as well as to some members of the press in the United States—that James Blaine's policies posed a threat to Latin America, especially to Cuba. The agenda of the new secretary of state was tinted with belligerence and assertiveness, two attitudes that in the press gained him the nickname "Jingo Jim" (Crapol 2000, 82–83). After a decade of opposing the acquisition of Cuba, Blaine now favored it, and in his closing testimony to the Congressional Investigative Committee, and later in a defense of his Latin American program published in September 1882, the statesman declared he was still convinced that the United States should maintain its trade dominance in the hemisphere and prevent European nations from taking advantage of a weak American diplomatic position: "If the commercial empire that legitimately belongs to us is to be ours, we must not lie idle and witness its transfer to others" (qtd. Crapol 2000, 83).

Throughout 1881, until his resignation after Garfield's assassination in September, Blaine spoke and wrote numerous times about the dangers that Cuba would pose to the United States in the event that, released from Spain, it fell to German hands.

On December 1, only eighteen days before leaving office, Blaine presented his concerns in a letter to the Senate: "That rich island, the key to the Gulf of Mexico, and the field for our most extended trade in the Western Hemisphere, is, though in the hands of Spain, a part of the American commercial system. . . . If ever ceasing to be Spanish, Cuba must necessarily become American and not fall under any other European domination" (qtd. in Crapol 2000, 83).

Although Garfield's assassination prevented Blaine from pursuing this agenda, his ideas on foreign policy became even more radical in the years that followed. On several occasions between 1884—during the presidential campaign—and 1890, the *New York Times* reported on Blaine's intentions to purchase Cuba for the sum of $500 million. The newspaper also addressed the candidate's concern that Cuba's foreign debt, mostly in German hands, could easily translate into a German appropriation of the island, creating an extremely uncomfortable geopolitical conundrum for the United States if it still wanted to project its political and economic influence over the Americas.[12]

By 1882, Martí felt that he had finally understood Blaine and the agenda behind his diplomatic maneuvers. In his columns and chronicles, but also from his position as a diplomatic envoy for Uruguay since 1887, he did as much as he could to prevent the realization of Blaine's annexationist plans and his ascent to the highest office via the election in 1884. Martí believed that, particularly after the presidency of Grover Cleveland, the United States could not accept as their leader a man like Blaine, such a "rapacious egoist, majestic [and] bold as an eagle" (qtd. in Karras 1974, 77). At first, the Cuban believed that there was a disconnect between Blaine's predatory intentions and the American people at large. But in 1889 he changed his mind. On March 16, the *Philadelphia Manufacturer* published a critical article titled "Do We Want Cuba?," which was later reprinted by the *Evening Post* in New York. The piece stated that

> the people of Cuba are divided into three classes, Spaniards, native Cubans of Spanish descent and negroes. The men of Spanish birth are probably less fitted than men of any other white race to become American citizens. They have ruled Cuba for centuries. They rule it now upon almost precisely the same methods that they have always employed, methods which combine bigotry with tyranny, and silly pride with fathomless corruption. The less we have of them the better. The native Cubans are not much more desirable: to the faults of the men of the parent race they add effeminacy and a distaste for exertion which amounts really to disease. They are helpless, idle, of defective morals and unfitted by nature and experience to discharging the obligations of citizenship in a great and free republic. Their lack of manly force and self-respect is demonstrated by the supineness with which they have so long submitted to the Spanish oppression, and even their attempts at rebellion have been so pitifully ineffective that they have risen little above the dignity of fare. To clothe such men with the responsibilities of directing this government, and to give them the same measure of power that is wielded by the freemen of our Northern States, would be to summon them to the performance of functions for which they have not the smallest capacity [added to this section copied literally from the *Philadelphia Manufacturer* is a second part penned by a writer of the *Post*]. All of this

we emphatically endorse, and it may be added that if we have now a Southern question which disturbs us more or less, we should have it in a more aggravated form if Cuba were added to the Union, with near a million blacks, much inferior to our own in point of civilization, who must, of course, be armed with the ballot and put on the same level politically with their former masters. [The only hope] we could have of opening Cuba to the dignity of becoming a State, would be to Americanize it in full, covering it with people of our own race. (qtd. in Martí 2002, 261–62; Kirk 1977, 284; my translation)[13]

Martí, furious, wrote a six-page rebuttal, "Vindication of Cuba," showing an immutable disillusionment with the American press, its politics, and its public opinion. The *Evening Post* published the letter in full:

This is not the occasion to discuss the question of the annexation of Cuba. It is probable that no self-respecting Cuban would like to see his country annexed to a nation where the leaders of opinion share towards him the prejudices excusable only to vulgar jingoism or rampant ignorance. [. . .] There are some Cubans who, from honorable motives, from an ardent admiration for progress and liberty, from a prescience of their own powers under better political conditions, from an unhappy ignorance of the history and tendency of annexation, would like to see the island annexed to the United States. But those who have fought in war and learned in exile, who have built, by the work of hands and mind, a virtuous home in the heart of an unfriendly community; who by their successful efforts as scientists and merchants, as railroad builders and engineers, as teachers, artists, lawyers, journalists, orators and poets, as men of alert intelligence and uncommon activity, are honored wherever their powers have been called into action and the people are just enough to understand them; those who have raised, with their less prepared elements, a town of workingmen where the United States had previously a few huts in a barren cliff; those more numerous than the others, do not desire the annexation of Cuba to the United States. They do not need it. They admire this nation, the greatest ever built by liberty; but they dislike the evil conditions that, like worms in the heart, have begun in this mighty Republic their work of destruction. They have made of the heroes of this country their own heroes [. . .] but they can't honestly believe that excessive individualism, the glorification of wealth, and the protracted exultation of a terrible victory, are preparing the United States to be the typical nation of liberty, where no opinion is to be based in greed, and no triumph or acquisition reached against charity or justice. We love the country of Lincoln, as much as we fear the motherland of Cutting. (Martí 2002, 263–64; Kirk 1977, 284–85; my translation)[14]

MODERNISMO, MARTÍ, AND A RADICAL RENOVATION OF THE SPANISH LANGUAGE

In December 1889, *La Nación* began to publish Martí's coverage of the Pan-American summit under the Cuban's usual header, "Escenas norteamericanas, cartas desde Nueva York" (North American scenes, letters from New York). The "Escenas," which ultimately amounted to more than four hundred chronicles that Martí submitted to different newspapers in the hemisphere but with particular frequency and quality to Argentina's *La Nación* between 1881 and 1890, were usually front-page features about life, culture, and politics in the United States. They reflected the political-journalistic tradition inaugurated by Domingo Sarmiento in Chile. In full, the chronicles constitute more than half of Martí's seventy-four volumes of published work and are central to understanding not only his political ideas but also one of the most dramatic changes in the Castilian language to take place since the times of Miguel de Cervantes (Rotker 1992b, 13–25; Gray 1963). They also contain examples of Martí's most powerful creative weapon: his ability to integrate genres, devices, formats, and points of view into a cohesive whole, at once unique to Martí and universal in scope.

The deeply political nature of Martí's chronicles and their undeniable urgency did not prevent them from becoming the most poetic and progressive forms of literature to be written in Spanish in centuries. And although Martí's writings do not show a delineation between aesthetic and political concerns or a clear divide between fact, fiction, and opinion, it would be virtually impossible to pigeonhole the Cuban as a literary aesthete, since writing was for him, first and foremost, a form of social service (Anderson Imbert 1953).

However, the poetic nature of Martí's prose, even in those chronicles that were political at their deepest core, was also accompanied by innovation, power, and elegance. In fact, the Cuban himself did not differentiate between his more literary writings and the militant ones. As proven in his testament, a letter sent a few days before his death to his secretary and friend Gonzalo de Quesada, Martí left instructions for his literary estate to be organized and published thematically in chapters that mixed, almost indiscriminately, his purely literary writings with the more political ones (Rodríguez-Luis 1999, xi). Poetry and essay, two genres read mostly by elites, had no more importance for Martí than the journalism preferred by the masses. Ultimately, all of these forms of literature served a higher purpose: the unification of a pan-Hispanic Latin America and Cuban independence. In many ways, the structure that Martí applied to the organization his own literary estate can be read as a testament—literal and figurative—to his will for the integration of a people.

The linguistic renovation that Martí spearheaded in the Castilian language took place in the context of an aesthetic movement called *modernismo*. Historically, modernismo was the literary acknowledgment of modernity, an era of speed, rapid change, and communication. Railroads, steamboats, factories, telegraphs, telephones, daily newspapers, and an array of technological and scientific developments opened what was until then local and communal to international influence. Internationalism, transcontinentalism, and cosmopolitanism, concepts that until then were only possible at an imaginary level, became the new reality. There was a general feeling that nature could be ruled, enhanced, and indefinitely corrected by artificial means, which in turn heightened expectations for a limitless and ever-improving future.

The main expressions of this technological era were the expansions in global communications, travel, and the extraordinary development of metropolitan areas (Rotker 1992b, 30–31; 2000, 1–3). In Latin America, Buenos Aires, Mexico City, and other urban areas grew exponentially. In the fifty years after 1880, "almost every capital city in Latin America doubled or tripled its population" (Romero 1976, 252). By 1890, Mexico City had 400,000 inhabitants, as many as Rome; Buenos Aires had more than 500,000, while New York City had close to 1.5 million, and London, the most important industrial center in western Europe at the time, counted 3.5 million (Romero 1976, 250–59). Cities became communication nodes, reached by waves of international information in the form of books, journals and newspapers, magazines, and new and different forms of journalism.

Due to the growth of metropolitan areas, a new division of intellectual labor became possible. This phenomenon, still in its infancy in Latin America, opened for those interested in intellectual pursuits a window of opportunity to turn away from careers in government and politics and instead become journalists, writers, and educators or a combination thereof (Henríquez Ureña 1949, 164–65). As Susana Rotker (1992b, 64–66) has noted, however, this division of labor did not mean that the new journalists had necessarily abandoned their political pursuits. And Martí, José Enrique Rodó, and Alcides Arguedas, among other *modernistas*, still worked as part-time diplomats or politicians and, in one way or another, stayed connected to politics and government affairs.

Modernistas, though, were not particularly fond of writing for the new urban masses, and the nature of their production was at least somewhat contradictory. On the one hand, many of them, like Rubén Darío, the most representative member of this movement, or Martí himself, produced extremely innovative avant-garde poetry and literature, sometimes only accessible to sophisticated critics and elite connoisseurs. On the other hand, these same authors spread their ideas and programs through the daily press, without concerning themselves with whether they would be understood by the populace. In the words of Darío, "The cries of three hundred geese will not keep you, woodsman, from playing your charming flute, as long as your friend the nightingale is pleased with your melody. When he is no longer there to hear you, close your eyes and play for the inhabitants of your interior kingdom" (qtd. in Rotker 2000, 22).[15]

In a way, many aspects of the modernist renovation became possible after Martí, forefather of the movement, relocated to New York. In the most modern metropolis of its time, the Cuban gained access to ideas, magazines, newspapers, books and fashion, and all the elements of a culture that, sometimes imported from France, sometimes originating locally and exported to Europe, was becoming more and more international. New York shaped Martí's idea of a mass public, and it did not take long for him to understand that in order to benefit from this exciting array of ideas and develop intercontinental refinement, it was necessary to overcome some archaic notions connected to nationalism, one of the ideological cores of romanticism. To become international, Martí believed, Latin American cultures had to first bypass the oppressive political and linguistic influence from Spain: "Knowing different literatures is the best way to get rid of the tyranny of some of them, just as there is no way to save yourself from the risk of blindly obeying one philosophical system if you don't get familiar with all of them," Martí wrote in a piece published by the Cuban newspaper *El Almendares* in January 1882 and reprinted by *La Nación* of Buenos Aires on December 10 of that same year (Martí 1991, 15:361; my translation).

As a literary tradition, modernismo appeared in Latin America in the early 1880s. After Martí, Uruguayan essayist José Enrique Rodó, Guatemalan diplomat and poet Enrique Gómez Carrillo, Colombian poet José Asunción Silva, Cuban poet Julián del Casal, Mexican writer Manuel Gutiérrez Nájera, and Mexican poet Amado Nervo, all of them journalists, continued the linguistic and literary renovation. In their writings, they all resorted to images of technology, urban development, and speed, combining them with *tropoi* anchored in the Spanish tradition of the Golden Age, as well as rhetorical techniques developed by medieval writers such as Santa Teresa de Jesús, Miguel de Cervantes Saavedra, Francisco de Quevedo, Baltasar Gracián, and Diego de Saavedra Fajardo. Characterized by its elegant prose, its openness to Anglicisms and Gallicisms, and a somewhat flamboyant style of versification, incorporating elements of French symbolism, parnassianism, and impressionism, and acknowledging that different forms of internationalization would become a norm for Latin American culture—and for culture in general—this linguistic and cultural revolution reached its maturity in the early twentieth century with the advent of Nicaraguan powerhouse poet Rubén Darío (Gicovate 1964; Schulman 1958; Rama 1983).

But Luis de Góngora's hyperbaton, Pedro Calderón's baroque phrasing, Baltasar Gracián's conceptual and lexical wit, and the abundant use of aphorisms, impersonal constructions, and neologisms were already present in Martí's chronicles. An example of this rhetorical arsenal can be seen in this fragment of an article Martí wrote about the execution of four anarchists held responsible for the Haymarket bombing in Chicago on November 11, 1887:

> Spies's face is a prayer; Fischer's is steadfastness itself; Parsons's radiant pride; Engel ducks his head and makes his deputy laugh with a joke. Each one in turn has his legs bound with a strap. Then hoods are flung over the four heads like candle snuffers putting out four flames: first Spies, then Fischer, then Engel, then Parsons. And while his companions' heads are being covered, Spies's voice rings out in a tone that strikes deep into the flesh of all who hear it: "The time will come when our silence will be more powerful than the voices you are throttling today." "This is the happiest moment of my life," Fischer says, while the deputy is attending to Engel. "Hurray for anarchy!" says Engel, who, beneath the grave-clothes, was moving his bound hands toward the sheriff. "Will I be allowed to speak, O men of America . . ." Parsons begins. A signal, a sound, the trapdoor gives way, the four bodies drop simultaneously, circling and knocking against each other. Parsons has died in the fall; one quick turn, and he stops. Fischer swings, shuddering, tries to work his neck free of the knot, extends his legs, draws them in, and dies. Engel rocks in his floating hangman's robes, his chest rising and falling like the swell of the sea, and strangles. Spies dangles, twisting in a horrible dance like a sackful of grimaces, doubles up and heaves himself to one side, banging his knees against his forehead, lifts one leg, kicks out with both, shakes his arms, beating against the air, and finally expires, his broken neck bent forward, his head saluting the spectators. (Martí 2000, 217–18)[16]

The scenic construction, the rapid succession of images, the interlaced dialogue, and the cinematic cadence in phrasing show Martí's groundbreaking literary techniques being applied to the coverage of current political events, using a completely new style of storytelling. Among the most stunning devices in this piece is the use of metaphor with political intention. In comparing the hoods to candle snuffers, the condemned are semantically linked to the power of light, enlightenment, and—to a degree—modernity, which had made light one of its most durable symbols. The interruption of Parsons's speech by the brutal act of his hanging reinforces the construction and renders the cruelty of the act even more barbaric and retrograde.

Although he was indeed an innovator, Martí was not an uncritical adopter or a purely slavish follower of social and technological changes. A profound admirer of science, technology, and progress, the Cuban was also one of its most vocal critics. In many of his pieces, but particularly in those written after 1884, admonitions and warnings about some by-products of American modernity, such as racism, exploitation, greed, and imperialism, abound.[17] Sometimes in these same pieces Martí even proposed wistful palliatives to the excesses, such as universal education, solidarity, and kindness (Jrade 1999, 3).

Modernismo was not only unique in its form and content. It was also extraordinary in the degree to which, as a movement, it depended on journalism to evolve and spread. Most Latin American modernistas relied on the press to publish their work, make a living, and reach their specific, sometimes minimal audiences. That is partly why many of these authors excelled at writing crónicas.

While criticizing the ephemeral nature of journalism and its impersonal style, which could turn a monarchist into a republican or a freethinker into a Catholic, according to the demands of the newspaper, the Cuban modernist poet Julián del Casal also praised journalism for being "the benefactor that puts money in our pockets, bread on our table and wine in our cup [although] it will never be the tutelary deity that encircles our brow with a crown of laurel leaves" (qtd. in A. González 1993, 86). Newspapers, the region's first mass media, were also the main vehicles for this new Latin American form of journalistic literature.

But although modernistas made use of newspapers, that did not mean they actually liked them. In his essay "Cómo ha de ser un diario" (What a daily newspaper should be like), Uruguayan essayist José Enrique Rodó argued that good newspaper craftsmanship responded in a way to "Herbert Spencer's theory of style," reducing "the secret of good literary form to an economy of attention" (qtd. in A. González 1993, 104). Mexican writer Manuel Gutiérrez Nájera, who also wrote for dailies, usually complained about the "brutal nature" of the telegraph, which had become one of the main tools in the newsroom: "Telegrams have no literature, no grammar or orthography" (qtd. in Rotker 2000, 33). Even Argentine writer Joaquín V. González characterized the daily press as a "monster that devours in one day enormous quantities of ideas [which are then melted and processed by journalists] as if it were a factory, [due to the populace's] scarce need for intelligent concepts." That was why, for González, "journalistic literature rarely rose to the heights of the sublime" (J. González 1936, 344; my translation). In fact, unlike their founding father Martí, modernistas as a rule did not take their journalistic texts too seriously; they gave more attention to their poetry, which they considered a real, innovative, and durable art form. But still, newspapers were for modernistas an effective means of establishing contact with a growing readership, helping connect their literature with the products of an incipient mass culture (Montaldo 2006).

In the late nineteenth century, it also became clear that a schism was developing between journalism and literature. In an editorial published in *La Nación* in 1889, some affirmations such as "journalism and letters seem to go as well together as the devil and holy water" or "a good journalist, on the other hand, cannot afford to let his pen stray in fields of fantasy" show to what extent these spheres had started to split (Rotker 2000, 36).

Early on, writing at the inception of modernismo, Martí too believed in the aesthetic limitations of journalism, and he expressed this eloquently during his stay in Mexico: "The newspaper writer cannot pretend to be sublime. The sublime is the essence of life: the mountain peaks in its summit: the sublime is the mountain's peak. [. . .] He who is not the owner of himself cannot wait the hour [of inspiration] to take advantage of it. The writer in a daily, who can sometimes be sublime, should be content being at least a pleasant writer" (Martí 1991, 21:251; my translation). However, his opinion started to change when he arrived in New York and became exposed to new, vibrant forms of journalism. One newspaper in particular, the *New York Herald*, revived the Cuban's enthusiasm for the narrative possibilities offered by the daily press. "There are no minor facts. [. . .] Every day can be a poem. [. . .] In a good newspaper everything beats and scintillates," he stated in early 1880 (qtd. in Rotker 1992a, 125; my translation). And only a few years later, in 1884, he would conclude, "Reading a good magazine is like reading dozens of good books" (qtd. in Fountain 2003, 15). In his New York years, Martí also became an avid reader of Jacob Riis, the Danish critic who wrote with style and distinction for both the *New York Tribune* and the *Evening Sun* and whose defense of New York's lower classes—a cause dear to Martí— later appeared as a book in *How the Other Half Lives* (Rotker 2000, 63).

Another newspaper that Martí found inspiring was Charles Anderson Dana's *The Sun*, a daily for which he would eventually write. Geared to a working-class audience, primarily immigrants and small merchants, *The Sun* did not compromise on literary quality or style. In fact, Dana's reporters resorted to an array of narrative devices in order to catch the reader's attention, while creating a vivid and accurate picture of daily events. The Cuban soon learned from *The Sun* that his rhetorical toolbox would be put to good use in daily journalism too, because "the facts would be there, but their point was as often to entertain as to inform" (Schudson 1978, 64). But probably one of the most important transformations in Martí's language takes place after his discovery of Walt Whitman, who, while initially an aspiring romantic, found in journalism the elegance and poignancy of facts.

Rotker (1992b, 129) marks the intellectual juncture between Martí's romantic core and ideas, and his modernist production: "Martí was romantic because of his longing for absolutes and his faith in the future, although more moderate: 'his thought falls back on the concrete and everyday; his absolutism widens to embrace the relative, [. . .] and the dreamy optimism is moderated by realistic caution.'"

Not surprisingly, Whitman, whom Martí related to both as a New York dweller and as a journalist, experienced a similar shift from romanticism to modernism. The American father of realism spent twenty-five years of his life as a journalist before publishing his first book of poems. Appointed as leading editor of *The Aurora* on March 28, 1842 (Fishkin 1988, 13), Whitman also wrote the "Walks" section, in which he detailed his wanderings across town for the newspaper. From this section, Shelley Fisher Fishkin argues, Whitman took the "subjects, styles, stances, and strategies" to which he would later return in *Leaves of Grass*:

> One Saturday night, not long since, a fantasy popped into our brain that we would like to take a stroll of observation through a market. Accordingly, sallying forth, we proceeded to put our wishes into execution. A short distance brought us to that large, dirty looking structure in Grand Street, where much store of meats, vegetables, et cetera, is daily dispensed to the sojourners of that section of our city.
>
> We entered. What an array of rich, red sirloins, luscious steaks, delicate and tender joints, muttons, livers, and all the long list of various flesh stuffs, burst upon our eyes! There they hung, tempting, seductive—capable of begetting ecstasies in the mouth of an epicure—or curses in the throat of a Grahamite. By the powers of cookery! The condition of the republic is not so grievous after all; we cannot be on the verge of despair, when such spectacles as these may be witnessed in the land!
>
> How the crowd rolls along! There comes the journeyman mason (we know him by his *limy* dress) and his wife—she bearing a little white basket on her arm. [. . .]

Notice that prim, red cheeked damsel, for whom is being weighed a small pork steak. She is maid of all work to an elderly couple, who have sent her to purvey for their morrow's dinner. How the young fellow who serves her, at the same time casts saucy, lovable glances at her pretty face; and she is nothing loth, but pleased enough at the chance of a little coquetry. (qtd. in Fishkin 1988, 16)

The subjects in this "walk" through the market, Fishkin notes, reappear in Whitman's 1855 *Leaves of Grass* and particularly in "Song of Myself." The wonder of the masses, the multiplicity of colors and shapes, the multitude, the anonymity of urban life—all these are elements that Whitman and Martí, a few years later, will claim in their writing.

On April 19, 1887, Martí published in Mexico's *El Partido Liberal* a piece on a talk Whitman gave in New York about Abraham Lincoln's death. While discussing Whitman's obituary ode to Lincoln, Martí wrote, "*It is more beautiful and strange* than [Edgar Allan] Poe's *The Raven*. The poet brings a bouquet of lilacs to the casket. / His entire work is like that. / There are no more willows weeping on the graves; death is now 'harvest, the one who opens the door, the great revealer'; what is being now, has always been and will be again; during a deep, light blue spring, oppositions and sorrows intertwine; a bone is a flower" (Martí 1991, 13:134; my italics and translation). The explicit separation from Poe's romanticism and the new approach to language are revealed by Martí later in the piece, where he writes, "Whitman's language, entirely different from the one poets have used till now, corresponds, by strangeness and vigor, to a cyclical poetry and a new humanity. [. . .] [I]t is all about echoing in words the noise of the masses settling, the cities bustling, of oceans tamed and rivers enslaved" (Martí 1991, 13:140–41; my translation).

Whitman, whose journalism and poetry Martí admired, offered the Cuban a taste for the concrete, for the detail, as well as a strategy to transport readers from individual, minute observations to universal realizations. Although Rotker argues that Martí was no follower of Whitman, it must be said that, in the context of the New York of that period, Whitman was unavoidable. American journalism was rapidly shifting the points of reference and the mechanisms of referentiality—first for Whitman, and probably in the same way for Martí. If romanticism was imbued with a Parnassus of universal ideas, modernism starts with the daily life of the markets, the fruit stands, the changing light, the seasons. Like Whitman, Martí navigates the transition from romanticism to urban modernism through language. His intermediate position between the life in New York and the Hispanic postcolonial world, his command of English and French, and his access to the cultures behind those languages gave Martí the tools to operate as a hinge between the West and Latin America, furthering the modernistic transformation of ideas much more deeply than any of his contemporaries.

A cosmopolitan at heart, Martí saw value in the dialogue of cultures and ideas while being a proponent of their singularity. He took a similar approach to the literary genres in which he worked: a fruitful conversation between poetry, the novel, crónicas, and interviews could only benefit and enrich the audiences. This may explain why he was able to open Latin American minds to the world, while keeping all the differentiating elements of the Latin American identity and ethos intact.

RETHINKING A MASS MEDIUM

"Martí was a masterful orator, and he used all the catchphrases and all the persuasion devices of which our language is capable," declared critic Enrique Anderson Imbert. "While writing, animated by that practical will or shaken by some declamatory impetus, he used to imbue his prose with the structure of a sermon, of a speech, of a proclamation, of a prayer. It is not classical architecture, not even the one used by our predecessors during the Golden Age [. . .] and yet there is in its eloquence the makings of a laborious architect" (Anderson Imbert 1953, 522; my translation).

It is also true, however, that Martí's prose feels at times like a succession of grammatical derailments in which new emotions and effects are delivered through different and totally new means. Ellipses, pleonasms, neologisms, hyperbatons, nominal phrases, and dispersed syntactic nuclei paint Martí's impressionistic, emotive imagery. A good example of this is his 1882 chronicle of the death of Jesse James in Missouri:

> These days in which New York has been a party, have been of great confusion in Missouri, where there was a bandit of high forehead, beautiful face and a hand made to kill, who didn't steal bags but banks, not houses but towns, and wouldn't jump balconies but trains. He was a hero of the jungle. His fierceness was so exceptional that the people of his land esteemed it above his crimes. He was not born of mean father, but of clergyman, didn't look like a villain, but like a knight, nor did he marry a bad woman, but a schoolteacher. And some say he was a political leader in one of his hideouts, or that he lived under false name and came as elected official to the last Democratic convention to vote for president. There are the lands of Missouri and those of Kansas, covered in woods and deep forests. Jesse James and his men knew the recesses of those jungles, the hiding places by the roads, the fords in the marshes, and the hollow trees. His house was armory, and another armory was his belt, because around his waistband he carried two cartridge belts loaded with handguns. He came'

to life during a war, and tore the life out of many a long-bearded man when he still had no beard himself. In times of Alba, he would have been [a] captain in Flanders. In times of Pizarro, his lieutenant. In these times, he was a soldier, and later a bandit. He was not one of those magnificent soldiers of Sheridan, who fought for this land to be one, or for the slave to be free, nor raised the flag of the North over tenacious Confederate forts. Neither was he one of those other patient soldiers of silent Grant, who rounded up the terrified rebels, like the serene hunter does the hungry boar. He was among the guerrillas of the South, for whom the flag was plundering booty. His hand was an instrument of killing. He'd leave the dead on the ground and, laden with booty, dole it out generously with his fellows in crime, smaller cubs that licked the paws of that great tiger. (Martí 1991, 13:237–41; my translation)

Martí's impact on language and culture was so durable and his vision so ahead of his time that an entire half century later, the same themes, rhythm, and tension, as well as many of the same devices (the oxymoron being a constant in Martí), would return in the writings of Jorge Luis Borges for the *Crítica* newspaper in Buenos Aires. (Borges would subsequently publish his *Crítica* pieces as *The Universal History of Infamy*.) Indeed, the selection of Billy the Kid as one of the characters in Borges's book should be read as a direct, if unspoken, tribute to Martí's eulogy of Jesse James.

In the Jesse James profile, cultural associations and extrapolations push the more mundane news content of a daily event into the terrain of a literary epic by introducing mythical elements, such as a comparison between the villain and a Spanish captain in Flanders or a lieutenant of Pizarro's army (Rotker 1992a, 206). These mechanisms make Martí's chronicles transcend the momentary relevance of daily journalism's fare to enter the perennial terrain of literature. Through this and other profiles, Martí meant to introduce the American character to the Latin American public. But when read years later, immediate references having receded, the epic elements persist and dominate the story, making it interesting, readable, and enjoyable to this day. Unlike other modernistas, Martí avoided the pitfalls of kitsch or absurdity, thanks in part to his nuanced understanding of culture across time and place. His references, vast as they were in range, were also always on point.

One of Martí's most commonly used literary devices was a metaphorical bestiary that ranged from terrestrial animals and insects, characterized as mostly carnal and weak yet sometimes humanely sublime, to the pure, aerial, and spiritual eagles and other creatures of the sky, which could also at times be base and grotesque. This interplay between high and low animals is key to understanding Martí's metaphorical apparatus, and it appears with eloquence in his introduction to Juan Antonio Pérez Bonalde's "Poem of Niagara": the *aguila rastrera*, or pedestrian eagle, is an oxymoron that speaks in the poem about certain types of political power that, when combined with greed, move against the current of public interest (Rama 1983, 113).

Although Martí was extremely concerned with the elegance of his prose, he was not—as discussed above—a pure aesthete. When in January 1882 the Cuban covered for *La Nación* the lecture that Irish writer Oscar Wilde delivered at Chickering Hall in New York, he portrayed Wilde as a dandy and was skeptical about his attempt to focus on "pure forms." In discussing Wilde—who was at the time the author of a slim volume of poetry with an impressionistic twist but had not yet achieved the notoriety he would reach years later—Martí emphasized the need for language to become a tool for social justice and the development of a just society. In that sense, contrary to Wilde's approach, which led to art nouveau and symbolism and a view of literature in which language as a sphere was completely separated from society—thus, symbolism's necessary response to realistic literature—the Cuban advocated for a stronger emphasis on reality (Pym 1992, 163). In that direction, the development of a stabilized form of Castilian in Latin America was for Martí a prerequisite to the development of objectivity and humanism (Rama 1983, 134). On a linguistic level, modernismo tried to adapt and incorporate a series of values, both fixed and stable, during a time of extreme dynamism, renovation, moral shifts, and uncertainty.

COVERING THE PAN-AMERICAN CONFERENCE

Martí considered himself an impartial journalist. However, it was also clear that he would not make any attempts to conceal his opinions about the Pan-American Conference: "From Independence down to today, never was a subject more in need of examination than the invitation of the United States to the Pan-American Conference. The truth is that the hour has come for Spanish America to declare its second independence," he wrote in one of his first pieces about it (qtd. in Karras 1974, 89). In fact, Martí had already prefigured a set of clear, direct, and strategic political goals for his coverage of the conference, and his articles were studded with sometimes open, sometimes more or less indirect warnings to attendees about the expansionist intentions of their host, Secretary of State James Gillespie Blaine, together with fragments of a political program for a future Latin America (Mañach 1950, 259).

Martí's chronicles from the Pan-American Conference had several political objectives. The first was that they were to serve as an alert to the Latin American attendees about Blaine's hegemonic intentions. In the Cuban's own words, the secretary of state was looking "for subsidies at Latin American expense" to secure via a series of commercial agreements access to Latin American markets for some US products that, due to high markups or excessive tariffs, did not find buyers in more traditional markets within the United States or Europe (Karras 1974, 78). This notion was not foreign to the local press. An article about reciprocity agreements published in the *New York Times* on July 24, 1890, referred to "[all] the reports from South America, and some of them very recent reports, too, [that] say that the chief obstacle in the way of increased consumption of American products is their great cost. Specified articles, of which samples and prices have been submitted from American manufacturers, are declared to be so much higher in price than similar articles sent from Europe that it would not be possible to sell the American articles in competition."

Martí's position regarding the creation of a pan-American customs union and the development of an inter-American common currency can be read as postcolonial criticism *avant la lettre*. The Cuban argued that free trade agreements between an economic power like the United States and premodern economies such as that of Cuba and other countries in Central and South America would hinder the potential for development of the smaller nations. And underdevelopment would, in turn, manifest itself in multiple forms of political dependency: "Whoever says economic union also means political union. [. . .] Commerce should be balanced to reassure freedom. [. . .] The excessive influence of one country over the commerce of another turns into political influence. [. . .] A people who want to be free, must also be free to conduct their own business" (Martí 1964, 254–55; my translation).

As a second goal, Martí's chronicles aimed to create a symbolic union of Latin American nations behind a common agenda based on progress and a shared identity. The goal was to eventually offset the United States' hegemonic and cultural claims on the region, gearing the nations south of it toward a new political and philosophical stance, critical of market individualism and the expansive capitalism proposed from the north. As part of that strategy, Martí coined the notion of "Nuestra América" (Our America), a claim for Latin American nations to acknowledge their past, heritage, and traditions and to take from other cultures only what might be useful in order to reinvent their own future. Martí's rejection of pan-Americanism in favor of pan-Hispanism was also a leitmotif in his essays (Kirk 1980, 131). The notion of Our America as a separate entity from, and opposed to, the United States was systematically outlined in an essay Marti published in 1891, toward the end of the Pan-American Conference, in *El Partido Liberal*, an influential Mexican daily. In it, he described the United States as a giant that was seven leagues tall and as an octopus with its tentacles wrapped around Latin America:

> These are not times for going to bed in a sleeping cap, but rather, like Juan de Castellanos' men, with our weapons for a pillow, weapons of the mind, which vanquish all others. Trenches of ideas are worth more than trenches of stone. [. . .]
>
> We can no longer be a nation of fluttering leaves, spending our lives in the air, our treetop crowned in flowers, humming or creaking, caressed by the caprices of sunlight or thrashed and felled by tempests. The trees must form ranks to block the seven-league giant! It is the hour of reckoning and of marching in unison, and we must move in lines as compact as the veins of silver that lie at the roots of the Andes. "[. . .] What are we like?" they ask, and begin telling each other what they are like. When a problem arises in Cojímar they no longer seek the solution in Danzig. The frock-coats are still French, but the thinking begins to be American. The young men of America are rolling up their sleeves and plunging their hands into the dough, and making it rise with the leavening of their sweat. They understand that there is too much imitation, and that salvation lies in creating. Create is this generation's password. Make wine from plantains; it may be sour, but it is our wine! It is now understood that a country's form of government must adapt to its natural elements, that absolute ideas, in order not to collapse over an error of form, must be expressed in relative forms; that liberty, in order to be viable, must be sincere and full, that if the republic does not open its arms to all and include all in its progress, it dies. [. . .] Standing tall, the workmen's eyes full of joy, the new men of America are saluting each other from one country to another. [. . .] America is saving herself from all her dangers. Over some republics the octopus sleeps still, but by the law of equilibrium, other republics are running into the sea to recover the lost centuries with mad and sublime swiftness. [. . .] But our America may also face another danger, which comes not from within but from the differing origins, methods, and interests of the continent's two factions. The hour is near when she will be approached by an enterprising and forceful nation that will demand intimate relations with her, though it does not know her and disdains her. And virile nations self-made by the rifle and the law love other virile nations, and love only them. The hour of unbridled passion and ambition from which North America may escape by the ascendancy of the purest element in its blood—or into which its vengeful and sordid masses, its tradition of conquest, and the self-interest of a cunning leader could plunge it—is not yet so close, even to the most apprehensive eye, that there is no time for it to be confronted and averted by the manifestation of a discreet and unswerving pride, for its dignity as a republic, in the eyes of the watchful nations of the Universe, places upon North

America a brake that our America must not remove by puerile provocation, ostentatious arrogance, or patricidal discord. (Martí 1991:6, 15, 20–22)

The notion of Our America had long been present in Martí's writings.[18] It was clear to the Cuban that after the United States acquired Florida and Louisiana, the American government had become well aware of Spanish colonial decadence and was eager to annex Cuba. In a letter to his friend and secretary Gonzalo de Quesada dated December 14, 1889, he wrote, "We don't have to make any effort for the island to become North American, because if we don't use well the little time that we have left to avoid it becoming so, that is what will happen due to its own disintegration. That is what this country [the United States, from where he writes] is waiting for and what we should oppose [because] once the United States is in Cuba, who would manage to get it out?" (qtd. in Rodríguez-Luis 1999, xvi).

Cuban independence, Martí wrote in a letter sent to his friend Manuel Mercado the day before his death, on May 18, 1895, would surely prevent the United States from "stretching out over the Antilles and falling, with added force, on our American lands" (qtd. in Rodríguez-Luis 1999, xvi).

Martí also believed that part of his duty as a foreign correspondent was to inform the Latin American public about the complexities of the United States as a nation and culture. If he could deliver the right message to the right audience, Blaine and his delegates would not be able to take advantage of potential factionalism between the new republics in the South or to set in motion a political and economic agenda contrary to their needs and traditions (Karras 1974, 77–99).

It was this feeling of an imminent danger dawning over the Americas that led Martí to apply the techniques he had developed for his literary journalism in order to create in his coverage of the Pan-American Conference an inclusive Latin American "us." This rhetorical movement entailed the exclusion and reification of the North and its attributes—reason, commerce, science, industry, profit—and the appropriation of aspects contrary to its character—beauty, disinterest, spirit, tradition, the subaltern—in the construction that would soon spread through the pages of the Latin American press: "Nuestra América" (Ramos 2000, 204). In his prose, Martí laid the groundwork for this mythic and ideological entity as a second foundation of Latin America, while his efforts toward the unification of the delegations were propped up and consolidated through concrete political actions (Rotker 1999; Kanellos 2005). In a sense, Latin America as an organized, demarcated territory with its corresponding identity did not exist prior to Martí's rhetorical construction (Ramos 2000, 298).

When "Nuestra América" appeared in Mexico in 1891 in *El Partido Liberal*, an official newspaper of the pro-development state, it was the peak of the Porfirian regime. Porfirio Díaz had opened his country to foreign capital, and the discourse of an autochthonous Latin America in "Nuestra América" can also be read partly as a critique of the alienating direction of Mexican modernization: "Over the heads of some republics the octopus is sleeping. Other [republics], which have forgotten that [Benito] Juárez once went about in a coach drawn by mules, hitch their carriages to the wind, with a soap bubble as their coachman; for poisonous luxury, the enemy of freedom, corrupts the lascivious man and opens the door to the foreigner" (Martí 1991:6, 21).

Clearly, Martí was concerned about American imperialism, and his fears were not unfounded. Despite Blaine's official pronouncements, which spoke to commercial agreements, the development of communications, arbitration, and other matters of little sensitivity, many articles in the New York daily press urged for a more aggressive role of the United States in relation to its southern neighbors. The *New York Tribune*, for instance, exhorted Americans to "reconquer their commercial supremacy . . . and to exercise a direct and general influence in the affairs of the American continent" (qtd. in Mañach 1950, 259). Martí was also aware of legislation, introduced in Congress by Sen. Wilkinson Call of Florida, that authorized the president of the United States to open negotiations with the Spanish government and induce it to consent to the independence of Cuba by means of an indemnity payable by the island. A month after introducing this legislation, the same senator had called Washington's attention to the dangers of Cuban debt falling into the hands of German financiers. To complete the picture, in February, when funding for a larger navy was being discussed in Congress, Sen. William Chandler of New Hampshire, a former secretary of the navy, urged the construction of an armada "[s]uperior to that of any nation in the Western Hemisphere and to that of the nation which owns the island of Cuba" (qtd. in Mañach 1950, 259).

A third goal for Martí's articles, and one that was perhaps more concealed in his chronicles, was to convince his fellow Cubans that, despite an unlikely alignment of Latin America behind the United States, the only option that would lead Cuba to its independence was a war. Spain was still holding on to its last colonial enclave in the Americas and was extremely unlikely to release from its orbit the jewel of its crown, an important source of income for the treasury, and the main producer of sugarcane in the world (Rodríguez-Luis 1999, xi). And although the reestablished monarchy had shown signs of goodwill toward the independentists—signs interpreted by a few of them as an open possibility to negotiate the terms of Cuba's independence without shedding blood—Martí was convinced that Spain's intentions were suspicious. As strongly as he opposed the negotiated independence with Spain, Martí was also against a growing annexationist movement supported by groups of Cuban exiles in the United States. His argument was mostly cultural: to impose the traditions and mores of Anglo-Saxon America on Hispanic-American Cuba would mean to obliterate, even despise, all that made the fabric of Cuban identity.

Only "iron and blood," he wrote, would set Cuba free from both Spain and the covetous eyes of the United States (qtd. in Karras 1974, 77).

On the way to a revolution, the Pan-American Conference was, in Martí's view, the last obstacle to overcome. It also proved to be the apotheosis of Martí's trajectory as a journalist thus far—harnessing all of his powers as a writer and all of his experiences as an exile for one clear, historical purpose.

MARTÍ'S REPUBLICAN PROGRAM

Martí did not operate on impulse or hunches. In fact, he detailed his plan for the constitution of a new Cuban republic in three documents that, before Cuban independence, also served as ideological guidelines for the formation of revolutionary republican groups in the United States. These ideas were brewing and coalescing around his journalistic works but were ultimately articulated apart from his daily dispatches. Being purely political, these texts show the extent to which Martí believed in journalism and literary writing as a guide to direct political action.

The first of these documents was *Resoluciones*, signed on November 28, 1891, by Martí and a party of Cuban exiles in Tampa, Florida; the second one, revealed on January 5, 1892, was *Bases y Estatutos secretos del Partido Revolucionario Cubano*, the cornerstone of the Cuban Revolutionary Party. The third and final one was *Manifiesto de Montecristi*, signed on March 25, 1895, by Martí and Gen. Máximo Gómez in the Dominican Republic (Gray 1963).[19]

Each of these documents stressed a different aspect of the future Cuban republic. For instance, in *Bases*, Martí stated the importance of a revolution conducted by all Cubans without regard to class or race: "The Cuban Revolutionary Party does not have as its object to bring to Cuba a victorious group that would consider the island as its prize and dominion" (qtd. in Gray 1963, 250).

Martí was aware of the historical role of military caudillos during the Latin American independence wars, so once the revolutionary process had begun he advocated against the formation of these militias in Cuba. Although the Cuban war had to be fought by an army, the actions of the revolutionary army and the development of republican institutions had to be headed by civilians: "The Cuban Revolutionary Party does not propose to perpetuate in the Cuban Republic, with new forms or with changes more apparent than real, the authoritarian spirit and bureaucratic composition of the colony, but to found in the free and cordial exercise of the legitimate capacities of a man a new people and a true democracy capable of overcoming through hard work and the equilibrium of social forces the dangers of sudden liberty in a society composed for slavery" (*Bases* qtd. in Gray 1963, 250). Martí's opposition to caudillism was sealed in 1884, when he rejected Gen. Máximo Gómez's revolutionary plans, putting distance between himself and the Ten Years' War commander due to the latter's caudillo-type aspirations. Martí expressed his disagreement in a personal letter to Gómez: "[It is] my determination not to contribute an ounce, for the sake of a blind love to an idea that is taking my life, with bringing into my land a regime of personal despotism, even more shameful and unfortunate than the political despotism that it now endures. [. . .] A nation is not founded, General, in the same way that you rule over a regiment" (Martí 1991, 1:177–81; my translation).[20]

In terms of identity, Martí also talked about the importance of developing governmental forms derived from the native traditions of Cuba, and this was a relevant theme in his *Manifiesto*: "Our country is to be constituted from its very roots with workable forms, grown in Cuba, in such a way that an inappropriate government may not end in favoritism or tyranny" (qtd. in Gray 1963, 251).

Martí also proposed an economic platform for Cuba planned for its new republican phase. And, although he was not an industrialist, he was a vocal critic of one-crop economies and economies dependent on industrialized nations. A nation wanting its political independence would also have to sell more than one product in the international market and, unlike the Cuba of his time, would have to develop diversified production capabilities to avoid dependence on the United States or Europe.

Finally, in order to prevent the dominance of a certain class or race over others, Martí constantly stressed in his articles the need for a cordial equilibrium between all the forces involved in the revolutionary process.

Many of these ideas appeared in his chronicles, articles, and editorials and were more directly expressed in *Patria*, the revolutionary publication he founded in New York. "[The] Republic . . . should not be the unjust predominance of one class of citizens over the rest, but the open and sincere equilibrium of all the real forces of the country, and of the free thought and desire of all the citizens," he wrote in 1891 (qtd. in Gray 1963, 250). By April

3 of that same year, the dissolution of the Inter-American Monetary Commission offered Martí his final victory over James Gillespie Blaine and his expansionist attempts.

More than sixty years later, during the early days of the communist revolution, after the 1953 Moncada uprising, Martí became again an ideological focal point. Fidel Castro, on trial for his attempted coup d'état, attributed to the journalist the intellectual authorship of the conspiracy. And seven years after that, Ernesto "Che" Guevara reiterated Martí's connection to the Cuban Revolution: "[Martí] suffered and died in order to realize the ideal that we are realizing today. [. . .] This is why we honor him, by trying to accomplish what he tried to accomplish. [. . .] Martí was the direct mentor of our Revolution, the man whose word is required to interpret with justice the historical phenomena we were living or the man whose word we have to remember every time we want to say or do something transcendent in this Motherland" (qtd. in Kirk 1980, 135, my translation). It would be virtually impossible, however, to prove whether or not Martí would have agreed with the ideas—let alone the methods—with which the Castro regime ruled over Cuba during half a century of communism.

PART II

• • •

LEVELING THE PLAYING FIELD

CHAPTER 4

· · ·

MODERNITY, MARKETS, AND URBAN BOHEMIA

The Southern Cone in the Early Twentieth Century

AT THE ASTOUNDING SPEED of eighteen miles an hour, it would take Juan José de Soiza Reilly only twenty minutes—stops included—to cover the six miles that separated the still bucolic neighborhood of Flores from the noisy and vibrant area of Plaza de Mayo in the traditional heart of downtown Buenos Aires.

Soiza's house at 95 Membrillar Street, surrounded by lush gardens, dirt roads, and open avenues, was only two blocks away from Flores Square. From there, an electric tram would take him directly to the office of *Caras y Caretas* magazine, at 151 Chacabuco Street, or to the informal editorial meetings held at the New Bar on Venezuela, on the corner with Bolívar. This type of mass transit commute, part of Soiza's everyday life, was a new phenomenon in an increasingly modern Buenos Aires.

Juan José de Soiza Reilly's parents were immigrants. The journalist did not belong to the downtown-dwelling Argentine upper classes, whose names dominated Buenos Aires's newspapers, the literary canon, and the official government ranks in Argentina and the subcontinent at the turn of the twentieth century. However, in the context of a rapidly expanding society, his background as a young writer from the suburbs was instrumental to his success as one of the first best-selling mass journalists in Latin America. Soiza's affiliation with the new urban middle classes and his intermediate social position—between Buenos Aires's underbelly and the city's enclaves of phenomenal wealth—were important elements behind his journalistic and literary success.

In his work, Soiza Reilly debated the elitist idea that journalism and literature were for the few. Instead, he embraced a growing middle-class public and professionalized his literary journalism, perfecting genres such as the interview and the *crónica* to a point where they became new forms of mass literature. He tapped into a growing audience eager for information and culture, one that had been overlooked by the lettered elites in the region. As a writer, Soiza became the emblem of an emergent publishing industry and the first true media personality in the subcontinent. He was a link between classes and an exemplar of success and class mobility, propelling modern ideas through his writings. Unlike Martí and Sarmiento, who spoke for the masses, Soiza *was* the masses, and he incorporated the voices of an as yet unheard audience into the public discourse.

In order to understand Soiza's ascent to media stardom, it is key to map his strategic position as an intermediary between *modernismo*, immigration, and the new urban readers, as well as his central role as an agent of a young mass publishing industry ready to experience an unprecedented expansion.

. . .

When Juan José de Soiza Reilly's parents, Juan José de Soiza and Catalina Reilly, first moved to Flores from neighboring Uruguay in the early 1890s, a commute of only minutes between their new neighborhood and downtown Buenos Aires was impossible. The distance between the city's center and its suburbs was spanned by a mix of sketchy, unfinished urban planning, a lack of wide, straight avenues, and a chaotic urban transit system comprising horse-drawn trolleys, carts, and expensive taxis that only sporadically connected the economic and financial center of the city with its outskirts. All that, however, was poised to change.[1]

The Soizas, like most immigrants at the time, had come from Europe. Juan José Sr., who was Portuguese, and Catalina, who was Irish, were employed in the meat-salting industry in Uruguay, but after a few years of hard work and having brought up five children (they would have five more), they decided to try their luck on the opposite bank of the river, in promising Buenos Aires. With migrant parents coming from two very different parts of Europe, Juan José de Soiza Reilly's cosmopolitanism was practically a birthright.

After the economic crisis of 1890, Buenos Aires, which had been declared the federal capital of the Argentine republic in 1880, entered its first phase of suburbanization. This process took place between the second national census in 1894 and the third in 1914 (H. Torres 1975). At the expense of heavy foreign investment and an increase in the levels of sovereign debt, the national government—also the administrative power in Buenos Aires—was committed to introducing a series of structural improvements in the city: paved streets with cobblestones brought from the island of Martín García, the first urban sewer system and the first electric grid, an efficient urban cleaning system, a social security network with world-class hospitals and clinics, and a reliable public transportation network, initially with horse-drawn tramways in 1870, followed by electric trams in 1898, and the first subway system in Latin America by 1913.

On a global scale, Argentina was considered to be on the cutting edge of modernity and capitalistic development. It received 8.5 percent of total foreign investments made by central nations (capital exporters) worldwide between 1860 and 1914. That was equivalent to 33 percent of the total foreign investment destined for Latin America and 42 percent of the total investment coming from the United Kingdom into the region (H. Torres 1975, 282–83).[2] Print capitalism, to use a term and concept coined by Benedict Anderson, was developing faster in Argentina than in any other nation in Latin America, which is why the consolidation of Argentina's literary journalism and its markets in this period can shed light on the expansion of the genre across the region.

The financial boost immediately made the suburbs of Buenos Aires more desirable, and thousands of working-class families relocated. This was accompanied by an intense wave of immigration that peaked between 1904 and 1914. In areas like Flores and Belgrano, west and north of the city, twenty thousand to thirty thousand plots of land were sold yearly in plans that called for 40, 80, or 120 monthly payments. Home ownership in Buenos Aires grew accordingly, from 8 percent in 1887 to 11.7 percent in 1914 (H. Torres 1975, 289).

The southern part of Flores, below Camino Real—renamed Rivadavia in the early 1900s—was one of those new suburban meccas. An area prone to floods and rich in marshes, it was also home to large *estancias*, which, after being subdivided and plotted, became the driving force behind a speculative real estate market that mainly targeted immigrants. The small parcels of land, still detached from the central sewer system and the electric grid, attracted the more entrepreneurial segments of the growing urban working class, who found in them an opportunity to establish permanent residency in the city by investing in land, building their first family (sometimes multifamily) residences, while realizing dreams of upward social mobility (H. Torres 1975, 288–89).[3]

The Soizas took advantage of this opportunity, as did their fifth son, Juan José de Soiza Reilly, after marrying Emma Martínez Lobato in 1908: following their wedding, the young couple moved into a house only a few blocks away from the Plaza Flores. By 1909 they had their first child, Rubén Darío, named after the powerhouse Nicaraguan modernist poet.[4] By 1919 they had a daughter christened after her mother, as was customary.

In those early days of the twentieth century, cultural associations and local societies sprang up all over the city and began helping to integrate the newcomers into communal and metropolitan life. The social gatherings and literary and political meetings in coffee shops, salons, and private residences, reported in newspapers, magazines, literary journals, and fanzines, became the springboard for more serious writers to join a growing number of more prominent professional publications (Saítta 2000a, 19).[5]

Soiza Reilly studied to be a schoolteacher at the Escuela Normal in Entre Ríos, and throughout his life he held positions as either a teacher or a librarian but also took an array of odd jobs ranging from newspaper delivery to security guard and justice of the peace, which probably contributed to his street-savvy personality. After moving to Buenos Aires, he soon started collaborating with some of the neighborhood newspapers (Escales 2008, 10).

By 1902, his byline and pseudonym, Agapito Candileja, began appearing in one of the most popular and innovative Latin American magazines of the period, *Caras y Caretas* (Cilento 2009, 67–86). Soon thereafter Soiza Reilly would become one of the most important journalists of his time in Latin America and a prominent face of the emerging written mass media in the region.

THE PUBLISHING BOOM OF THE 1910S

By the end of the first decade of the new century, Argentina was poised for one of the most vertiginous changes to be experienced by any Latin American country over the next one hundred years. A democratic consolidation resulting from the 1912 passage of the Sáenz Peña Law—establishing universal and compulsory male suffrage by secret ballot—led in 1916 to the presidency of Hipólito Yrigoyen, the first popularly endorsed Argentine head of state after decades of electoral fraud.[6]

A sustained increase in population, helped by steady migration from Europe—actively promoted by the government—created a workforce broad enough to complete the full integration of Argentina's economy into world trade markets as a first-tier provider of raw materials (Furtado 1970, 50–51; Halperín Donghi 1969, chap. 3). The incorporation of new workers into Argentina's political life was facilitated in part by the Láinez Law, or National

Education Law, passed on June 26, 1884, which granted free, secular primary education to all residents on Argentine soil. The Láinez Law was also instrumental in the professionalization of workers, triggering a pronounced drop in illiteracy rates—which fell from 78 percent in 1869 to 35 percent in 1914—while fostering a new reading public (Eujanian 1999, 21).[7]

These changes had an impact on the development of a new reading market in several ways. With the technical ability to read and write but without the skills, habits, or a developed interest that would lead them to navigate a book catalog or browse a public library, the new readers, eager to partake in a changing and ever more exciting new world, found it easier to purchase newspapers and magazines readily available on newsstands. On December 6, 1924, when launching Biblioteca Crítica, a series of cheap books published by the daily *Crítica*, an editorial in that newspaper reinforced this idea: "The man who, weighed down by his hard day's work, wishes to enliven his leisure time with some reading, stumbles into a big dilemma: What can he read? He lacks the time to search a library for what best suits his temperament. He recognizes neither authors nor titles; he is no erudite, and would want a book that is enjoyable and instructive at the same time" (qtd. in Saítta 1997, 74; my translation). In Argentina, as well as in the rest of Latin America, the mass media would play, despite its intrinsic limitations, a key role in opening the world of written knowledge to the new reading public. Purchasing a morning newspaper for twenty cents, twice the price of a tramway ticket in Buenos Aires, the daily commuter would gradually start to develop new reading habits, accessing and consolidating a new imagined community of readers (Eujanian 1999, 24).

Aside from the news sections, which were heavy on crime and human-interest stories, popular newspapers at the turn of the twentieth century also included serialized novels and other types of easy reading. The transformation of the political press model into a modern, information-based press was under way. Interested in the city and its occurrences, the new mass reading public rejected the opinionated political style preferred by the elites, a style that coincidentally was also being challenged inside newsrooms by the new information paradigm that was spreading from newspapers in the United States and Europe. An editorial in *La Nación* on April 3, 1914, shows the growing concern over separating objective fact from opinion: "Our reviews are not the result of judgment of, nor are they under evaluation by, a committee; our sympathies or our disagreements don't force us to assimilate, nor to promote or resist current or upcoming opinion forces. [...] We were once, openly and frankly, in days of great and famous debates, a party newspaper, but we have stopped being so, especially since the virtue inspired by our gospel has closed the circle of its own action" (qtd. in Sidicaro 1993, 150; my translation).

By adopting new styles and genres, newspapers gained access to a broad new public. Buenos Aires had 663,854 inhabitants in 1895 and 1,575,814 by 1914, and this growth was also echoed in an increasing number of daily publications. In the first decade of the twentieth century the number of daily newspapers in Buenos Aires more than doubled, from only six dailies in 1895, to fourteen by 1914 (Saítta 1999, 29).

But newspapers were not the only thriving players in the new mass media landscape. By the dawn of the 1910s, mass magazines had already added to the supply of reading options for the daily commuter (Eujanian 1999, 22–51). Between 1900 and 1941 at least 1,039 titles were published in the province of Buenos Aires and 637 in the rest of the country. And in the city of Buenos Aires alone, the number grew from 36 in the first decade of the twentieth century to 552 in the 1930s (Fernández 1943, cited in Eujanian 1999, 30). These new magazines not only offered an array of information unrelated to current events, but, unlike newspapers, their content was especially geared to—and suited for, their editors believed—women and children. These magazines created a new relationship with their audiences, one that mass newspapers like *Crítica* would start to tap into by the mid-1920s.[8]

There were also some sectors in the publishing business that lagged behind, especially those connected to the book industry. From 400 titles released annually between 1900 and 1910, to 750 by 1931, the expansion in book publication remained negligible in Argentina. On June 30, 1932, the passing of Law 11,588 exempted from taxation all imported paper destined to newspaper, book, and magazine printing, as well as other types of public interest publications (García 1965, 58). The new printing law, which accompanied the early stages of the import-substitution industrialization process—a trend that gained full force during World War II—had a clearly beneficial impact on book publishing. From there being only a few printing houses in the late 1920s, almost 2,000 were in operation in Buenos Aires by the end of 1932. These new publishing operations employed at least twenty thousand specialized workers (García 1965, 78–132).

A few years later, the Spanish Civil War had an even more potent effect. Between 1936 and 1939, a large number of Spanish editors and publishers immigrated with their businesses to both Argentina and Mexico, fueling an astounding increase in book exports: between 1933 and 1941 the number of titles shipped from Argentina grew from 68,960 to 121,670. Mail orders for books also increased, from 291,000 titles in 1942 to 339,000 in 1950 (Eujanian 1999, 27).

Despite modernization and the changes taking place in the news paradigm, information-centered newspapers would have to wait until the mid-1920s to incorporate the new style embodied in the mass press. It was in 1923 that, after an extensive revamping, *Crítica*, the daily newspaper founded in 1913 by Uruguayan journalist Natalio Botana, became the "voice of the people." Its importance in Latin America would be equivalent to Joseph Pulitzer's *New York World* and William Randolph Hearst's *New York Journal* in the American newspaper industry thirty years earlier.[9]

THE MASS PRESS IN ARGENTINA AND MEXICO

Although the effects of modernity and integration on world commerce were felt all over Latin America, a confluence of circumstances put Argentina substantially ahead of the curve, thus making its changing media landscape central to any understanding of the development of the mass media in the entire region. In fact, compared to Argentina, most other countries still lagged behind in the political process of democratic consolidation and its consequent development of a mass audience. Argentina had three key advantages that created beneficial conditions for the press: a booming economy, political stability guided by a democratic impetus, and the incorporation of new audiences into the reading public. By examining the contrasting conditions in Mexico, the second most important Hispanic literary market in the region at the time, it is possible to see how Argentina, and in particular its most important urban center, Buenos Aires, was a perfect micro climate for the expansion of a free press.

Mexico was closest to Argentina in the development of this type of news market. But it is important to briefly discuss certain political and social conditions that delayed the full development of its mass media for decades. During the Porfirian years—the period from 1881 to 1911, when Porfirio Díaz was Mexico's head of state—dissent and opposing political parties were generally banned from public debate, and elections, when held, were either fraudulent or suppressed. Díaz was efficient at eliminating all centers of institutional and political opposition and ruling over the various Mexican states by means of economic inducements (Negretto and Aguilar 2000, 385–86). But the lack of a political opposition and his hold on power debilitated some core democratic tendencies, slowing down some of its accompanying processes, such as an increase in literacy levels, the development of a politically active reading public, and the consolidation of a vibrant political public sphere and free press.

Unlike Argentina, where the gap between the elites and the lower classes had started to shrink and continuoúsly narrowed until the early 1930s and where political participation, with the ascent of the Unión Cívica Radical party, was based on the inclusion of popular sectors in political life through education and the expansion of the public sphere, the Porfirian regime pushed Mexico into world commerce by opening the national economy to foreign investment in key sectors like transportation, communications, and oil production. The inclusion of the masses in public life was secondary.

During the thirty years of the Porfirian regime, illiteracy in Mexico remained at an average of 80 percent, education was generally conceived as a privilege of the upper classes, and new schools were opened only in big cities and urban centers (Ortiz Marín and Duarte Ramírez 2010, 3). There were, however, some isolated efforts to make education accessible to the popular sectors. After the First National Education Congress of 1889–1890, secular primary schooling was declared mandatory and free for every child between six and twelve years of age, and by 1901 there were forty-five normal schools in the country to train teachers (4).

The absence of a reading public kept the Mexican publishing industry in its infancy until the late 1920s, when the dust of the revolution finally began to settle. In the early twentieth century there were at least 2,579 newspapers in Mexico, of which 579 were sold in Mexico City. Most were published irregularly and distributed erratically. Still geared to political opinion rather than information, newspapers were also expensive, with prices ranging between one cent and fifty cents.[10] But that was not the only reason newspapers were luxury goods: at the end of the Porfirian regime in 1910, barely 30 percent of the population could read and write (Ortiz Marín and Duarte Ramírez 2010, 5).

At the turn of the twentieth century, the largest Mexican newspapers were *El Imparcial*—the first mass newspaper in Mexico—*El Monitor Republicano*, and *El Universal*. They issued between fifteen thousand and twenty thousand copies a day, with no more than a dozen pages. These figures were well behind the circulation of most Argentine national newspapers: *La Prensa*, by then the most important one, was well above ninety-five thousand daily copies, *La Nación* was close to seventy thousand, and *La Razón* was also above sixty thousand. Articles in the Mexican press usually appeared unsigned, and when they covered political activities, Porfirian government officials were described in laudatory terms. In contrast, critical views were common in the Argentine press, and the tradition of reporters bylining their own articles was in ascent.

With technical improvements in the printing industry, newspapers like *El Imparcial* started to incorporate photographs, also without credit lines, and for certain special events up to one hundred thousand copies a day might be printed. Those improvements, however, were overwhelmingly offset by the strict control that the Porfirian regime exerted on the press, which made for sluggish growth in the industry, at least until after the Mexican Revolution (Ortiz Marín and Duarte Ramírez 2010, 6).

The picture was bleaker in the rest of Latin America, except for Argentina, where the publishing industry was consolidated and booming. During the period from 1900 to 1930 a new type of mass newspaper was born in the Southern Cone, focused on information and grounded on a new, dynamic relationship with its audience. And this new relationship was directly imported from the popular magazines of the early 1900s.

In the first decade of the twentieth century, magazines had been the stars of the printing business in the Southern Cone. And among several big players, like *Don Quijote*, which claimed circulation peaks of sixty-one thousand in the 1890s, as well as *PBT* and *Fray Mocho*, *Caras y Caretas* was undoubtedly the most emblematic, relevant, and influential of all Argentine—and Latin American—new publications in those early years of the new century (Eujanian 1999, 28).

In fact, it was thanks to his articles in *Caras y Caretas* that Juan José de Soiza Reilly caught the public's eye. His constant presence in magazines and mass newspapers soon turned him into the most renowned journalist of his generation.

CROWDSOURCING JOURNALISM FOR *CARAS Y CARETAS*

Although it was a cornerstone of the Argentine magazine boom in the early twentieth century, *Caras y Caretas* was born neither in Argentina nor in the twentieth century. Indeed, it was not even conceived by an Argentine. Perhaps it was this outsider origin that gave the periodical its independent spirit and led to its irreverent mandate for mass media: to foster an intimate rapport and complicity between magazine and reader. The magazine swiftly realized its vision by introducing innovations such as photography, science coverage, human-interest stories, and reader competitions. In so doing, *Caras y Caretas* defined not only the kind of relationship readers would have with mass media but, more importantly, the type of reader the new media demanded: curious, engaged, and upwardly mobile, in pursuit of middle-class status.

Caras y Caretas was first published in Montevideo, Uruguay, in 1890, by thirty-year-old Spanish poet and humorist Eustaquio Pellicer. The Uruguayan version of the weekly was short-lived, and by 1892 Pellicer had been invited to Buenos Aires by his friend Bartolomé Mitre y Vedia, son of former

Argentine president Bartolomé Mitre and codirector with his father of the influential newspaper *La Nación* (Pignatelli 1997, 274).

Pellicer and Mitre y Vedia planned to publish *Caras y Caretas* in Buenos Aires with Pellicer as director. But the revolutionary war in Cuba and the growing pro–Latin American sentiment in the region made it unwise for a native Spaniard to direct a mass publication. The role would have naturally fallen to Mitre y Vedia, but his father believed that *La Nación* and the family name would be compromised if Bartolito—as he was known—became the editor of a satiric publication.

Mitre y Vedia thus declined any further association with the weekly, and *Caras y Caretas* appeared on Saturday, October 8, 1898, under the direction of the journalist and writer José S. Álvarez, best known by his pseudonym, Fray Mocho. The first issue included a letter from Mitre y Vedia in which he apologized to readers for "having mistakenly considered [himself] strong enough to commit to an endeavor that, [he] soon learned, largely exceeded [his] abilities" (qtd. in Pignatelli 1997, 281; my translation).

Alvarez had started his newspaper career at *El Nacional* in 1879 and had acquired vast experience in crime reporting by working for *La Patria* in Argentina and *La Razón*, the largest Argentine newspaper of the early twentieth century. He had also penned a few serial novels, and for a brief period of his life, between October 16, 1896, and August 3, 1897, he was commissioner of investigations for the Buenos Aires police department. In that year he published *Galería de ladrones de la capital 1880–1887* (Gallery of thieves of the capital city 1880–1887), a treatise that included two hundred portraits of the most famous thieves in Buenos Aires, "accompanied by a description of each individual, an enumeration of their crimes, their criminal record, and a summary of their personal habits" (Pignatelli 1997, 277; my translation). Also in 1897, under his pseudonym Fabio Carrizo, Alvarez wrote *Memorias de un vigilante* (Memoirs of a street cop), which consecrated him as the foremost interpreter of Buenos Aires's underbelly.

Alvarez's editorial line separated *Caras y Caretas* from other magazines and newspapers in Buenos Aires by focusing on human-interest stories rather than politics. Known, among other things, for having interviewed Sgt. Andrés Chirino, responsible for the death of popular gaucho hero Juan Moreira, it was probably Alvarez who first invited Soiza Reilly to collaborate with *Caras y Caretas*. Born in Entre Ríos like Soiza, Alvarez had a similar interest in pickpockets, street criminals, and hookers and wrote about them as frequently as he could (Cilento 2009, 72).

The relationship between *Caras y Caretas* and its readers was radically new, embodying an unprecedented rapport based on complicities and shared expectations that had not previously been pursued by any Latin American medium. The relationship was also permeated by a growing democratic feeling, as well as a tendency to put writers and readers on an even field.

El Caricareta, as it was called by the boys selling it at newsstands, on tramways, and in the most populated corners of Buenos Aires, received a warm welcome by publishers and the most influential newspapers of its time. *La Prensa*, with a national daily circulation of 160,000 copies (90,000 in Buenos Aires and the rest in the provinces) and deemed the "most powerful press institution of South and Central America, and one of the leading newspapers worldwide" (Saítta 1999, 30), published a cordial editorial welcoming the magazine on October 8, 1898:

> The festive weekly, announced with so much grace by its founders, has just appeared, and its first issue has not only delivered on the promises they had made, fulfilling the hopes of our public, but it has done so exceedingly. Mr. Bartolomé Mitre y Vedia, who was meant to be its director, has announced in this first number that he has decided, with a great deal of sadness, to resign his position due to external forces and the demands of his multiple occupations. [. . .] Illustrations, text, and even the vignettes that accompany the ads, everything in this new weekly is original, varied, and effervescent. (qtd. in Pignatelli 1997, 275; my translation)

El Nacional joined the general excitement on October 9 and 10: "With some delay, *Caras y Caretas* has reached our hands. Its first number has lived up to the high hopes the public had heaped upon it, and it's to be expected that this satirical-humorous weekly will find its mark among those of its genre. We kindly salute it, wishing the magazine a happy and prosperous life" (qtd. in Pignatelli 1997, 275; my translation).

The *Caras y Caretas* motto—*semanario festivo, literario, artístico y de actualidades* (festive, literary, artistic, and current events weekly)—presented the magazine as a lighthearted, ironical publication along the lines of the late *El Mosquito* (1863–1893) and *Don Quijote* (1884–1905), which had heavily relied on graphic humor. *Caras y Caretas*, however, was much more innovative than its predecessors. The magazine was probably the first print mass medium in Latin America to use photography and photo engravings for illustration and photojournalism as a storytelling device.

Caras y Caretas was "an encyclopedia of its time" (Ludmer 1999, 251). It blended high and low culture, science, literature, politics and global journalism, fact and fiction, written and graphic journalism, advertising and the market. These distinctive markers of modernity, the professionalization of photojournalism, the innovative use of genres such as the *crónicas*, investigative news stories, and the abundance of interviews all flourished, providing a radically different way of reaching the public. *Caras y Caretas* thus prepared the new field of the mass media for the founding in 1913 of the revolutionary newspaper *Crítica*.

On November 26, 1898, an announcement appeared in *Caras y Caretas* inviting all amateur photographers in Argentina and abroad to submit their photos of unique and curious events, to be considered for publication. The request crystallized a new rapport that the periodical was establishing with its public. The announcement was also an indication that the increasingly professional and tech-savvy Argentine audience was starting to be perceived as a partner in an equal, balanced relationship. The mass public was no longer an abstract entity, a void that needed to be filled in with information or guided with ideas. The new audience was educated, prepared, ready, and able to make informed decisions about what was worth its attention and what was not. Furthermore, it had acquired a number of technical skills that would become instrumental to collaborating with the publishing business. This leveled playing field was another direct consequence of an increasingly democratic Argentine society:

> Despite the fact that our weekly has a full team of correspondents in the country and abroad, the pursuit of guaranteeing the most complete graphic information coverage has led us to request the collaboration of all amateur photographers in Argentina and abroad under the following conditions: (1) *Caras . . .* will pay 5 pesos for photographs of 8 × 9 to 13 × 18, and 10 pesos for 13 × 18 to 18 × 24; (2) Photographs should reproduce events, or anything that represents a curious topic; (3) Copies will be printed on paper, without prejudice to their clarity; (4) It is imperative that the photographs have not been reproduced by any other publication; (5) Published photos will show the author's name at the epigraph. (qtd. in Pignatelli 1997, 280–81; my translation)

For the first time in Latin America, photographs were incorporated into a news publication as material of journalistic interest. As a practice, photography required not only a basic knowledge of optics, physics, and photometry but also a more sophisticated understanding of electromagnetism and chemistry in order to control chemical reactions, mix and manipulate emulsions, and develop film. These scientific and practical skills, seldom taught in schools, were generally learned from technical manuals and magazines, such as those printed by the Italian publisher Hoepli and widely read by hobbyists in Buenos Aires during the first decade of the twentieth century. Those skills represented a know-how that had little to do with the education of the upper classes (Sarlo 1992, 23). Labor-intensive and requiring manual skills, this was a craft that eluded the elites by its very nature. The monetization of these new technical skills thus spoke not only to the professionalization of the journalistic field—which now paid photographers for their work, incorporating the discipline as a new facet of the journalistic profession—but also to the integration of a modern, middle-class practice into the sphere of remunerated activities within an increasingly modern society.

The growing importance of science became apparent in those years, when Soiza Reilly and other authors and journalists such as Horacio Quiroga and Roberto Arlt began to incorporate it into both their journalistic and fictional stories. Soon enough science became not only a topic of news articles but also—in the figure of the expert and the scientist—a way to validate ideas, claims, observations, and positions.

To engage its public in conversation, *Caras y Caretas* kept introducing editorial innovations that went beyond photography. Some of them, such as drawing contests, offered prizes in cash—payable in French francs—or in kind. Many of these competitions were developed around national symbols or heroes. The participants, generally children, were asked to send sketches of an Argentine founding father or some other patriotic icon. These pictorial representations of national symbols in magazines and newspapers had a strong institutional value and were instrumental in the consolidation of the Argentine national identity (Varela 1994). In addition to receiving a prize, the winning artists would have their drawings featured on the cover of *Caras y Caretas*. One of these amateur contributions was chosen to illustrate a special issue commemorating the centennial of the May Revolution of 1810; the press run for that issue was more than four hundred thousand (Pignatelli 1997, 317).

At the beginning, *Caras y Caretas* ran no more than two dozen pages, a quarter of which were advertising. But the page count soon increased to an average of 100. Some special issues, however, came out with even four times as many pages. The special May 1910 issue included 372 pages, 87 of which were ads. On the editorial page, the publishers flaunted their satisfaction, saying that, had the copies been piled on each other, they would have reached an altitude of ten thousand feet, or thirty-five times the height of the National Congress building. And had they been laid out end to end, the line of magazines would have stretched thirteen thousand miles, the distance between the North and the South Poles (Eujanian 1999, 29).

Caras y Caretas was a hit. Its circulation grew astoundingly and consistently, from 80,760 in 1904 to 111,800 in 1912, stabilizing at around 100,000 in 1913. It then began a slow decline that would lead to its closure in 1941. Between 1898 and 1912, the weekly used its cartoons for political humor and opinion. In fact, much of the editorial line rested in the hands of the *Caras y Caretas* political cartoonists, including Manuel Mayol and José María Cao Luaces (known simply as Cao), both of Spanish origin; brothers Cándido Villalobos and Francisco Redondo, also Spanish; Mario Zavataro, who was Italian; and an Argentine, Aurelio Giménez. They all considered themselves *periodistas dibujantes* (journalist illustrators) and not just illustrators (Pignatelli 1997, 279). But in 1912, probably as a consequence of the increasing political tensions in Europe, the editorial line started to veer in the direction of international news. With this shift, the style of *Caras y Caretas* also changed, as illustrations lost ground to information and the magazine moved closer to the information model practiced by the international news services frequently consulted in the newsroom.

The change did not go unnoticed. Some of the founding members argued that a neutral position and the emphasis on international news were contrary to the original spirit of the weekly, so when an agreement with the editorial board proved impossible, a key sector of the staff set sail for two new magazines: *PBT* and *Fray Mocho*, the latter founded by Cao, the chief illustrator for *Caras y Caretas*, and named after José Alvarez, the magazine's renowned and recently deceased first editor. Even Eustaquio Pellicer, the original director of the publication, stepped down from the editorial board to found *PBT*, which would carry on the tone and original editorial style of *Caras y Caretas*.

The expansion of the international section and an increased emphasis on the informative approach presented a superb opportunity for experimentation for those who stayed with the publication. New, avant-garde narrative forms and the Great War would offer writers like Soiza Reilly the opportunity, the tools, and the substance to explore fresh ideas and topics and to develop their writing in the context of modern journalistic genres and styles.

THE MASS PUBLIC AND THE MODERN CITY

Since its beginnings, *Caras y Caretas* had been conceived as a magazine for the people, and that was reflected in its cover price. Until its thirteenth issue, *Caras y Caretas* cost twenty-five cents on newsstands, a little more than twice the value of a two-way working-class tramway ticket, the *boleto obrero*. But starting with the fourteenth issue, its price was reduced to twenty cents, and it stayed the same until 1939 (Pignatelli 1997, 281).

Matching the *Caras y Caretas* cover price to the cost of a round-trip tramway ticket was not a random move. Public transportation had become a central aspect of urban life in Buenos Aires. New forms of metropolitan transportation were not only changing the urban landscape; they were also instrumental to the incorporation of the suburbs and their inhabitants into the life of the city, while drastically changing the way people accessed culture and information. Publications became accessories for the mobile middle class, a means not only to gather information but to communicate, in turn, one's taste, ideology, and status to other riders.

Buenos Aires's electric tram network was inaugurated on April 22, 1897, and had only two sections at first: one that ran between Canning Avenue and the zoo in Plaza Italia on the northern side of town, and another in the west, running along Avenue Primera Junta—formerly known as Camino Real and later renamed Rivadavia. The northbound line, managed by Tranvía Eléctrico de Buenos Aires, was built by American engineer Charles Bright. The westbound section, inaugurated in December of that same year and connecting the corner of San Juan Avenue and Entre Ríos with Plaza Flores, was managed by Tramways La Capital.

Electric streetcars, one of the clearest signs of modernity in a city that by the 1900s was already considered among the most advanced metropolitan centers in the world, had not only started to change the pulse of the town but also helped incorporate a large mass of immigrants, mostly living in the peripheries, into the workforce. At ten cents per round-trip, the *boleto obrero* was a sign of the transformation about to occur in Buenos Aires. Upward social mobility and the rapid development of new economic sectors like services and finance were two aspects in the consolidation of a vibrant mass culture already showing signs of tremendous vitality.

In the two decades that followed, the tram network spread at full speed, and by the mid-1920s, when it reached its maturity, it extended 550 miles, ran more than 3,000 tram cars, employed 12,000 workers, offered 99 urban routes, and on average was used for 650 million commutes on an annual basis. Buenos Aires soon earned a new moniker, the City of Tramways, and the system became instrumental in connecting a growing middle class during an expansion that was unprecedented for Latin America.[11]

Urban public transportation was also a boon for the consumption of mass media. People started to use their daily commute as a time to read. And, as a new space in the public sphere, buses and trams opened different types of social interaction, anonymous and sometimes purely based on appearances. External signs became increasingly relevant markers of cultural, social, and political identity. Newspapers and magazines were seen as emblems of status and social association, helping define expectations, affiliations, and interests. It was not only important to be seen reading on the bus or the train. Different types of reading also defined different ideological, political, and social interests and ranks.

La Novela Universitaria, one among the many popular magazines in those years, advertised itself as a "sign of good literary taste. When you carry *La novela universitaria* in the train or the tramway, there's no reason to hide it: those who see it will know that you are an intellectually distinguished person, a person of culture" (qtd. in Mizraje 2006, 46–49; my translation).

The title of avant-garde poet Oliverio Girondo's first book, *Veinte poemas para ser leídos en el tranvía* (Twenty poems to be read in the tramway), published in 1922, also spoke to the habits and nature of this developing mass public, which took advantage of long urban commutes to gain access to the new forms of modern culture while displaying its objects as symbols of class and identity.

THE JOURNALISM OF SOIZA REILLY

Soiza Reilly's articles made good tramway reading. During his many years with *Caras y Caretas*, he consolidated his ascent in the new journalistic circles with extraordinary success. His first stories for the magazine focused on the outcomes of Buenos Aires's rush to modernity and also on some of the most blatant contradictions of his time: the emergence of an urban underclass, the new poor, the rejects and oddballs, and the world of crime in a city that, unlike the rest of Latin America, was becoming cosmopolitan at a fast pace.[12] In covering for the first time subjects that members of the public at large were seeing in their daily life, Soiza was using the mass media as a lens to discover and acknowledge uncomfortable realities, giving it a new level of intimacy and credibility in the eyes of its audience. During 1905, using both his name and his pseudonym, Agapito Candileja, Soiza Reilly published five stories in *Caras y Caretas*, four of them journalistic crónicas and the fifth a philosophical short story (Cilento 2009, 72).[13] After World War I, however, Soiza's interests started to veer toward money-related crime narratives.

In his early writings, Soiza Reilly produced one of the first journalistic records of gay activity in Latin America in the early twentieth century. In those years, immigration, deviance, and crime were widespread preoccupations in growing cities around the world. A massive migratory influx from Europe, the consolidation of the legal apparatus, and the development of notions of citizenship and civil norms triggered a taxonomical, classificatory interest that fostered the development of such disciplines as eugenics, positive criminology, and phrenology (Ludmer 1999, 130–47). Realism and naturalism in literature were clearly connected to these preoccupations.

Soiza was among the first modern Latin American journalists to tap into those topics. Magazines and newspaper articles—but also certain forms of literature—started to reference science and legal terminology to back up stories and ideas, connecting with a public increasingly interested in those new types of knowledge (Sarlo 1992). In "Ladrones vestidos de mujer" (Thieves dressed like women), an article published in *Fray Mocho*, Soiza reported on an underworld clique of three thousand transvestite thieves he called the "manly Eves," who dressed like high-class women in order to rob men in downtown Buenos Aires—one of the first modern accounts of cross-dressing in the Latin American mass press.[14]

Using his encounter with an old friend–turned-thief as a narrative stepping stone, Soiza began his journey into the world of this guild of pickpockets, blackmailers, and thieves who lurked in the dark corners of the fanciest streets in town:

> "Initiated." "Aesthetes." They exploit their effeminate looks to take advantage of the naïve vanity of the provincial Don Juan. . . . Their operation is extremely simple. Young boys, neurotic and sickly, some of them with beautiful features, dress up like women, with elegance. Even with *chic*. . . . They walk the dark streets. They see someone coming, unsuspecting. They approach him. They say they have lost their way . . .
>
> —Dear sir, I am lost. You look like a kind and distinguished gentleman. Couldn't you walk with me? I am scared. I'm a widow.
>
> Deep inside every gentleman there is a knave.
>
> —Of course I can escort you home, Madam—the "distinguished gentleman" answers. And so he does.
>
> They jump into a taxi car. And while the false lady softly sighs and cries, she steals her Don Juan's wallet.
>
> Soon thereafter, Don Juan will complain to his family or to a police agent:
>
> —Someone in the trolley stole my wallet. (Soiza Reilly 2006, 232–33; my translation)

Through a technique that both Sarmiento and Martí had perfected, Soiza subtly traced the genealogy of this "unholy" profession back to ancient Greece, the Bible, and the European kingdoms of France and England, presenting it in the context of a larger series of human activities:

> Theft by "men dressed as women" is, in fact, nothing new. If this type of perverse delinquent wanted to claim an illustrious origin, it would not take much of an erudite inquiry. [. . .] Saint Paul in his letter to the Christians of Rome mentions some of them and says "they deserve to die." [. . .] Moses had to pass very severe laws against Midianite thieves. [. . .] Among the false divinities, the Holy Scriptures mention Baal-Fagor, who dressed as a woman to steal stars from Jacob. [. . .] Henry VIII of England was proud of his buffoon: Will

Summers, an effeminate fellow and the "court's burglar." Henry admired him so much that he requested Holbein, the premier portrait artist of the sixteenth century, to work on two paintings of the great buffoon in women's attire. [...] Both remain in London—one in the Antiquarian's Hall, the other at the British Museum. (Soiza Reilly 2006, 234–35; my translation)

To back up his facts, Soiza quoted authoritative scientific and legal sources. His medical sources described cross-dressing as a pathology, and his police sources shared with him statistics of burglaries recently committed by cross-dressers in Buenos Aires. Soiza ended the article with two cases, one about Luis Fernández, also known as La Princesa de Borbón (the Bourbon Princess), and the other about Culpiano Álvarez, also known as Bella Otero. "For the most part, these thieves are refined and educated men. [...] Almost all of them love music, flowers, sewing and poetry," he states. "They play the piano. They live off of stolen property" (Soiza Reilly 2006, 236–37; my translation).

By revealing the dark side of Buenos Aires's modernity while at the same time inserting the city into a larger, universal context, Soiza was gearing his narratives toward a new reading public. Like Martí, he was expanding the scope of Latin American modernity beyond the subcontinent and across class boundaries drawn earlier by the *modernistas*. In many ways, Soiza could be read today as one of the last modernistas, on par with Enrique Gómez Carrillo of Guatemala and Manuel Gutiérrez Nájera of Mexico. But due to his origins and his connections, Soiza chose a different slice of modernity to reveal—that of the marginal, the dispossessed, and the outcast. These were the rejected classes that were forming at the city's core and in the peripheries alike. In his articles, Soiza wrote for the new urban workers, who were exposed to these emergent subcultures firsthand. Not acknowledging them would have amounted to a lie, an omission apparent to readers, and a breach of the journalistic and literary contract with the audience.

In his stories, Soiza offered scientific, technical, and legal information useful for the masses in interpreting the city within the larger frame of universal culture—information immediately useful to the technically able new urban publics.

For the first time in Latin America, a journalist used the mass media as a lens through which to see the world.

.   .   .

Soiza was not an uncritical defender of modernity. Compassionate toward those who were left on the margins of progress, he was also a strong critic of superfluity and greed and had developed a somewhat romanticized view of the urban poor. In fact, in his idealization of the underclasses, he channeled some of his mistrust of science, progress, and the market.

Soiza usually portrayed the penniless as voluntarily distanced from mundane temptations and the vices of modern society. He called them dogs, which was not only a reference to Diogenes the Cynic, his dog-like behavior, and his usual companions but also an allusion to Saint Rocco, the mendicant pilgrim and Catholic saint:

> Surrounded by the filth of his rags, his cans, his dogs, and his madness, the hirsute tramp lives the legendary life of his brother Rocco—the pilgrim saint—and of his other brother Job—the sad and dreadful. Far from the clownish laughter that reigns over the city of progress; free from contact with people who suffer the dementia of living a sane life; immune to the cramps triggered by the thirst for vain ambitions; fugitive of noise, he sees the hours pass one by one. He sees them pass with patriarchal indifference, indolent, serene as a cat. . . . He sleeps outdoors, on his rags. He eats the crumbs that he can find in the garbage. And he lives happily, feeding his soul with the pleasure of a unique love. The love of his dogs. He loves his dogs with feminine passion. Listen. He is talking to us:
>
> —See, sir. I dearly love my dogs because they have offered me the tenderness that not even my mother gave me. . . . Do you even know who my mother was? No? It's funny, but neither do I. . . . But who cares. I know many other things. (Soiza Reilly 2008, 143–44; my translation)

This motif appears again in "Un pueblo misterioso" (A mysterious town), this time much less idealized. Published by *Caras y Caretas* on November 4, 1905, the article described the precarious conditions in the town of Las Ranas (which means "the frogs") and the daily habits of some three hundred people living behind the former cattle corrals of the Abasto market, in a place that had become the municipal dumpster (Gayol 2004, 224; Soiza Reilly 2008, 233–36). "It would be more appropriate to call it the city of swine," Soiza writes. "Located where garbage is incinerated, behind the corrals of the Abasto, far from the vibrant streets and their luminous signs, this mysterious town has the sad face of any town that sleeps in the arms of death. [. . .] [B]ehind the warm garbage smoke, there are the buzzing lives of a beehive of people. Very bad people who carry the instinct for crime in their blood and the sweet fatigue of sluggishness in their muscles" (Soiza Reilly 2008, 233; my translation).

Although Soiza's take on social disparities was constantly present in his early articles, he did not frame them as political or class asymmetries. What actually seems to be always present in Soiza's journalism is the naturalized notion that, in a vibrant city like Buenos Aires, extreme wealth and poverty both exist as the consequence of purely personal, individual choices. And surely enough, it was this point of view that helped Soiza establish a direct connection with his ascending, immigrant, middle-class readers.

Soiza Reilly was one of the first mass journalists in Latin America. But in a time when living off of one's writing was not well regarded by Latin American elites and literature was perceived as a prerogative of the leisurely upper classes, writers, journalists, and the market did not coexist peacefully. Soiza's solution to this conundrum was simple: he turned his back on the idea that literature was for the few, and he embraced the mass public, professionalizing his journalistic and literary activities. By the early 1910s, after having published several of his novels in cheap editions that were sold at newsstands for sometimes much less than a peso, he had been able to successfully monetize his work. *El alma de los perros* had at least twenty-four printings, and as a journalist and a writer Soiza lived comfortably, his journalism and his novels and stories in constant demand.

His ubiquitous presence in popular mass magazines such as *Caras y Caretas*, *Fray Mocho*, *PBT*, *Revista Popular*, *Nosotros*, *La Novela Semanal*, *La Novela Universitaria*, *La Novela de Hoy*, and *La Mejor Novela*, as well as in penny papers like *La Razón*, *La Nación*, and *Crítica*, undoubtedly helped Soiza become a coveted commodity in an industry geared to satisfying a growing mass public. This position, antagonistic to the Argentine literary avant-garde, not only turned him into one of the first heroes of the mass media but also earned him the antipathy of writers like Jorge Luis Borges. In *Martín Fierro*, the literary magazine founded in the mid-1920s by Evar Méndez, Borges wrote that Soiza produced only "nonsense" (*ñoñerías*) and suffered from "literary diarrhea" (Escales 2008, 12–13; Mizraje 2006, 35–36).

To give an idea of how antagonistic the avant-garde authors published in *Martín Fierro* were toward Soiza Reilly's commercial success, it suffices to note that Borges took pride in having to pay out of his own pocket for the publication of his first book of poetry. Borges used to quote a conversation about Arturo Cancela, a writer who denied that his books sold much, "because if other writers thought that [they had sold well], they would also think that the books were written for the populace and held little [literary] value" (Borges 1972; my translation).

Market failure was, for the Argentine avant-garde, a sign of literary success. In those early years of the mass media, consecrated writers like Borges and Cancela still looked at the masses with contempt and mistrust. Any kind of literature—fiction, nonfiction, poetry—geared toward the general public was not to be taken seriously. *Martín Fierro*, for instance, constantly referred to Soiza Reilly's books as a "sub-class of [. . .] Journalistic Literature" (Miz-raje 2006, 36). Their attacks reached a point where, in 1924, some of those same writers—hidden behind pseudonyms—wrote Soiza Reilly's "literary epitaph."

Soiza, however, largely ignored the attacks. He had already chosen sides. In 1906 he had cofounded the Writers' Society with Roberto Payró and Alberto Gerchunoff; by 1910 he had published *Cerebros de París* (Parisian brains), and around that time he was also awarded the gold medal in a San Francisco exhibit for *El alma de los perros* (The soul of dogs). Soiza also received several distinctions for his work, such as the title *Commendatore de la corona de Italia*, one of the highest honors conferred by the Italian government, while his fame and popularity kept growing (Mizraje 2004).

"My books, my travels, and my friendship with some celebrities in Europe have given my name a sonorous prestige," he acknowledged in the prologue to *Cerebros de París*. "Because of that, I have been called imbecile, dunce, jerk, lunatic, liar, hypertrophied, insolent, pedantic, slanderer, anarchist, catholic, weeping willow, oriental, bohemian, Brazilian, numb-skull, and other equally flattering adjectives" (qtd. in Escales 2008, 12–13; my translation).

During the years between 1905 and 1914, Soiza Reilly consolidated his position in the Argentine journalistic Parnassus. In 1907 he became *Caras y Caretas*'s star reporter in Europe, where he interviewed some of the most important personalities in the world of politics, science, and culture. And traveling back and forth between France and Argentina, he progressively started to focus on the developing conflicts that would lead to World War I (Ludmer 1999, 308).

By 1914 a long list of books had cemented Soiza Reilly's ever-expanding fame. *El alma de los perros*, which turned him into a favorite of the mass public, first appeared in Spain in 1907, having been edited by the famous novelist Vicente Blasco Ibáñez. Published by Casa Sempere, in Valencia, with a prologue by Manuel Ugarte, an Argentine diplomat, Latin American activist, and writer, the book sold out its first three consecutive printings of fifty thousand units each. *El alma de los perros*, soon translated into French, Italian, Czech, Yiddish, and several other languages, was then published in Argentina in 1917 and released in numerous subsequent editions until the early 1950s (Ludmer 1999, 308–9; Mizraje 2004, 173–78). His *Cien hombres célebres: Confesiones literarias* (One hundred famous men: Literary confessions), published in Buenos Aires in 1908, became the second best-seller in the history of Latin American literature. A compilation of 533 interviews and profiles, with illustrations by Paola Lombroso-Carrara—daughter of Cesare

Lombroso, famous founder of the Italian school of positivist criminology—the first edition sold twenty thousand copies and brought Soiza 5,000 pesos in royalties (Ludmer 1999, 189). In 1911 Soiza published again, this time back in Barcelona, his *Crónicas de amor de belleza y de sangre* (Chronicles of love, beauty, and blood), a title that may very well have inspired Horacio Quiroga's 1917 *Cuentos de amor de locura y de muerte* (Stories of love, madness, and death). The book was followed in 1914 by *La ciudad de los locos: Aventuras de Tartarín Moreira* (The city of the insane: The adventures of Tartarín Moreira), a novel and five essays on Europe and America, with illustrations by José Friedrich and dedicated to Soiza's colleagues at *Fray Mocho* magazine. In the prologue that Zeda—or Francisco Fernández Villegas, PhD—wrote for *Cerebros de París* (1912), the famous literary critic elevated Soiza to the status of a virtuoso of the crónica (Escales 2008, 20).

Soiza also published collections of his chronicles and interviews for magazines and newspapers. In *Cuentos de amor de belleza y de sangre*, dedicated to his colleagues at *Caras y Caretas*, Soiza explained,

> I've been living among famous men and women for quite some time now. Currently, I am the writer who has seen the most illustrious personalities of these times up close. . . . My books *One hundred famous men: Literary confessions*, *Men and women from Italy*, *The soul of dogs*, and *Parisian brains* include details of a thousand and one visits that I paid to the greatest geniuses as well as the most insignificant men in the world. . . . I was the first writer in South America to talk about some of the big names in Europe. My books have served to spread the word about many talented artists who, despite being popular in the Old World, were still unknown in America. Creating an audience for yet another book is equivalent to enlightening yet another man. I have enlightened many. (qtd. in Ludmer 1999, 190; my translation)

The volume included conversations with writer Edmundo D'Amicis, Spanish literary critic Menéndez Pelayo, and various performers, poets, and authors, including Gabriele D'Annunzio, Florencio Parravicini, Max Nordau, and Julio Herrera Reisig, whom a *Caras y Caretas* photographer captured on film shooting heroin (Ludmer 1999, 193).

Life in Paris was good. In *La juventud intelectual de América hispana*—with a prologue by Rubén Darío—poet Alejandro Sux described Soiza Reilly's Parisian apartment on the rue Clichy, with its overwhelming photographic gallery, irreverent statues, and collection of rare books: "On his desk could be found a few grinning skulls and Japanese monsters performing homely duties, while behind a mountain of papers you could see his impertinent eyeglasses and his Voltairean smile. [. . .] I am sure that in Latin

America there's no one so well suited for this genre of long reportage. If we were the nephews of Uncle Sam, we would definitely say that [Soiza Reilly] is the king of *reporters*" (qtd. in Ludmer 1999, 285; my translation).

His articles and interviews for *Caras y Caretas*, written in a colloquial yet insightful tone combining highbrow Buenos Aires culture and lowbrow street slang and usually shifting between first- and second-person narration, made him so immensely popular that magazines like *El Hogar* and *Fray Mocho* and mass newspapers such as *La Nación*, *Crítica*, and *La Razón* paid handsomely for his services.[15] When war broke out in Europe, there was little doubt he would become the first Latin American international correspondent to cover it.

DISPATCHES FROM THE GREAT WAR

On August 18, 1914, after a short trip back to Argentina, Soiza Reilly embarked on another voyage to Europe, this time commissioned by *La Nación*. Whatever he learned about writing from the class trenches of Argentina, he would see it dramatically tested in the war trenches of Europe. Along with his passport he carried a document issued by *La Nación* that stated, "D. Juan José de Soiza Reilly is invested with powers as special envoy for *La Nación* to Europe, with the purpose of informing this newspaper about the development of current events. He is hereby authorized to invoke its name when serving as its official representative in every circumstance that so requires, in order to better perform his mission. *La Nación* thanks in advance all people, colleagues, individuals, journalistic outlets, and public employees for the assistance provided to Mr. de Soiza Reilly in the success of his undertaking" (qtd. in Mizraje 2006, 32; my translation).

The contract with *La Nación* was not exclusive, so Soiza was also able to send dispatches to *Caras y Caretas* and *Fray Mocho*. In those articles, he generally avoided discussing the geopolitical aspects of the war in order to focus on his area of expertise: the human-interest story and local color. This is apparent in the following excerpts from two articles published in *Fray Mocho*. The first one, titled "Cómo se divierten los ingleses" (How the English amuse themselves), datelined France, October 14, 1914, explores a Babelic gathering of soldiers of all colors, languages, and religions:

> Every step of the way you find uniforms of the most fantastic colors and the
> most extravagant shapes. This war has turned out to be so extraordinary, so
> impossible, that it has gathered soldiers of all races and languages. All in all,
> they fight for the same cause. The spirit that unites them is one. Thanks only to
> their uniforms would you know where they come from. Catholics, Protestants,
> Muslims, Buddhists, non-believers.

Side by side with the Belgian soldier who—except for his rubber-lined cap—looks almost identical to the French, we see the Sikh from India, with his white turban, and by his side, in blue or red jackets and multicolored pants, the skilled Algerian snipers, who compete in blackness with those dexterous men from Senegal. Every type of weapon has its corresponding uniform. And the more African the soldier, the more colorful his attire. . . . The only ones who possess a real "war uniform" are the English. Theirs is khaki-colored, like the soil, which makes them pass unnoticed in the trenches. They don't even have badges. Officers are indistinguishable from their troops. Those golden laurels that both in France and Spain are used even by chiefs of train stations, the English have given up for modest black cords. And in the battle field they are almost invisible. (Soiza Reilly, 1914; my translation)

Soiza's reporting from the front lines was often based on second-hand sources, observations, and even rumors, and its goal was mostly to entertain rather than to inform. By humanizing the conflict, Soiza made the war more relatable to mass audiences in Argentina, who perceived the conflict as distant and rather incomprehensible.

Can you imagine—Lieutenant Helene said to Gómez Carrillo and myself yesterday—that these English devils, while they are holding a position—with the enemy fire strong and the bodies piling up at our feet—they pinch each other's legs to crack a laugh. . . . During truces, instead of lying down to rest, they play football, tennis, or they wrestle. . . .

[. . .] Undoubtedly, the English take war as a joke. I have also seen them, at Soissons, pounding at each other. I have witnessed the comfort with which they furnish their trenches. They are not satisfied with digging a ditch in the ground. They are not happy with a shelter good enough to shoot at their enemy. No! They don't believe that men go to war to die like heroes but rather to have fun like Englishmen. Once they have built their trench, they keep on working and dig out entire caves to live in. If the cave gets flooded, they develop a drain system to dry it out. They carpet the ground with hay, they build their bunks with four sticks of wood and interlaced string. They line their uniforms with newspaper. They brew their own whisky with water-soluble pills. The pills are condensed whisky, and each pill is equivalent to a quart.

A curious thing—the young lieutenant continued—is that they never look giddy. . . . It's amazing to see how sharp their aim is, and moreover, the moral and physical strength that drives them. I haven't heard a single English soldier complaining of fatigue. . . . Plus, they don't suffer from the ailment that makes French soldiers so miserable: nostalgia. (Soiza Reilly, 1914; my translation)

Through the use of the first-person narrative voice, Soiza appropriated the experiences of his subjects. As narrator, his voice became entangled with, and was often indistinguishable from, the voices of his characters. A mix of direct observation and interviews complemented with information obtained in local newspapers and second- or third-degree sources, Soiza Reilly's reporting technique was unorthodox in the eyes of American and European reporters. By focusing on people, and on long series of bizarre situations, he gripped the attention of an Argentine public far removed from the realities of the war. In his articles the human aspect of the conflict also took precedence over military and strategic details.

Soiza stayed in Europe until 1916, developing his reportorial technique and expanding his range of subjects. His most common topics were love ("French women are falling for the [English] allies with delirious enthusiasm"), class, and social differences in the battlefield. But he also focused on other narratives he was sure would captivate the growing middle-class readership in Argentina, whose interest in the purely political was limited. For example, "The organization [of English companies] is also quite strange. Men enrolled in the same province, or in the same city, stay in their own unit, so camaraderie bonds them very closely. Battalions are made of people of the same social condition, who belong to the same guild or profession. So, there's a battalion of rich noblemen, another of bank clerks, one of undergraduate students, and yet another of chauffeurs and butchers. The teachers at the 'London County Council' have their own battalion too" (Soiza Reilly, 1914; my translation).

On the German side, Soiza Reilly visited the Polish front in Kowal and Gostynin, where, in rain and snow, he witnessed the dismal life of the troops. In "La estrategia de los ratones" (The strategy of mice), an article published in *Fray Mocho* on April 23, 1915, he described the experience: "Polish snow isn't the white snow of the Russian steppes, or the snow of the Carpathians in Hungary. It is a snow that, when falling from clouds, presents the milky whiteness of snow, but as soon as it touches the ground, turns dirty gray, ashy, and melancholic. Realizing that it has fallen so unfortunately on the motherland of the poor persecuted Poles, perhaps it dreads having to face a scene of total desolation. And, unable to lift itself back to the clouds, it ages in sorrow and grays" (Soiza Reilly 1915; my translation).

After setting the scene, using dense layers of description, Soiza Reilly goes on to recount how the two German military encampments in Poland, located beside the frozen Vistula, were the daily scene of a human tragedy: desperate, hungry, and cold, some German soldiers walked on the thin ice of the river to escape the torments of war by drowning in its frozen waters.

Soiza presented the scene as if he had observed it firsthand, with profiles that are usually psychological, interpretive, and sometimes almost scientific:

> In fact, that afternoon we witnessed a deadly scene that looked like a suicide.
>
> A Red Cross soldier, a twenty-year-old man, bored with inaction, made a bet to amuse himself. He ventured he would walk across the Vistula, in the region of Gostynin, where that deep river is forty-five yards wide. It was four in the afternoon. It was getting dark.
>
> The young man started to walk on the vitrified surface, open-armed, mocking Jesus's walk on the water. . . . He laughed. He took slow steps. . . . However, when he had ventured some sixteen yards away from the bank he felt, undoubtedly, that the ice layer was solid enough. Emboldened by the accomplishment, he did a pirouette and started walking faster with a triumphant grin on his face, marking each step with the fierce emphasis of the Prussian style.
>
> He will win his bet!—his comrades cried out—The ice is hard today!
>
> That was what I thought too. But when he reached the middle of the river, we saw him stop. His right foot plunged. He jolted violently to liberate it. He couldn't. The ice cracked and the young man began to sink while swinging his arms trying to reach the small ice blocks that slipped from his hands like bars of soap. Without yelling or theatrics, three friends came downhill and started to walk on the frozen river to help their colleague. It was in vain. The young man sank, disappearing from the surface. And while sinking, the crack closed back over him, like the solid slab of a cold grave. (Soiza Reilly 1915; my translation)

Like most reporters of his time, Soiza Reilly was also fascinated with the technological advances of modern warfare. With technology becoming a topic of interest to the new mass public, the use of devices such as telephones, gas masks, and periscopes was frequently described in his stories. But Soiza also left room in his articles for other, more obscure aspects of war, such as spiritualist séances, ancient war history, and the physical and psychological consequences of sustained combat and life in the trenches.

Back in Buenos Aires in October 1916, Soiza received a hero's welcome. His dispatches had been read so widely that his three speaking engagements—on the topics of war, the battles in France, and the German people—completely sold out the Teatro Coliseo. Soiza had become so popular that even his homecoming was newsworthy. On October 2, 1916, *PBT* magazine's 623rd number welcomed the correspondent with an exultant editorial:

> Famous writer and brilliant journalist J. J. de Soiza Reilly has returned to Buenos Aires after a two-year tour around the European battlefields. Soiza, as the public is well aware, has been publishing his columns in our peer publication

La Nación, his ideas drawn directly from the source of such enormous and painful tragedy. [. . .] Soiza brings back a suitcase full of notes, and will take advantage of them during his conferences at the Coliseo theater. [. . .] It is our great pleasure to salute Soiza Reilly and wish him the success that both his talent and heart deserve, and we also would like to point out that he has gained his laurels not only thanks to his brain, but also thanks to his soul. (qtd. in Mizraje 2006; my translation)

It was clear by then that Soiza had succeeded at understanding and positioning himself in this new niche between journalism and mass literature, one generally frowned upon by the elites who had until then dominated both the Latin American and the Argentine literary canon.

BUENOS AIRES, BOHEMIA, AND THE MASS PUBLIC

Although many of Soiza's topics and ideas were akin to those that had interested members of avant-garde literary movements, such as the modernistas (topics like technology, the new metropolitan life, spiritualism, science fiction, internationalism, and science), unlike the modernistas Soiza did not write poetry or resort to publishing obscure editions just to be accepted by his peers. Indeed, he disregarded what the mouthpieces of the literary elites had to say about him and his work and focused on perfecting a popular genre that many of the modernistas had despised and considered merely a necessary evil: the crónica.

"Despite the fact that he doesn't want to be anybody's disciple and wishes to walk without a cane, a guide, or a professor," as the critic Zeda stated with poignancy in his prologue to Soiza's *Los cerebros de París*, "it is apparent that [Soiza Reilly] follows in the steps of the French masters who are behind the powerful literary genre we call 'cronica'" (qtd. in Escales 2008, 20; my translation). One of Soiza's short stories from 1909, "Psicología de una nota policial" (Psychology of a crime story), constitutes almost a writing manifesto, a theorization about the connections that crónicas established between the world of literature and the world of journalism (Terranova 2006).

In the story, a young writer explains to his girlfriend how to read a newspaper crime story: "If you want to satisfy your curiosity by learning about cruel, savage, horrible events, you shouldn't just expect for newspapers to give you the full story, with their shocking details of burglaries, suicides, and murders. If you do, you will be endlessly disappointed. [. . .] Tragedy isn't always in the grand, the noisy, or the bloody. Sometimes it lies in the insignificant. . . . In every line of a crime crónica there is drama. You only have to guess it. And feel it" (Soiza Reilly 2008, 220; my translation).

This approach was the one that Soiza followed between 1916 and 1920. In those years, he also became interested in the emerging world of radio. The colloquial style of his writing blended seamlessly with the new medium, and with journalists Josué Quesada and Clemente Onelli he started a show on LOX Radio Cultura, a private station owned by Francisco del Ponte (Mizraje 2006, 38). Soon Soiza's voice could also be heard on Radio Stentor, Radio del Pueblo, Radio Belgrano, and Splendid.

Although his journalism was never partisan or militant, it would be accurate to say that Soiza Reilly did have a political stance. In his early works he appeared to sympathize with socialist or anarchist causes, and his articles showed compassionate support for the workers and the dispossessed. In 1919, during what was known as the Tragic Week of January 7, popular strikes, marches, and protests that started at the British-owned Vasena metal works were violently confronted by an anti-Semitic paramilitary group known as the Liga Patriótica. The violence resulted in seven hundred deaths and more than three thousand wounded. In response, Soiza voiced his disgust in an article titled "El martirio de los inocentes" (The martyrdom of the innocent) and published in *Revista Popular* in February 1919: "I saw innocent old men whose beards were torn out [. . .] an old man lifted his undershirt to show us two ribs. They came out of his skin like two needles, bleeding. . . . A woman was forced to eat her own excrement. . . . Poor girls of fourteen or fifteen . . . [were] raped. I saw Jewish workers with both legs broken, broken in splinters on the sidewalk. And all this executed by gunslingers carrying the Argentine flag" (qtd. in Escales 2008, 15; Mirelman 1975, 63).[16]

 But it was not what he said that was political as much as how he said it: the profile method that Soiza Reilly had developed and the subjects he chose equalized his literary characters before the mass public—it put nobles and literates, artists and tramps on a level playing field. Soiza's use of the profile was a political, democratizing act.

In fact, Soiza extended this equalizing approach to other literary mechanisms. Many of his profiles start with a second-person narrative invocation, a direct appeal to the reader that brings narrator, public, and subject to the same plane. This happens, for instance, when he describes the inhabitants of a tenement in the underbelly of Buenos Aires: "Let's go in. . . . Is it disgusting? Well, you can wait at the door. You won't get to witness this lovely spectacle. . . . Lovely? Yes. It's the loveliest tableau, that of humble poverty, which frolics and rejoices in the dark of the tenement. . . . [. . .] Look over there at that lovely old lady. She is withered meat. Look at how she washes. Those filthy clothes. But you will never see her grimace in disgust. Why should she? She is washing her son's clothes!" (Soiza Reilly 2008, 147; my translation).

Some of Soiza Reilly's profiles also open with a few lines of dialogue between narrator and character, a device that delivers the same leveling effect. The profile of this *provincianita*, a woman who comes from the provinces and whom he contrasts with the cosmopolitan *porteña* (referring to the inhabitants of the port city of Buenos Aires), effectively demonstrates this technique:

—Be careful, young lady. The fire in the stove can be treacherous. It would be a shame if such beautiful hands . . .

—There is no problem, sir. We women from the provinces, we are strong.

—You? From the provinces? I would have bet you were . . .

—Argentine? Yes! To you people from Buenos Aires, the women from the provinces aren't Argentine: *we are from the provinces*. You talk so much about the elegance of the *porteñas* and about the intelligence of the *porteñas*, that anything that isn't *porteño* in the republic you deem deplorably *provincial*. (Soiza Reilly 2008, 275)

Many of Soiza Reilly's profiles also linger on the description of the dead. Death, looming or present, menacing or desired, conjures on a thematic level the same narrative effect as the second-person voice and the dialogue: it equalizes the rich and the poor, the famous and the unknown. A good example of this strategy is Soiza Reilly's story about the death of the Cuban violinist Claudio Brindis de Salas, who had risen to the pinnacle of the European musical aristocracy of the late nineteenth century, only to die in dire poverty in the streets of Buenos Aires in 1911.

—Hello! Am I speaking with Public Assistance?

—Yes, sir, who am I speaking to?

—This is "Aire dei vini" Inn, at Paseo de Julio, 294. Could you please send an ambulance for someone? He is a black bum, and he is sick, he is dying.

The ambulance left. It came back with the wretch. He was laid out on the examination table. He was black. Two nurses started to undress him. The jacket and the pants of his suit were dirty and torn. His shoes were worn out. His underwear . . . What a shame! Disgusting! It was shameful and disgusting at the same time, all that misery. [. . .]

Who could this man be?

A hobo, no doubt about it.

Here, in this pocket, he has a few papers. There's a ticket. There's the program of a concert in Ronda. A card. A passport. . . . What do they say?

Lord of Brindis, Baron of Salas! . . .

When he heard his name, the dying man experienced a moment of clarity.

He opened his eyes. He writhed in agony. And slowly, quietly, he began to turn cold. Hard. Rigid. Dead! (Soiza Reilly 2008, 129; my translation)

Although Soiza did prefer popular causes to those of the elites, and the voices of the street to those cultivated in the ivory tower of the Argentine literary canon, after the war his range of interests broadened. His articles, written with modernistic flair and vivid imagery, in a style somewhat close to American hard-boiled fiction, started to pay special attention to the other side of the coin of Buenos Aires's modernity: the upper classes and the rich.[17] Soiza would seldom reveal the names of the protagonists in his upper-class chronicles, but thanks to these articles, for the first time in the short history of Argentine journalism, writers began to take a peek into the lives, vices, and eccentricities of the new urban rich. Soiza's stories of those years featured the "vices (gambling, drugs and so on) that are made possible by an overabundance of money" (qtd. in Mizraje 2004, 175).

La muerte blanca: Amor y cocaína (White death: Love and cocaine) from 1926 and *Las timberas* (Female gamblers) from 1927 were both by-products of Soiza's magazine reporting. Published as novels, they compiled series of journalistic chronicles turned into moral fables that read like detective stories.

One of those chronicles, "Paraísos artificiales" (Artificial paradises), showed Soiza Reilly on the prowl for a story at an all-night party in the beach town of Mar del Plata, where socialites and powerful members of the Argentine aristocracy indulged in the hedonistic consumption of "the three paradises of an artificial heaven": morphine, cocaine, and opium (Soiza Reilly 2008, 263): "Today nobody reads Baudelaire. However, smoke paradises are at their apogee. Junkies don't just silently shoot their mysterious injections at home or in the restrooms of luxury department stores. Now there are nests for the aristocracy where devotees of both sexes get together around fatal drugs like bees around gardens. They shoot morphine with Pravaz needles set in gold. They snort cocaine as if it were the Archbishop's snuff. They smoke opium in Venice crystal hookahs" (Soiza Reilly 2008, 262; my translation).

Soiza populated the scene with somber characters, in just a few masterful strokes:

In harmony with the space, a woman's silhouette—long, gracious, slim, gray— moves across the room with a tray covered with small plates. On each plate there's a Pravaz syringe and a glass vial with morphine. . . . Behind her comes another woman, thinner and more delicate looking, all dressed in white like a nurse. . . . She is in charge of administering the shots. Not everyone accepts the morphine.

I can see a lady, whose hands are a constellation of shiny rocks, nodding nonstop to conceal her cough in a handkerchief. She promptly accepts the tray. A slight smile illuminates her eyes. . . . The woman dressed in white approaches her and is ready to inject her in the arm. But the lady stops her.

—No!

Then, the hierophant kneels at her feet. She lifts the woman's skirt an inch. She unties her pink stockings. . . . The lady reclines her head on the headrest, as if she were about to sleep. . . . The shot paints a smile of happiness on her lips. (Soiza Reilly 2008, 266; my translation)

By becoming a character in the scene Soiza Reilly gave credibility to his story and offered a front-row seat to his readers. Even though he never revealed the names of his real-life characters when they happened to be socialites (as he did, sometimes, when he reported about the poor), his stories were accurate enough to give him a terrible reputation among the Argentine elites—so much so that his 1925 book *Pecadoras* (Female sinners) was shunned by newspapers like *La Prensa* and *Sociedad* because some of the characters "resembled too closely many of the figures of Buenos Aires' aristocracy" (Mizraje 2006, 46). The attacks on the book reached the Commission of Morality, which finally censored it in 1925. *Criminales: Almas sucias de mujeres y hombres limpios* (Criminals: Dirty souls of clean men and women) from 1926, also based on his journalistic chronicles, claimed in the foreword that, after its publication, Soiza Reilly was on the brink of excommunication from the Catholic Church. And, again according to the prologue, several efforts were made to ban the book, and Soiza reported at least one attempt at stealing the manuscript (Mizraje 2008, 37).

These attacks reveal just how threatening Soiza Reilly's writing had become to the status quo and the elites. Profiles and interviews of both the rich and the poor had such an equalizing effect before the mass public that his very use of the profile had turned into a radically political act.

Confronted by Buenos Aires upper classes, Soiza raised the stakes, and in 1927 he published *Las timberas: Bajos-fondos de la aristocracia* (Female gamblers: The underbelly of aristocracy), followed by a direct take on censorship in the prologue to his 1927 *No leas este libro* (Don't read this book):

I know what happens. In my book I have portrayed, with an excess of truth— and truth is always excessive to the timorous—characters well known in Mar del Plata, in Avenida Quintana, in Calle Florida, and at the "Vogue" Club. . . . Those characters belong to the *haute*, to high society, where there may be many decent women and many decent men, but . . . My God! How about those little women I saw drunk with morphine, cocaine, and champagne?

The rich always find protectors. The poor, the police . . . And, if the police and the newspapers are so focused on revealing the places where cheap cabaret women and men gather to snort cocaine, why on earth would I be banned from revealing the aristocratic places, and the private apartments where milady Cocó and milord Fifí, or Madame Pola gather with their friends to celebrate their Sapphic masses and their ardent follies? What is vice for the poor, is *chic* culture for the rich. (Soiza Reilly 2008, 243–44; my translation)

As a professional writer isolated from Buenos Aires powerbrokers, Soiza Reilly clearly would not be associated with what Ángel Rama called the "lettered city," that stratum of Latin American intellectuals intimately connected with the political power and the social elites. In the mass public Soiza Reilly found his primary audience and interlocutor. And the ubiquitous growth of these audiences over the years that followed paved the way for Soiza's relative independence from the old models of both journalism and literature.

EXIT THROUGH THE RADIO

In the 1930s, Soiza was already one of the main figures in the bohemian subculture of Buenos Aires, and he had become an influential figure in the emerging world of the mass media, with friendships that can be traced back to the many prologues he wrote, for writers such as Alejandro Sux and Nicolás Granada, and for tango singer and composer Enrique Cadícamo. Soiza's career as a writer was stable and blooming. His crónicas and interviews, the two genres he had mastered, were among the most read and commented on in the Argentine press, and through popular editions and collections he had also released a long list of books—more than a dozen—in his particular genre that bridges fiction and nonfiction, all sold in cheap thirty-cent editions.

Many of those books and most of his journalism could be characterized as literary journalism, particularly because it was in fact Soiza Reilly who had coined that notion to define his own work. Like Soiza himself, literary journalism stood in between two traditions: the leisurely writing activity that, for several years, had been a prerogative of the high bourgeoisie, and journalism, which in the first decades of the twentieth century had started to become a professional activity for the middle classes.

In an interview with Eduardo Scarfoglio, an Italian "millionaire journalist," writer, and entrepreneur, that *Caras y Caretas* published on March 23, 1909, Soiza Reilly explored not just the idea of journalism as a lucrative profession, one that, just like many other liberal activities, was now regulated by the laws of the market. He also insisted on mentioning that "any journalist—that is, any journalist with writing talent—can write a good novel. But not every novelist, no matter how talented, can write a good news article. . . . [Today's] journalism is not the barren profession of years past. It is no longer a profession. It is not a craft. It's an art. A delicate and profound one. An art of goldsmiths. Of poets. Of philosophers. An art that has its heroes and victims. I imagine that you don't believe in what I say, but I am talking—with utmost devotion—about literary journalism" (qtd. in Cilento 2009, 81; my translation).

By the mid-1930s Soiza's presence in mainstream written media had started to wane, perhaps as a consequence of the military coup of Gen. Félix Uriburu. It is also conceivable that two of his books of that period, one commissioned by Standard Oil and a second one by Firestone, had cast a shadow of suspicion over his name, while eliciting some questions about the connections between journalism and powerful corporations, as well as the relationship between mainstream media and the market.

Written in 1934, *La República Argentina vista con ojos argentinos: El problema del petróleo* (The Argentine republic seen with Argentine eyes: The problem of petroleum) welcomed the Standard Oil Corporation to Argentina after the Argentine government had privatized its national oil reserves. Both the reserves, as well as the Argentine national oil company, YPF, had until then belonged—by law—to the Argentine state. But after the coup of September 6, 1930, the de facto government overruled the democratic law and moved ahead with an unconstitutional privatization.

Desde la lágrima del caucho hasta el ala en que volamos por los caminos (From the tear of the rubber tree to the wing that drives us down the roads), published in 1935 and commissioned by Firestone, was also an open welcome to an American corporation entangled in shady businesses with de facto government officials.[18]

Curiously, after these two books Soiza practically quit writing to become a full-time radio personality. Fascinated with the power of the medium, he embraced his new role and became the host of one of the most popular shows on Radio El Mundo: *Arriba los Corazones*. Years later, in 1954, during a short appearance on LR4 Radio Splendid, he would describe his lifelong passion for journalism:

> My beginnings in journalism can be traced back to the day I was born. I came out of the womb yelling the news of my birth. What is journalism? An eternal announcing cry of what's new.

I have sailed through all the fatigues in the world, but I never stopped being a journalist. What did I do in my youth when I started as a paperboy in the University of the Streets? Journalism. What did I do during my forty years as a chair at a certified teachers school? Journalism. What did I do in forty-two published books? Journalism. What have I been doing on radio for twenty-three years? Journalism. When God wants to find out my profession, it will be enough for him to ask me:

—Show me your hands.

He will see the callus that the pen left on my fingers after sixty years of writing. And God will say with his merciful tenderness:

—Journalist!

And will send me to hell to teach the devil about the most delicious suffering on earth: journalism. (Soiza Reilly 2006, 515–16; my translation)

Soiza Reilly's literary journalism served as a bridge between immigrants, middle classes in formation, and the established aristocracies of Buenos Aires; between literature as a prerogative of the patrician bourgeoisie and journalism as a rented and lucrative profession; between the lowlifes, the marginals, and the vices of the upper urban classes; between European wartime experiences and Latin America's new world order. An outsider to all these groups, and also to the Latin American literary canon, Soiza personified the mass mediated journalism in Latin America in the first two decades of the twentieth century, turning his extraordinary powers as chronicler and writer into an equalizing force for an emerging modern audience.

CHAPTER 5

• • •

THE MASS PRESS

THE LIFE OF A tabloid crime reporter in the 1920s and 1930s was no bed of roses. To hobnob with Buenos Aires's pimps, to schmooze with the police, and to produce a readable, sensational drama each day out of abhorrent murders, petty crimes, arsons, and garden-variety accidents was only the first part of the job description. Reporters for *Crítica*, *La Prensa*, and *El Mundo* also had an acquired obligation that stemmed from the implicit reading contract their newspapers had forged with the mass audiences. In a way, to be a reporter for a newspaper in those years was to enter public service, to become a guide and an aide to the readers, to tend to their multiple needs and wants—often even on a personal basis—while simultaneously convincing them to become visible and active players in the new experiences of democracy and the mass media.

Argentine writer and journalist Roberto Arlt was by 1927 a staff reporter with the evening newspaper *Crítica*. Although he had already published a very successful novel, *El juguete rabioso* (*The Mad Toy*), winner of the 1926 Editorial Latina award with almost unanimously glowing reviews, Arlt could not make a living off his literature alone. In his first full-time job as a journalist, he found the means for sustenance, a source of inspiration, and sometimes even more: "Today [April 5, 1927] one of our news writers, Roberto Arlt, and photographer José Chiapetti, called in by a pre-suicidal woman to her apartment on Uruguay street, prevented her death by disarming her while she tried to shoot herself in the temple. Given the extraordinary development of the adventure, we present this illustrated chronicle to our readers, who will see that the profession of a journalist isn't a bed of roses" (Saítta 1998, 207; my translation).

The article was accompanied by photos of Arlt struggling with the woman for her gun, and it described how, at the beginning of the "rescue," both writer and photographer were held at gunpoint and threatened by the woman, who had called *Crítica* herself to announce her suicidal intentions.[1]

Although somewhat atypical, the story illustrates a type of conversation established between audiences and mass-circulation newspapers that, inaugurated by *Caras y Caretas* a few decades earlier, was now at its peak. Readers were no longer passive recipients, pure consumers of a commercial product, but partners—direct participants in a mediation in which, many times, relative positions would change.

An immigrant whose family lived in the suburbs, Arlt was deemed an unrefined writer by the literary elites of Buenos Aires who shared their ideas and opinions in two magazines: *Martín Fierro* (1924–1927) and *Sur* (1931–1970). He was frequently criticized for his language, which was considered substandard and low by the highbrow critics, but he was adored by the Buenos Aires public, and his books and plays regularly sold out. A product of the welcoming policies of the turn of the century introduced by Sarmiento's generation, Arlt was also the embodiment of the free education law, which had benefited the new urban classes. In many ways, he opened the gates for a type of language and a set of narratives that originated in the growing sections of the modern city. In his texts, Arlt made a point of challenging the purism of the Castilian language, whose proponents he mocked. He also furthered a renovation in the Spanish vernacular of the Río de la Plata, which was directly connected to the incorporation of Anglicisms, Gallicisms, and Italianisms—new forms created by the integration of immigrants into society. Arlt was an active agent for a new vernacular open to argots and foreign voices, and a language experience more permeable and therefore more available to be used and molded collectively and spontaneously. In this sense, Arlt channeled the mutability of the new urban masses through his literature and journalism. Much like Juan José de Soiza Reilly, he showed the narratives of cultural appropriation—the working classes taking over high culture—in his novels and his literary journalism, incorporating the tastes and the ideas of the new reading publics into the zeitgeist. But, unlike Soiza Reilly, Arlt had experience in muckraking, a form of journalistic practice that involved the infiltration of institutions in disguise. Arlt was, in more ways than one, a cultural reformer and an infiltrator.

Just like Arlt, who would become a towering figure among Latin American novelists of the early twentieth century, Jorge Luis Borges, one of the most praised fiction writers of all time, also spent the early days of his career immersed in the world of journalism. But Borges had his own way of reaching out to the new audiences in the context of an ever-expanding modernity.

A son of the lettered elites of Buenos Aires, Borges was a different kind of integrator. Educated in Spain, he viewed with curiosity and enthusiasm the potential of the new urban publics blooming in Latin America. Much like Domingo Sarmiento sixty years earlier, he sought a specific type of reader, a "blacker and rarer swan" (Borges 1975, 15), and he tried to shape that reader with his first works in narrative prose published in *Crítica*, one of the most innovative and sensationalist mass-circulation newspapers in Latin America in those years. The boom of the new press and the popularity of the tabloids also gave Borges room for literary experimentation, at a time when the avant-gardes used journalism as a medium.

The reading masses were for Borges a sounding board. In his early works in prose, the writer built complicity with his readers based on irony, contextual interpretation, antiphrasis, and humor. But these strategies are only visible today through very close, historical reading. Without understanding Borges's journalism first, it would be virtually impossible to see the direction, trajectory, and development of his later fiction.

While Borges aimed at multiplying possible references and connections between modern Buenos Aires and the world from the pages of *Crítica*, Arlt strove to understand Buenos Aires as an enclosed system. By tapping into certain classificatory tools—Marxist categories among them—Arlt documented, described, and quantified Buenos Aires's types on more or less their own terms. Arlt's effort was that of a taxonomist, and through literary journalism he succeeded in painting modern Buenos Aires in its unique and strange colors.

Separating themselves from the *modernistas*, the journalists of the new mass press contributed to turning the writers' adventure into an adventure *with* the readers by sharing one of the rarest experiences in the new urban world: intimacy. Intimacy helped bring a previously top-down approach to literature—educating the public—to eye level. Working alongside the masses, these writers catered to one of the main social functions of the new press: integrating the public into the democratic game.

A DIFFERENT KIND OF POPULAR PRESS

Although *Crítica* established the sensationalistic trend that many newspapers in Latin America would follow during the second half of the twentieth century, its main competitor, *El Mundo*, a daily tabloid founded in 1928 by Alberto M. Haynes—the owner of Editorial Haynes—appealed to its readership through a more restrained strategy catering to families. Arlt had cut his teeth with the flamboyant content he wrote for *Crítica*, but it was not until he moved to the more serious atmosphere of *El Mundo* that he found the conditions in which to explore his voice as a narrative journalist.

El Mundo was Argentina's first tabloid, a friendly format for commuters. Its layout featured headlines in large fonts and photographs on the cover. But unlike its broadsheet competitors, it was conveniently well organized for a reader on the move, with fixed national and international "panorama" sections on the cover, and social events and comics on the back. *El Mundo*'s tone was light and sober, as it was geared toward "family-type" readers. And although it was technically a tabloid, *El Mundo* was nothing like its American counterparts. The newspaper was devised to compete against the two most traditional Argentine morning broadsheets: *La Prensa*, the largest, and *La Nación*, second in circulation yet most traditional among the nationals.

Conceived as an alternative to solemn morning newspapers, *El Mundo* based its strategy on slashing its cover price to five cents (half that of its competitors), distancing itself from politics, resorting to the informative paradigm rather than an entertainment one, and employing a number of young writers with little experience in journalism—and thus less familiar with the clichés of news copy—in order to improve the quality of its writing. *El Mundo* crusaded for morality in a city it described as threatened by vice and corruption (Saítta 1998, 20–21).[2]

In 1928, Roberto Arlt left *Crítica*, where he had been one of the four writers "in charge of the [daily] bloody, truculent article" (Arlt 1998, 426). Moving to *El Mundo* to be a general assignment journalist, he was excited to join a team of respected young reporters, including Leopoldo Marechal, Francisco Luis Bernárdez, Amado Villar, and his longtime friend and confidant, poet Conrado Nalé Roxlo. *El Mundo* soon gifted Arlt with fame and recognition, as well as a fresh start as a star journalist.

Although he had already published his first novel, *El juguete rabioso* (*The Mad Toy*) in 1926, Arlt's experience in journalism was limited. His first job for the mass media had been as a collaborator on *Don Goyo*, a general-interest magazine published every Tuesday and directed by Nalé Roxlo. The magazine, a flagship publication at Editorial Haynes, put out stories by Eduardo Mallea, Luis Cané, Manuel Ugarte, Leopoldo Marechal, and poet Alfonsina Storni—many of the writers who would also join *El Mundo* in 1928 (Saítta 2000a, 37).

In his first year with *Don Goyo*, Arlt wrote twenty-two articles, one every two weeks, all in a personable, autobiographical tone. Always using the first-person narrative voice, tapping into highly codified genres like the sermon, the open letter, and the apology, he also produced for *Don Goyo* semifictional stories which, on occasion, caused problems for the magazine's administration. "When I was the director of *Don Goyo*," Arlt's friend Conrado Nalé Roxlo (1978, 37) wrote, "I published one of Arlt's *short stories* that talked about the grotesque love encounters of a couple of prosperous bakers in Flores whose obesity was the living proof of the succulence of their pasta. A lawyer asked me for an appointment; they wanted to sue the magazine for defamation" (my translation and italics).[3]

These pieces, read as factual narratives by *Don Goyo*'s audience but still considered short stories by Nalé Roxlo, evolved in tone and character and were the prequel to Arlt's *Aguafuertes* (Etchings), the short human interest features he would present on a daily basis in his column for *El Mundo*. Since 1928, and in a very short period of time, "Etchings" turned Arlt into the most famous journalist of his generation.

TALENT AND COMPENSATION IN THE DOUBLE LIFE OF ARLT

Arlt was first and foremost a fiction writer, novelist, and playwright; being a journalist came in at a distant fourth place. Nalé Roxlo, a neighbor during Arlt's formative childhood years in Flores, described his friend's original passion for and dedication to writing: "[I am referring] to the years before *Mad Toy*, the formative years, his literary prehistory. His life, for him, had only one meaning: to become a great writer. I have never witnessed such strong will—persistent, obtuse. It was a violent and conclusive passion, as are those of passionate young men" (Nalé Roxlo 1978, 86; my translation).

That passion was partly fueled by Arlt's need for transcendence and his desire to put his origins behind him (Masotta 1982, 9). In a quest for uniqueness that would accompany him his whole life, Roberto Arlt, the son of Carlos Arlt, a Prussian army deserter from Posen, and Ekatherine Iobstraibitzer, a peasant from the Italian Tyrol, pledged allegiance to two kinds of writers: the talented and the economically successful.

On the side of the talented, a short autobiography published in *Crítica* magazine after the success of *The Mad Toy* showed Arlt's preference for Gustave Flaubert and Fyodor Dostoyevsky. His choice was part sincere, part provocation. By expressing equal admiration for the greatest among the French romantic realists and the Russian father of psychological existentialism, Arlt positioned himself in a neutral zone between the two main writing schools in Buenos Aires at the time: the socialist realists of Boedo—writers like Leónidas Barletta, Nicolás Olivari, Elías Castelnuovo, Álvaro Yunque, and César Tiempo—and the avant-gardists of Calle Florida, with writers like Jorge Luis Borges, Oliverio Girondo, Conrado Nalé Roxlo, Leopoldo Marechal, Raúl González Tuñón, Eduardo González Lanuza, and Arlt's own mentor, Ricardo Güiraldes, in its ranks.

In his "Letter to the Geniuses of Buenos Aires," which appeared in *Don Goyo* a few months before the publication of *The Mad Toy*, Arlt explained his double allegiance: "If you wander around [the writers of Calle] Florida, you will communicate with frightening detail the reasons for which Dostoievsky [*sic*] was a degenerate and Tolstoy a whiner; if you socialize with [the writers of] Boedo, you will badmouth Flaubert, that 'bourgeois,' and that other aristocrat, D'Annunzio. You, in Florida, [. . .] will tear apart Dostoievsky and reduce Tolstoy to the size of a lentil, while you, in Boedo, will explain how Flaubert wrote his novels and how easy it would be for you naturally, if you wanted, to become a writer as great as Flaubert" (Arlt 1996, 63–65, my translation).[4]

On the side of the economically successful, Arlt expressed devotion to the French feuilleton writer Pierre Alexis Ponson du Terrail and—a little closer—to an old neighbor from Flores who was instrumental in his becoming a full-time working journalist: Juan José de Soiza Reilly. Soiza Reilly was Arlt's only local journalistic hero and his direct media mentor.

In Ponson du Terrail, Arlt found the image of a successful, prolific writer—someone who could, through sheer willpower, reap the rewards of multiple best sellers and the acclaim of the mass public:

> Let's not try to find novelistic technique [in his work]. [Ponson du Terrail] solves the trials and tribulations of his dramas mathematically, through the most outrageous procedures, and despite the truculence of his resolutions, despite how laughable Rocambole feels to us [. . .], he simply nails our interest to the burning grill of curiosity. The novel finished, the characters immediately start to fade away, because the French Vice Count is rabidly a novelist, a novelist with the power of a sledgehammer, meaning an expert in the art of playing with the easiest human frailties. [. . .] Rocambole is alive . . . and to be alive is the first among the qualities necessary to aspire to immortality. As soon as a character becomes alive, although his father has created him with mutilated pieces, lame or stupid, he has reached what a classicist would call the doors of eternity. (Arlt 1940, qtd. in Saítta 2000a, 39; my translation)

Yearning for mentorship and inspiration, Arlt found Soiza Reilly only a few blocks from home. In "Éste es Soiza Reilly" (This is Soiza Reilly), an "Etchings" piece he wrote in Río de Janeiro and published in *El Mundo* on May 31, 1930, Arlt told in third-person narrative voice the story of his first encounter with his admired neighbor. It was a winter morning in "1916 or 1917" when a teenage Arlt showed up at Soiza Reilly's house in Flores, on the corner of Membrillar and Ramón Falcón. Arlt recalled he was welcomed by a housekeeper, who let "the poorly dressed boy in" to "read one of his pieces to the great Soiza Reilly" (Arlt 1960, 221–24).

Arlt was elated:

> He was going to talk to the author of *The Soul of Dogs* and *Men and Women from Italy and France*. Soiza Reilly was, at the time, famous among young writers. His chronicles about Paris [. . .], about Verlaine, have shaken the souls of those poets in shorts and of those redeemers of the world who still don't have a driver's license.

The young writer was escorted to a room upstairs, and marveled at what he saw:

> Through the window he looks at the street, then the bookshelves and thinks: "Living like this, it's a pleasure to be a writer. With a room like this, books, a maid. Will he read what I brought? Maybe . . . from his chronicles you can tell he is a good man." (Arlt 1960, 221–22; my translation)

When Soiza Reilly showed up, wearing "a fur coat as he cleaned his glasses with a handkerchief," Arlt introduced himself as a "writing aficionado" and recited by heart the beginning of *The Soul of Dogs*—which the elder acknowledged as the work of his young self. Arlt then asked Soiza Reilly if he could read one of his own pieces for him. But Soiza told him to leave the manuscript and promised that, if he liked it, he would publish it in *Revista Popular*, a magazine he edited at the time. A month later, the piece appeared as a short story titled "Jehova" in a section Soiza Reilly named half-jokingly "Prosas modernas y ultramodernas" (Modern and ultramodern prose). Arlt never forgot the gesture:

> I believe that men and women are naturally ungrateful creatures, both jovial and ferocious. . . . I also believe that these animals never forget whatever sears them with terrible pain—or happiness. That's why I have never forgotten Soiza Reilly. He was the first generous hand to offer me the most extraordinary joy in my teenage years.
>
> Two months later, the magazine went bankrupt. But I knew that if I kept writing it was because in that article, fixed to my bedroom wall with four nails, I saw the invisible promise of success in the grandiose title "Modern and Ultramodern Prose." A title that a mature author had put there as an admonition to the younger one who believed that the more "convoluted" the words he used, the more artistic his prose would be. (Arlt 1960, 223–24; my translation)

A few years later, Soiza Reilly wrote the prologue to Arlt's first book (now lost), *Diario de un morfinómano* (The diary of a morphine maniac), published in the city of Córdoba in 1920. Soiza Reilly continued to cross paths with Arlt in newsrooms and publishing houses, and he remained one of Arlt's greatest inspirations throughout his life. This was not only because the older writer represented the honorable, good-spirited mentor who sided with the dispossessed and the voiceless but also because he embodied a successful model of journalism, a new type of writing professional devoted to facts. Soiza Reilly's productivity and personal sacrifice had been rewarded by the masses and the markets with a comfortable financial position. That position of success would be one to which Arlt would aspire throughout his career.

THE SECRETS OF SUCCESS AND THE RHETORIC OF NUMBERS

Like no other writer in those years, Arlt took pride in his productivity and the sheer volume of his journalistic production. As if locked in a perpetual race against time to prove his worth, knowledge, and relevance to his peers and the mass public, he also strived to quantify and measure his cultural intake and output, identifying hard work as one of the keys for success in the modern mass market. "I have read many novels," he stated in an article headlined "El cementerio del estómago," which ran in *El Mundo* on January 29, 1929. "I started reading them when I was twelve years old, and I am twenty-eight. So, for sixteen years I've been reading an average of fifty books a year, which means six hundred novels. I have read many more, but at least that many" (qtd. in Goloboff 2002, 111–12; my translation).

Sylvia Saítta has identified Arlt's need to "flaunt" his acquired competences as part of the writer's class inferiority complex, which places him in a long tradition of boasting that began with Sarmiento. Unlike many of his peers, who came from patrician families and literature, Arlt felt that behind his name there was nothing—no titles, no ancestors who had fought in the war of independence, no illustrious writers. There was only an immigrant past of uncertain origins (Saítta 2000a, 62).

However, the topos of *quantity* in Arlt also has other roots that should be explored, especially in light of his communist sympathies—specifically, Arlt's collaboration with publications such as *Bandera Roja*, house organ of the Argentine Communist Party. In fact, after 1930, Arlt was systematically associated with Argentine socialism and communism. "Sometimes I think of the yards of prose that I have written," he mused in a piece published March 9, 1929, in *El Mundo*. "One hundred and forty-five yards of prose to date. One hundred and forty-five! When I die, how many miles would

I have written?" (Arlt 1981a, 1:225; my translation). Arlt had a penchant for "measuring" his oeuvre, but the quantification of his production was no different than what, for instance, the magazine *Caras y Caretas* had done in the past. In an editorial for its special May 1910 number, the publishers of *Caras y Caretas* boasted about the two miles of altitude that all the copies of that special issue would have reached had they been piled on top of each other. Aligned next to each other the copies would have stretched thirteen thousand miles, the distance between the North and South Poles (Eujanian 1999, 29; see also chapter 4 of this book).

The topos of quantity was also frequently used by *Crítica*'s editor, Natalio Botana. Exactly like Arlt, who saw himself as a writer without a tradition, *Crítica* presented itself as a newspaper without one, a publication that was absolutely new, a unique occurrence in the history of Latin American journalism. "*Crítica* is *Crítica*. It has no grandparents," it editorialized in "*Crítica juzgada por la revista Nosotros*" on October 12, 1925. "It was born by spontaneous generation at a time in the century when communications have torn down so many old walls and have unveiled fresh new sources. It is a worthy child of this century" (Saítta 1998, 158).

To validate *Crítica*'s leverage in the public discourse, Botana constantly had to measure its worth by quantifying its interactions with the audience. Numbers—of readers, editions, participants in a tango competition, of stories submitted to a writing contest, of published articles and books read and written—granted both *Crítica* and Arlt the means to bypass tradition as a criterion of legitimization. Modernity was, first and foremost, commensurable. Prestige, relevance, talent, legitimacy, and social worth could all be quantified, numbered, charted, added up, divided, and multiplied.

In that spirit, Arlt, who was particularly inclined toward the rhetoric of numbers, was indirectly questioning José Martí's (2002, 93) notion of quantity. "These people eat quantity; we, class," was no longer a valid statement to Arlt, in part because in *quantity* Arlt also—and especially—saw *class*.

Arlt's take on quantity, however, was not based purely on the virtues of sheer accumulation. Influenced by some Marxist notions, the author of "Etchings" equated production volume with the power of labor, as he wrote in "¡Con ésta van 365!," which appeared in *El Mundo* on May 14, 1929: "One year. Three hundred and sixty-five articles, meaning one hundred and seventy yards in newspaper column, which is equivalent to 255,500 words. *If these one hundred and seventy yards were cashmere, I would have suits for the rest of my life*" (Arlt 1981b, 132; my italics and translation).

The mental operation of converting prose into cashmere required that both products (treated by Arlt as commodities) be expressed in quantities of the same magnitude. And for Arlt—likely via Marx—that magnitude was "abstract human labor," the productive expenditure of human brains, nerves, and muscles (Marx 2000, 432). Any increase in quantity was, therefore, the by-product of an increase in human labor. Hard work (or human labor) being an Arltian precondition for accessing culture, accumulation—of any kind—was consistently viewed by the writer in a positive light. Knowledge accumulation, but also the accumulation of words or any other type of material stock, was the result of human work and therefore the by-product of a positive human quality.

Arlt, however, was not strictly a Marxist, and his approach naturalized historical-social constructs such as property and culture, while overestimating the power of self-sacrifice and drive. His take on Marxism was in fact severely criticized by the higher echelons of the Argentine Communist Party during the writer's brief collaboration with *Bandera Roja* (Saítta 2000a, 105–33).

This quasi-Marxist approach to journalism and literature was for Arlt more classificatory than revolutionary, however. Marxism served him primarily as a taxonomical instrument, much more so than as a revolutionary weapon. In his "Etchings" Arlt did not strive to create social transformation but simply to make sense of Buenos Aires's modernity. Through the lens of certain Marxist constructs Arlt developed a classificatory system, which he displayed with eloquence in his columns for *El Mundo*.

ARLT'S "ETCHINGS" AND THE PRESENTATION OF THE ARGENTINE CHARACTER

Mass-circulation newspapers like *El Mundo*, *Noticias Gráficas*, and *Crítica* positioned themselves as the interpreters of progress and change in the new city. From their pages, professional journalists addressed their audiences by classifying, describing, and enumerating a new cast of social types in an array of innovative writing formats, genres, and styles. Among these new formats were Arlt's "Etchings" for *El Mundo*. These daily columns of literary journalism, in which Arlt described, analyzed, and typified new urban professions, activities, and trends, were also instrumental in the legitimization of a new language: a modern "Castilian" from a Buenos Aires in perpetual transformation, the language of a city wide open to immigration and in constant flux.

Arlt's "Etchings" were part of a strategy developed by *El Mundo*'s editor, Carlos Muzio, to appeal to new audiences and increase its advertising revenue. Muzio, who had been responsible for slashing *El Mundo*'s cover price to half that of most morning newspapers, also added comic strips on the back, including Otto Messmer's *Felix the Cat*. And on August 5, 1928, he introduced a new section called "Aguafuertes Porteñas" (Buenos Aires etchings), written by Roberto Arlt (Saítta 2000a, 55). The strategy paid off, and *El Mundo* rapidly became the morning newspaper with the third-highest circulation in Argentina, trailing only *La Prensa* and *La Nación*. Among the tabloids it reigned supreme, growing from 40,000 copies in October 1928 to 127,000 only a year later (Saítta 2000a, 71).

At first, Arlt's columns appeared unsigned. But on August 14, little more than a week after "Etchings" was introduced, the writer's initials popped up at the bottom of the page, and on August 15 his full byline was featured for the first time. The prominent appearance of his name affected not only Arlt's popularity, which skyrocketed in a matter of days, but also the tone and content of the columns. With his name on the page, Arlt started to shift from the distant third-person narrative voice to the first-person and sometimes second-person voice. The second person in Arlt's "Etchings" broke the fourth wall of the mass press. Using his own name and appealing to the reader as "you," he created a shift from anonymity to individualization, building a reading contract based on the power of intimacy and an implied personal relationship between writer and reader.

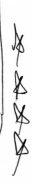

For fourteen years, until the day of his death, Arlt would write his daily column for *El Mundo*. His topics were varied, but they could easily be grouped in a few general categories: the Argentine and Buenos Aires types, which included profiles of professionals and artisans of all kinds, as well as social and criminal characters; places and traditions in the city; the language of Buenos Aires, a quasi-philological approach to the changing language in an increasingly cosmopolitan city; and civility, because Arlt, a communist writer, was explicitly banned from proselytizing in his pages. "I've been ordered not to get into politics," he wrote in one of his columns in 1930 (Arlt 1992a, 121; my translation).[5] The "Etchings" columns also dealt with relationships and every now and then introduced autobiographical notes.[6] This array of categories appearing in a daily column created multiple, juxtaposed layers of analysis and classification.

The Argentine writer and critic Pedro Orgambide described Arlt's "types" as an intermediate point between the men and women Arlt the journalist observed in the streets, and the characters Arlt the writer created in his literature: "[Arlt] imported the intensity with which these *people-characters* lived using the devices of a professional who had already written some of his best pages as a novelist" (Orgambide 1960, 12; my translation).

The cross-pollination between journalism and literature in Arlt's work was best revealed in the character of Haffner, the Melancholic Pimp, of *The Seven Madmen*, or the maid who is the main character in Arlt's play *300 millones* (300 million). Haffner was inspired by anarchist Noé Trauman. Arlt had met Trauman while covering the crime beat for *Crítica*, and he held a long series of interviews with him at Las Violetas, a fancy teahouse in the Almagro neighborhood. A Polish immigrant, Trauman had arrived in Buenos Aires in 1906 and was the founder of Varsovia, or the Israeli Society of Mutual Assistance, soon renamed Zwi Migdal. The association was a front for a powerful prostitution network managing thousands of brothels in Argentina, with branch offices in Brazil, New York City, Warsaw, South Africa, India, and China (Saítta 2000a, 53; Ragendorfer 1997).

The maid of *300 millones* was also based on a real person pulled from one of the many crime stories Arlt wrote for *Crítica*. She appeared again as the main character in one of Arlt's "Etchings" columns:

> As a crime reporter working for *Crítica* in 1927, one September morning I had to write a chronicle on the suicide of a Spanish maid, single, twenty years of age, who had killed herself one morning at 5:00 a.m. by jumping in front of a tramway that passed by the house where she worked.
>
> When I arrived, the dismembered body had already been removed. I would have attributed no importance to the event whatsoever (during those years I saw dead bodies on a daily basis) had it not been for the fact that, after visiting the house during the investigation, I was confronted with a number of striking details.
>
> The lady who owned the house told me that the night before the suicide, the maid hadn't slept. A visual examination of the maid's bed allowed me to establish that she hadn't even lain down, which also made me think that she had actually spent the night sitting on her travel trunk (she had emigrated from Spain a year before). When she walked out of the house to leap in front of the tramway, the maid had also forgotten to turn off the light.
>
> All these details together made a deep impression on me. For months on end I walked around daydreaming, picturing the spectacle of a sad young woman sitting on the edge of a trunk, in a room of whitewashed walls, thinking of her hopeless destiny under the yellow incandescent glow of a 25-watt bulb. (Arlt 1960, 13; my translation)

In the "Etchings" column about Argentine places and traditions, Arlt described innumerable hangouts in Buenos Aires, either very well known or totally hidden—shady pensions, glamorous coffeehouses, dirty brothels, suburban plazas, loud soccer stadiums, and kitschy German bars:

> [But] not those types of German bars where you go during the winter, with ordinary interiors, deer heads, and grotesque Tyrolese landscape paintings

hanging on the walls: a carrot-haired guy, exposed knees, wearing green socks, courting a grocer in a Theodiscus market, she wearing a hat that looks like a basket, with a nose like a trumpet. No, I'm not talking about that, nor about this other German bar mainly visited by Spanish chauffeurs and literates who tell each other that they are either overlooked or predestined geniuses. No, no! I want to tell you about another bar, one that deserves to be called a place of solace, one that blooms with unusual exuberance in the neighborhood of Belgrano; a bar decorated with little lights hanging between the branches of cypresses and a Germanic orchestra scratching a few of Strauss's Viennese waltzes on its violins. (Arlt 1960, 315; my translation)

In many regards, these narrations tapped into—and sometimes colored in a few strokes—the identity of certain Buenos Aires places and the habits of some of its characters, such as the old retired ladies hanging out in sunny suburban streets: "The suburban dweller, particularly the one who wanders around at one in the afternoon, can, if he makes an effort, discover neighborhoods where 'old ladies' spend hours on the streets, their backs covered with a foulard, their arms crossed while sipping a mate" (Arlt 1992b, 42; my translation). Or the old drunkard at a downtown bar:

I know you, old drunkard.
    Like many other unfortunates you have had a wonderful life. Like every sad person, you too could recite an Iliad of misfortunes and an Odyssey of sorrows. You have crisscrossed the earth, you have gotten drunk in every tavern, you know the lingo for "pint" in every bodega of the world, in every saloon in the universe, in every cantina on the planet. And without a drinking buddy, you choose to tell your life story to the waiter who looks at you with contempt, and your philosophy to the owner who would have already had you kicked off the premises if he didn't need your coins. (Arlt 1992b, 45; my translation)

Other times, Arlt turned his "Etchings" into a formidable tool for journalistic investigations. In December 1932, after receiving several letters complaining about the catastrophic state of public hospitals in Buenos Aires, he singlehandedly started a crusade to denounce the municipal government for its incompetence and inaction. Working undercover as a medical student, he spent forty-five days infiltrating several municipal hospitals and scrutinizing their practices. When the investigation was completed, *El Mundo* published an impeccably documented series of articles titled "Hospitales en la miseria" (Hospitals in shambles). The series combined meticulous data on understaffing, a below-par bed-to-patient ratio, and the scarcity or unavailability of certain drugs and presented the exposé in a vivid, narrative, realistic-naturalistic style. For example, in "Hablan los leprosos," published in *El Mundo* on January 15, 1933, Arlt wrote,

> The lepers' pavilion is hell. If one ever had the courage to visit it, he should also make the utmost effort not to faint. There are certain instances when it feels like the visitor will fall to the ground. . . . But the fear of rolling on leper-infested floors is such that it keeps everyone on their feet. You don't even dare breathe. There's filth everywhere. Filth on the floors, on the walls, on the stairs. There are beds in the corridors. Lepers fry eggs or an omelet in a Primus perched on a mattress. . . . Body parts decomposing, turning purple. [. . .] Human corpses, living, rotten to different degrees, showing the entire color spectrum of organic putrescence, piled up at God's will, simply waiting to die in one way or another. (qtd. in Saítta 2000a, 65; my translation)

Arlt, of course, couldn't channel all of his discoveries and interests through *El Mundo*, a popular, family-friendly mass newspaper that crusaded against immorality and vice in the big city. Thus, many of his ideas and stories, superficially presented and discussed in the "Etchings," were promptly repurposed into literature and drama for an expanded readership.

El Mundo catered to an audience interested less in politics and the volatility of sensational current events and more in a need for stability and understanding. Arlt's "Etchings" helped *El Mundo*'s readers identify, order, classify, and ultimately make sense of the new urban types created by the modernity around them.

But despite the many differences between *El Mundo* and the more sensationalist newspapers, like *Crítica*, the new press inevitably resorted to innovative genres and styles, vivid, realistic, and sometimes even cinematic narrations, and solidly crafted stories to engage readers in a new type of collaboration.

In the seedbed of the mass media in Latin America, literary journalism became a central tool for the emerging popular press. It was one of the most effective devices attracting the new publics and interacting with them at eye level. It shaped and consolidated national and local identities and mediated between readers and governments, renewing and perfecting its traditional role as a channel for social and political commentary.

CRÍTICA AND THE NEW, COLLABORATIVE AUDIENCE

In 1926, the Buenos Aires police issued an information blackout against *Crítica*, accusing the newspaper of fueling a wave of suicides by cyanide through its relentless coverage. Cut off from its police sources, *Crítica* turned to the public directly, asking its readers to share with the newsroom any information on events, suicides, or private matters that might make a publishable story. On December 13, 1926, the editors invited readers to join them in thumbing their noses at the police: "*Crítica*'s public, which has always informed us about resonant events earlier than the police, will continue communicating with us about any occurrence in the city and anywhere else. The public will be our collaborator, always the effective and unbiased collaborator. The police will see how, invariably, we will know even more, and much sooner" (qtd. in Saítta 1998, 206; my translation).

Crítica took collaboration with its public to a new level. The relationship between the newspaper and its public went much further than the popular competitions, a genre initiated in Latin America by the magazine *Caras y Caretas* at the turn of the century. On occasion, as during the coverage of the assassination of millionaire Alberto de Álzaga—found dead, throat slit, in his residence on Charcas Street—*Crítica* asked readers to contribute directly to the investigation. For that coverage, the editors asked readers on August 4, 1933, to mail in their theories on the motivations and possible perpetrators of a crime that "seemed [pulled from] a Conan Doyle novel" (Saítta 1998, 208). Several questions ensued:

> Who was the author [of the crime]? What were the motives that induced the crime? *Crítica* has offered a substantial amount of information about this mysterious issue. Now it offers the readers an opportunity to test their opinions and hypotheses regarding the questions we are asking. Send us your theories, and we will publish them tomorrow, to contribute [with the police investigation] and shed some light on the mystery that surrounds this crime. The victim's personality, his lifestyle, his economic situation have added a sensational twist to the death of millionaire Álzaga. We hope that our readers collaborate as they have done in the past, helping the authorities who are actively pursuing all possible clues to find out what happened. (qtd. in Saítta, 1998, 208; my translation)

The readers' theories were published, as announced, on August 5, 1933. As a follow-up, on August 9 the newspaper also featured a photographic reconstruction based on these speculations, as reenacted by professional thespians José Gómez (as Alberto de Álzaga), Enrique Roldán (as Nicolussi), and José Guisone, portraying the murderer (Saítta 1998, 208–9).

Reenactments, reconstructions, writing contests, speculative resolutions of real crimes, and a close rapport with the public were only some of the strategies used by *Crítica* to consolidate its dominant position in the Argentine media market of the 1930s. It is unclear whether Natalio Botana, *Crítica*'s famous founder and editor, was directly influenced by the late nineteenth-century sensational and participatory journalism of William

Randolph Hearst and Joseph Pulitzer in the United States. However, it is well documented that Botana traveled with his family to Europe and New York in 1928 and 1929, after the death of his adopted son, Carlos Natalio. During that trip, the newspaper reported on March 15, 1929, "he was able to observe the operations of some of New York's largest dailies and adopt [. . .] some practices he considered convenient to implement among us [in *Crítica*]" (qtd. in Saítta 1998, 287). By the late 1920s, however, the gilded age of sensationalism and yellow journalism was long gone from New York, and the new paradigm of objectivity as "consensually validated statements about the world," associated with specialization and interpretive journalism, was now in fashion (Schudson 1978, 122, 144–59).

In fact, it would be difficult to pigeonhole *Crítica* during the early 1920s within the templates of traditional American journalism of that time. Due to the unique social and political circumstances under which *Crítica* bloomed, it would be inaccurate to compare it one-to-one with the tabloid newspapers of the penny press era or with the factual journalism of the early 1900s in the United States. *Crítica* was, by origin and evolution, an amphibian between these two worlds.

In those days, for instance, *Crítica* began to develop a style of crime reporting that molded the information provided by the police, or gathered by the reporter, into the narrative framework of classic crime fiction (Saítta 1998, 198). The reporter, usually young and energetic, asked the right questions, dug deeper, outsmarted the police, and ended up solving the mystery. The structure was very similar to the one popularized by Hearst's *New York Journal* with the lurid Guldensuppe murder case in 1897. In the 1930s, when detective novels had consolidated their narrative formats and established a new genre, *Crítica*'s reporters continued to skillfully exploit some of those same strategies, frequently bordering on fiction writing.

But it was in the reenactment of crime stories that *Crítica* reigned unsurpassed. In April 1923, *Crítica*'s journalists became convinced that the police were responsible for a crime wave in Buenos Aires; they blamed the department's incompetence, nonresponsiveness, and perhaps even corruption. To corroborate their suspicions, a group of reporters and collaborators went out to the streets to "act out" crime scenes in different parts of town, using innocent bystanders as mock victims. As they reported on April 25, 1923, the group first stopped in Plaza Once, where they learned that a burglar had just mugged a woman, knocking her out by pressing a chloroform-soaked handkerchief to her nose. Immediately, the reporters jumped into character:

All six people in the group cross the street and reach the square. In the middle of the block, on Rivadavia, we spot a nice old lady walking slowly.

—Here's the main character . . .

—Let's get her!

The photographers grab their equipment and ready their magnesium. The designated person moves forward and puts a handkerchief violently on the woman's face. She shudders, screams, and falls back. . . . The magnesium flash goes off and the scene is captured. When she comes to, we explain to the nice old lady our motivation for using her as the main character in our article. We convince her that this [reenactment] is aimed at improving public safety. A few curious bystanders approach.

—And the police? . . .

We look around in every direction. A block away we see two agents chatting in the middle of the street. Last night at 8:30 p.m., in the center of Plaza Once, we reenacted a robbery, including every gritty detail, without getting bothered in the least by the authorities. (qtd. in Saítta 1998, 200; my translation)

These experimental strategies made *Crítica* a strange amalgam of solid factual reporting and writing, narrativization and sometimes fictionalization of the news, the manufacture of pseudo events, and participatory journalism, all primarily focused on human-interest stories but with a tremendous resonance in the political world.

CRÍTICA AND THE AVANT-GARDE

Crítica was as open to literary avant-garde movements as it was to journalistic experimentation. In 1922, it welcomed the first issues of *Proa*, and in 1924 it saluted the creation of *Martín Fierro*, both literary magazines cofounded by Jorge Luis Borges, Leopoldo Marechal, and some of the most innovative Argentine writers of the period (Saítta 1988, 160). But *Crítica* not only welcomed these movements; it also hired their most talented representatives to become part of its newsroom. By doing so, Botana's newspaper renewed its writing techniques and approach, incorporating literary innovation and original styles, while opening entirely new areas of interest to its already groundbreaking repertoire of sections.

Between 1925 and 1933 many writers and artists associated with *Martín Fierro* became part of *Crítica*'s staff. Roberto Arlt, brothers Raúl González Tuñón and Enrique González Tuñón, poet Conrado Nalé Roxlo, Edmundo Guibourg, painter Enrique Pettoruti, Ulyses Petit de Murat, and Jorge Luis Borges were all invited to work with *Crítica* and to consolidate an aesthetic renovation in which not only literature, poetry, and the arts but also journalism would play a central role.

Crítica anchored this renovation, and its ties to the avant-garde movements, in two special supplements. Starting on November 15, 1926, and continuing every Monday until May 30, 1927, the newspaper published twenty-nine consecutive issues of *Crítica Magazine*, a cultural pullout geared to connect *Crítica* with a more sophisticated public, while establishing its role as an innovator in the news-entertainment business. A second insert, *Revista Multicolor de los Sábados* (Multicolored Saturday magazine), directed first by Raúl González Tuñón and later by Jorge Luis Borges and Ulyses Petit de Murat, appeared between March 14, 1931, and February 13, 1932 (Saítta 1998, 173). The *Revista Multicolor* played a central role in the development of an Argentine literary avant-garde that would gain international acclaim in the 1940s and 1950s.

It was in the *Revista Multicolor de los Sábados* that Jorge Luis Borges published his first narrative work, later edited into a single volume as *Historia Universal de la Infamia* (*A Universal History of Infamy*). This collection of sixteen short stories, some nonfiction and some "literary forgeries"—as he called them—was Borges's first iteration of the narrative genre that would consecrate him as one of the most innovative writers of the twentieth century.

In the context of a popular daily newspaper deeply committed to the renovation of the arts, literature, and journalism, Borges's groundbreaking nonfiction work found its first natural habitat and was introduced to the mass public.

HARNESSING THE MASSES

"Universal History of Infamy" was, Borges once said, "the true beginning of my life as a writer" (qtd. in Burgin 1970). The *Revista Multicolor de los Sábados*, the pullout section where the series appeared, was the equivalent of any Saturday or Sunday magazine in a mass-circulation newspaper at the time, with long, entertaining reads, humor, and games. However, *Crítica* brought its special flare to the *Revista Multicolor*. The newspaper was, after all, unique among its peers.

A daily evening broadsheet created in 1913 by Uruguayan journalist Natalio Botana, *Crítica* enacted a reading contract based on a sometimes dialogical, sometimes tongue-in-cheek complicity between readers and writers. Through *Crítica*, Botana introduced the techniques of serial novels in news-writing in Argentina, adding a dramatic effect close to what we now know as yellow journalism. However, the most innovative element of Botana's contribution as publisher was his search for a literary voice in newswriting. As part of this quest, in the early 1930s Botana hired a team of professional, well-established fiction writers and poets to improve the quality of *Crítica*'s prose and, ultimately, its journalism. It was only three years later that *Crítica* would start publishing the *Revista Multicolor*.

Botana used the evening newspaper to become a key political player in Argentina by catering to his public in the most unorthodox ways, Sylvia Saítta (1998) argues. In 1916, for instance, *Crítica* started offering free medical consultations and assistance to its readers. And on September 1, 1927, after moving to its new building on Avenida de Mayo, the newspaper expanded the medical practice, incorporating three specialties: otorhinolaryngology, pulmonology, and internal medicine.

As early as 1923, Botana's newspaper had also started presenting itself as "the voice of the people." "In the amazing success of *Crítica*'s 5th edition," the editors wrote on April 18, 1923, "we see the love and the striking sympathy of the people toward our paper. [We] think with the people's mind, and we vividly voice their ideas, *we speak with the voice of the people*, and it is its soul, grand and noble, which gives eloquence to our voice" (qtd. in Saítta 1998, 61; my italics).

The privileged position as a mediator between "the people," the authorities, the government, philanthropic institutions, and society at large allowed *Crítica* to become a political voice on the basis of its market success. In the minds of *Crítica*'s editors, a circulation of eight hundred thousand during the newspaper's peak in popularity was equivalent to eight hundred thousand votes.

However, though *Crítica* usually sided with the poor and the humble, most of its articles naturalized the divide between rich and poor, the powerful and the dispossessed, thus leaving unquestioned the social structure upon which those differences were built and the policies that had fostered them (Saítta 1998, 136). This was not the case with mass newspapers such as *El Mundo* or *La Vanguardia* (house organ of the Socialist Party), which articulated their discourse around Marxist, anarchist, and unionist *topoi* frequently used in certain intellectual circles in Argentina during the 1920s and 1930s.

Thanks to his newspaper, Botana became a feared political player and was thus always consulted by governors and presidents. To remain a powerful opinion leader, Botana paid special attention to charity actions. For example, *Crítica* donated "one hundred thousand toys to children in need" and "*Crítica* will grant a Merry Christmas to the unemployed. We have collected a donation of 400 kilos [900 pounds] of Pan Dulce for them" (qtd. in Saítta

1998, 138, 154). He also focused on sustaining the newspaper's growth in distribution and readership. Ultimately, Botana built a media empire around *Crítica*, with a radio station and correspondents in all the Argentine provinces and abroad. Its constantly growing circulation numbers legitimized *Crítica*'s claims to political relevance and grounded Botana's intentions to present the paper as representative of the people.

Paradoxically, in the quest for political relevance, *Crítica* had to enter the cultural arena. As Jorge B. Rivera (1976) writes, "[Natalio Botana] thought that there was a type of literature that was vital, real, that the people had to know directly and not by proxy. . . . I think he wanted to take advantage of the enormous circulation of the newspaper to make accessible a number of values that were not within everybody's reach, just as he did with his popular book editions" (22; my translation).

Just as he gave mass audiences access to new ideas, the relationship that Botana promoted between the literary avant-gardes of Buenos Aires and the mass public also helped relatively unknown Argentine literates in turn gain access to the growing mass audiences (Rivera 1976). When in the 1930s Botana hired a roster of the most innovative writers in Latin America to cover the arts, literature, and even crime, he opened the gates for a literary and journalistic revolution in Buenos Aires that spread all over the continent. As Rivera writes, "[They] were pure literates, poets for the most part, who read the most innovative writers in literature in their native tongue. Nobody ever dreamed that they would jump from the modest, almost family editions that were given away to friends to *Crítica*'s huge circulation" (Rivera 1976, 22).

Borges's own work for the Saturday supplement of *Crítica* had its initial genesis in Botana's quest for an improvement in the literary quality of his newspaper. Immediately successful and ubiquitously praised, Borges's short stories for the *Revista Multicolor* garnered the attention of the most important critics in the Americas. Amado Alonso's "Borges narrador" (1935), one of the first studies of Borges's prose, was published by the legendary literary magazine *Sur*, edited by Victoria Ocampo. Until then, it would have been inconceivable for a self-respecting literary magazine to review any type of work appearing in a mass-circulation newspaper.

One of the most unusual aspects of Borges's early narratives—nonfiction stories written for *Crítica*'s readers—is their connection to the political context of 1930s Buenos Aires. A triangulation between the historical background in which these stories took place, the medium Borges used to share them (the *Revista Multicolor*), and the type of reading activity Borges promoted based on a particular writing mechanism (the antiphrasis) reveals that Borges resorted to a genre with which he has not until today been associated: the hoax.[7]

"UNIVERSAL HISTORY OF INFAMY" AND *CRÍTICA*

During the week of August 12–19, 1933, the two most important evening newspapers in Buenos Aires, *El Mundo* and *Crítica*, were concerned with a gruesome and fatal event. The assassination of millionaire Alberto de Álzaga—his body having been found, throat slit, in the family apartment on Charcas Street, a wealthy neighborhood of downtown Buenos Aires—was the focus of *Crítica's* front page during that entire week and headed *El Mundo's* local section.

The headlines following the investigation, the doubts about Álzaga's will, and questions about the whereabouts of an unknown assassin took over most of the editorial space of *Crítica's* front page, which was shared on Sunday, August 13, with only one sports piece; on August 16, with news about a newly appointed business minister in Argentina; on August 17, with an international headline about Bolivia; and on August 18, with another international piece about the collapse of diplomatic relations between Germany and Austria. With these exceptions, *Crítica's* front page was almost entirely devoted to the Álzaga case.

During the coverage, as mentioned above, *Crítica's* reporters asked readers to contribute directly to the investigation by sending their own hypotheses. The crime, the editors wrote, "seemed [pulled from] a Conan Doyle novel" (qtd. in Saítta, 1998, 208). An analysis of *Crítica's* full coverage of Álzaga's assassination and a detailed examination of the newspaper during that entire week shows the extent to which its readers were prompted to interact with the newspaper. They were expected to be immersed in a crime story not only as passive receptors but as amateur Sherlock Holmeses—contributors on an investigative level, which was equivalent, in *Crítica's* reading contract, to the connection detective novelists would have had with their stories.

It is into this context—while a real murder was being presented as a "Conan Doyle novel"—that Borges introduced his story "El proveedor de iniquidades Monk Eastman" (Monk Eastman, purveyor of iniquities). Asking *Crítica's* audience to separate speculation from fiction and exaggeration from fact, while discerning some deep political subtext, was a usual requirement for any average reader of the newspaper. When "Monk Eastman" appeared in its pages on August 19, Borges must have known that navigating his story's nuances would not have constituted a deviation from the usual engagement required by the newspaper. In fact, Borges was likely using the reading expertise of *Crítica's* public to test-drive his own direction as a writer.

But how can we determine whether the readers of *Revista Multicolor*—

and of Borges's stories in particular—were the same ones who read the rest of the newspaper? More than eighty years after this piece was first published and without a direct ethnographic study of its audience, Borges's early work and its initial newspaper context can only point to one indicator that may yield an answer.

Advertising for the *Revista Multicolor* during its first two weeks appeared in *Crítica*'s sports section, the most popular in the paper. It was therefore meant to appeal, with its simple prose, to the common denominator of its readership. The first advertisement for the *Revista Multicolor* ran on August 11—a week before the publication of "Monk Eastman"—and described its forthcoming articles as "true stories," "real stories," "articles," or simply "stories." Curiously enough, only a few of the pieces were described as "fictional accounts."

In the second ad, appearing on August 18, 1933—again on the cover of *Crítica*'s popular sports section—only six out of the seventeen stories were described as short stories or fiction. In that announcement, "Monk Eastman, Purveyor of Iniquities" was not classified as fiction or nonfiction but simply as "Universal History of Infamy," one chapter of the magazine section.[8]

FACTUALITY AND THE MASS PRESS IN THE INFAMOUS DECADE

Jorge Luis Borges's fictional narrative works have gathered the obsessive attention of experts and academics around the world from the moment he started publishing them. The secondary bibliography that his fiction has generated can, on its own, fill entire libraries. But Borges's early narrative exercises, which could be generally classified as nonfiction, have only recently started garnering the critics' interest. "Universal History of Infamy," the writer's first narrative effort, comprises a series of short stories that the Argentine published in installments between August 12, 1933, and January 20, 1934, in the *Revista Multicolor de los Sábados*. The stories then appeared in a single edited volume in 1935 as *Universal History of Infamy* (abbreviated here as *UHI*) and were revised and republished by Borges in 1954.[9]

The relevance of *UHI* to storytelling and journalism is multifaceted. These narrations show the formative exercises in prose of an author who would go on to become one of the most influential fiction writers of the twentieth century. *UHI* also opens a window onto Borges's approach to factuality, storytelling, and the role of the mass press in a young, modern democracy. Finally, the stories in *UHI*, as well as Borges's recollections of the time when he wrote them, reveal his process as a journalist, a factual storyteller, and the editor of a Saturday magazine in the Latin American mass press of the early 1930s—specifically, his highly experimental, conceptual, and groundbreaking techniques in engagement with and formation of his readership, foreshadowing a trajectory of unparalleled innovation in the field of literature.

This foundational decade for Borges coincided in Argentina with the Década Infame, as christened by journalist José Luis Torres. Riddled with innumerable acts of government corruption, fraud, and political crime, the quasi-homonymous "Infamous Decade" resonates very closely to the journalistic series "Universal History of Infamy" in *Crítica*'s pullout section. It was a name that Borges had chosen himself. Clearly, Borges's writing arose in a specific political context and for a specific readership trained by the media to engage with it.

From the time these narratives were published in book form, however, Borges sought to and successfully did erase their contextual roots, doing so in the forewords of editions released in 1935 and 1954, so that his stories could transcend time and become "universal." But that does not mean those roots should not be considered when reading Borges today, a process that can take on new depths and reveal not just unusual qualities in his writing but the scope of the readers with whom he chose to engage.

A CONTEXTUAL READING OF "MONK EASTMAN"

If there is one story in *Universal History of Infamy* that could be considered pivotal for the development of Latin American literary journalism, that story is "El proveedor de iniquidades Monk Eastman" (Monk Eastman, purveyor of iniquities). The piece—only the second to appear in *Crítica*'s "Universal History of Infamy" series, after the inaugural "The Cruel Redeemer Lazarus Morell"—is Borges's take on the biography of one of the most violent gang leaders in New York at the turn of the twentieth century. Borges's text follows very closely historian Herbert Asbury's 1928 book *The Gangs of New York*.

Based on the similarities between these two texts, Daniel Balderston (2003) has correctly identified a number of factual alterations and omissions that Borges undertook after he encountered Asbury's biographical piece:

> In "El proveedor de iniquidades" the added details have largely to do with Eastman's relations to his cats and pigeons, a detail mentioned by Asbury. In other words, the grand epic scenes—the battle of Rivington, for instance—are closely based on the Asbury book, but Borges adds a few telling details to make the story more vivid. An example of this technique is the mention of the dead after the "battle of Rivington." Asbury writes:
>> It was not until the reserves from several stations charged down Rivington street with roaring revolvers that the thugs left their dens. They left three

dead and seven wounded upon the field, and a score were arrested before
they could get away.
Borges ends the section with this incident:

> Debajo de los grandes arcos de ingeniería quedaron siete heridos de grave-
> dad, cuatro cadáveres y una paloma muerta (Under the great engineering
> arches seven were left behind seriously injured, four bodies and a dead
> pigeon).

The addition of the dead pigeon is a reminder of Eastman's tenderness with
his pets, who accompanied him everywhere; it is a sign of Borges's fascination
with the cinematic detail at the time of this writing. (Balderston, 2003, 28–30)

After a few other interesting observations (e.g., Borges altered Monk
Eastman's death date—December 26—to make it coincide with Christmas
Day), Balderston concludes that the changes Borges made to the original
narrative were aimed at augmenting the entertainment value of the story
while enhancing its visual impact and cinematic quality.

This analysis is plausible, if limited. Reading from the point of view of
Borges's own erasure, Balderston is effectively dismissing the influence of
the journalistic context within which Borges first published the piece, and in
so doing he is denying the dialogue with the readership, which serves as the
story's dominant framework. Indeed, Balderston completely omits in his article the initial section in which the narrative framework is established. The
framing device section appears before the biographical account and totals
513 words in the Spanish original and 566 words in the English translation—
almost a quarter of the full story. (It will be examined in detail below.)

Balderston's decontextualized reading is understandable, especially giv-
en Borges's own efforts in his later forewords of 1935 and 1954 to erase that
very context, but this approach has a price. It denies the complex conditions
in which a writer like Borges first found his voice, and, more importantly,
it ignores the profoundly effective strategies with which he responded in
his writing to a political newspaper like *Crítica*: participating in subtle ways
with his readers, encouraging them to discern and decide for themselves
what was true and what was false, what was real and what was fiction—a
decision-making skill that would prove pivotal for the mass publics entering
political life in Argentina in the early twentieth century. By omitting this
paragraph, Balderston misses an opportunity to interpret the entire series
of "Universal History of Infamy" on a historical level, as one of the political
devices that a popular mass newspaper put in place to establish a new type
of democratic dialogue with its audience. And it is precisely by focusing on

this device that part of Borges's literary work can be reconnected to Latin America's long lineage of political writing.

Missed by Balderston, these elements would have been immediately noticeable to the readers of *Crítica* in 1933 and are key to understanding Borges's approach to journalism in those years. They would also have revealed an emphasis on two literary devices—the oxymoron and the antiphrasis—refined by Borges in his treatment of factuality and fiction in the context of an incipient Argentine democracy.

These devices had been used as structuring mechanisms by another important figure in both journalism and literature in Latin America—José Martí—and they place Borges squarely in the tradition of Latin American literary journalism. In fact, although no formal connection has been established between Borges's and Martí's work, it is important to note that *UHI*'s "The Disinterested Killer Bill Harrigan," a story about Billy the Kid, bears a close structural and aesthetic resemblance to Martí's "Jesse James, gran bandido" (Jesse James, great bandit), starting with the oxymorons in both titles.[10] Martí's obituary for the train robber was written for *La Opinión Nacional* of Caracas in 1882 and was republished by *La Nación* of Buenos Aires. The piece was part of a series of antiheroic, reverse hagiographies by the Cuban author that were included in his column "Letters from New York," a source to which Borges would have had access and which could have influenced his direction in journalism. The antihagiographic tradition—one in which *UHI* can also be inscribed—has a long history in Latin America in its own right. Stories of antiheroes and antisaints were a constant in modern Latin America, starting with Sarmiento's *Facundo* (1845).

THE GANGS OF BUENOS AIRES AS A FRAMING DEVICE

Crítica was the perfect testing ground for Borges's first narrative stories, which employed a number of literary devices that had already been present in the emerging journalistic tradition of Latin America and come to the fore when the stories are read in their original context.

The pieces in the "Universal History of Infamy" series can be read as interacting with the reader by enhancing the news stories that appeared in the newspaper throughout the course of a week. Raquel Atena Green has discussed the structural similarities between *Crítica*'s news features and the stories in "Universal History of Infamy"—the divisions in subsections, for instance, or the sensational use of the subtitles, a technique common to the news sections of both *Crítica* and the *Revista Multicolor* (Green 2010).

Aside from narrative enhancement and inventions, several other aspects of the "Universal History of Infamy" connect Borges's style of storytelling with those of Sarmiento and Martí. As suggested by some observers (Alonso 1935; Alazraki 1971; Balderston, 1993), *UHI*'s foundational figure of speech is the oxymoron, a rhetorical device that juxtaposes terms of opposing meaning. The oxymoron appears in the title of the series, "Universal History of Infamy"; again in the title "The Cruel Redeemer Lazarus Morell," which was the first of the narrative pieces bylined by Borges; in the second title of the series, "Monk Eastman, Purveyor of Iniquities"; and in most of the other stories in "Universal History." As noted earlier, this device was already present at a structural level in Martí's writings.

Borges used another narrative strategy that was also frequently found in the new Argentine mass press (Soiza Reilly resorted to it often, as did the modernistas): comparisons that project local references to a universal level. By equating automobiles with gondolas, for instance, Borges triggers a series of intercultural, transhistorical references that project what is local and specific onto a universal, cultural, and essential plane. This helped readers connect occurrences in Buenos Aires with the larger frame of modernity. It was, moreover, a means to symbolically integrate faraway Buenos Aires into the *civilized* world.

But there are other contextual clues that invite an enhanced way of reading Borges's stories. The mechanism of antiphrasis, for instance, is apparent only when reading the story in its original context. Published the week of Álzaga's murder and sharing editorial space with the coverage of that crime, "Monk Eastman, Purveyor of Iniquities" starts with a framing section that works as a comparison on a grand scale, between "Those of This America" and "Those of the Other" (both subtitles are added to the 1935 book edition of *UHI* and were not included in *Crítica*'s version of "Monk Eastman"). The motif is undoubtedly rooted in a topic already developed by Martí: the notion of "Our America" as a cultural entity separate from and opposed to the United States (Rotker 1992a; Calvi 2012; and others). We can only speculate that, by adding these subtitles to the story in the book, Borges was emphasizing his connection with Martí's motif.

In comparison to the ruthless, dizzying, clumsy, barbaric, and inept New York underground, Borges portrays Buenos Aires's underworld as stylized, sober, honorable, elegant, and clean. For the purpose of illustration, I quote the passage at length:

THOSE OF THIS AMERICA

Standing out sharply against a background of blue walls or open sky, two hoodlums dressed in close-fitting suits of sober black and wearing thick-heeled shoes dance a deadly dance—a ballet of matching knives—until a carnation starts from the ear of one of them as a knife finds its mark in him, and he brings the unaccompanied dance to a close on the ground with his death. Satisfied, the other adjusts his high-crowned hat and spends his final years recounting the story of this clean duel. That, in sum and substance, is the history of our old-time Argentine underworld. The history of New York's old underworld is both more dizzying and more clumsy.

THOSE OF THE OTHER

The history of the gangs of New York (revealed in 1928 by Herbert Asbury in a solid volume of four hundred octavo pages) contains all the confusion and cruelty of the barbarian cosmogonies, and much of their giant-scale ineptitude—cellars of old breweries honeycombed into Negro tenements; a ramshackle New York of three-storey structures; criminal gangs like the Swamp Angels, who rendezvoused in a labyrinth of sewers; criminal gangs like the Daybreak Boys, who recruited precocious murderers of ten and eleven; loners, like the bold and gigantic Plug Uglies, who earned the smirks of passersby with their enormous plug hats, stuffed with wool and worn pulled down over their ears as helmets, and their long shirttails, worn outside the trousers, that flapped in the Bowery breeze (but with a huge bludgeon in one hand and a pistol peeping out of a pocket). [. . .] All these go to weave underworld New York's chaotic history. And its most famous hero is Edward Delaney, alias William Delaney, alias Joseph Marvin, alias Joseph Morris, alias Monk Eastman—boss of twelve hundred men. (Borges 1975, 51–52, 53)

Monk Eastman was the leader of one of the most violent gangs in New York at the turn of the twentieth century. But for *Crítica*'s new mass audiences, who had been following coverage of the gruesome murder of Alfredo de Álzaga for an entire week—while at the same time reading page after page filled with stories of murderers and pimps, thieves, burglars, assassins, drug dealers, and lowlifes of the most diverse origins and lineage—New York's "weeks of riots" and "burned out buildings" were probably not so foreign. "This America" and the "Other America" were, for *Crítica*'s readers, perhaps even alike. The dissonance between what *Crítica*'s readers were told by Borges and what they understood by reading the entire newspaper must have produced an effect of shock, a disorientation that forced them to interpret, decipher, and decide the deeper meaning of the piece.

If the reader decided that Borges was being literal, the story was simply a biography of Monk Eastman. But Monk Eastman's activities "during elections [as the] captain of an important ward" hired by "Tammany politicians" to "stir up some trouble" were, again, only too familiar to Borges's readers. Such activities were common currency in the Argentine politics of the Infamous Decade, especially when considering that, by the early 1930s, electoral fraud was endemic, supported and practiced by local caudillos, and condoned to some extent by the police and the regulators.[11] If, on the other hand, the reader interpreted the story within the context of Argentine politics and *Crítica*'s reading contract (with the framing device serving as a strong cue—after all, the "clean duels" that Borges describes were far from a reality in the Buenos Aires of the time), then "Monk Eastman" acquired a deeper meaning. It became a politically loaded joke.

In the edited *UHI* volume of 1935, Borges tapped into Martí's motif of both Americas, only to re-signify it. A factual story about New York published in the pages of an Argentine popular newspaper must necessarily be read as an internal pun between writer and reader. As an internal joke about Argentine politics, it makes particular sense in terms of *Crítica*'s reading contract. The comparison between this America and the other America can be understood only by those who can read the context correctly. Making sense of this antiphrastic device separates those who are "in" from those who are "out"—the good readers from the bad. When Borges denotatively establishes a separation between Buenos Aires's and New York's underworlds, he is allowing his best readers to connect these underworlds, and the two cities, in one tale. In so doing, he integrates Buenos Aires into the larger universe of modernity. The final effect for *Crítica*'s readers is that of alignment, equivalence, familiarity. New York and Buenos Aires become—by the artifice of a literary ruse, as understood by a well-informed audience—parallel and level.

THE HUMBUG, THE HOAX, THE INS, AND THE OUTS

Borges understood his *UHI* as a playful book. He made this clear in his prologue to the 1935 edition. In that text he describes good readers as "even blacker and rarer swans than good writers" and reading as "an activity which comes after that of writing; it is more modest, more unobtrusive, more intellectual" (Borges 1975, 15). In the pages of the *Revista Multicolor*, Borges tried to find, maybe create, that perfect reader, a highly trained decoder of subtle interactions and subtler messages.

"[All] the stories in that book were kind of jokes or fakes," Borges said years after the release of the second edition of *UHI*, in conversation with Richard Burgin (1970, 28). "But now I don't think very much of that book, it amused me when I wrote it, but I can hardly recall who the characters were," he stated.

Borges's statement, however, should not belie the purpose of the book's stories, originally published in a popular newspaper.

In *Froth and Scum*, Andie Tucher (1994) discusses the role of the hoax, a common practice in the penny papers of the Jacksonian era; false or apocryphal stories ran side by side with "real" news stories. It was left to readers to decipher the stories' authenticity or their utter falseness.

"Working through and solving a hoax, in short, demanded from every citizen the democratic duty of judgment," Tucher explains. She continues: "It offered to every citizen the democratic satisfaction of participating in public life. [. . .] In one important sense, however, a humbug does resemble a lie. There are victims. They are not actively injured; they pay no penny, ruin no dessert. Often they don't know they are casualties. Yet, without them there would be no humbug. They are the ones who do not catch on" (Tucher 1994, 57). Of course, the very act of questioning whether a story is a hoax requires democratic conditions of dialogue.

When I learned some twenty-five years prior to writing this chapter that Borges had written his first work in prose for *Crítica*, I went straight to my grandfather, who had been a voracious newspaper reader and a devotee of *El Mundo* and was also acquainted with *Crítica*. The son of Asturian immigrants, he had made his way into retail and in the 1930s had reached the peak of his career as a salesman for the downtown Buenos Aires store Harrods Gath & Chaves. When I asked him whether he'd read Borges, his answer was terse and unequivocal: "He was a comic. He wrote the funnies." I believe that is how Borges's first narrative work was read by people like my grandfather—people exposed to the gory and corrupt Infamous Decade, who witnessed assassination attempts in the National Senate and suffered the bullying of local strongmen on election days. Borges's "Universal History of Infamy" was understood by *Crítica*'s readers as a hoax. And, like the hoaxes and humbugs of the American Jacksonian era a hundred years earlier, it served a higher purpose: by producing a sophisticated reader, it aimed at the consolidation of a democratic dialogue in the cafés and the hallways, the buses and the plazas of a young, urban, and vibrant democratic nation.

Read in the context of *Crítica* of the early 1930s, Borges's "Universal History of Infamy" regains a political edge that follows the editorial line of Botana's newspaper—an edge that Borges meticulously tried to erase throughout the forewords he wrote for the subsequent edited collections of his newspaper pieces.

In the most interesting example of such an erasure, the preface for the 1954 edition of *UHI*, Borges defined these factual stories as the "game of a shy man who dared not to write stories and so amused himself by falsifying and distorting (without any aesthetic justification whatever) the tales of others" (Borges 1975, 12). In what has often been read as a *captatio*, Borges separates the stories in the book from their original historical context and the political situations to which they could have easily been linked by disqualifying the narrator as unreliable.

"[T]he word 'infamy' in the title is thunderous, but behind the sound and the fury there is nothing" is another of Borges's pronouncements in that foreword (Borges 1975, 12)—one that, by pointing at Shakespeare's *Macbeth*, tries again to dismiss potential connections between the politically loaded word *infamy* in the title of this 1935 book and the Infamous Decade. A period of political fraud, extreme corruption, state terrorism, and a succession of de facto governments, the Infamous Decade followed the 1930 coup d'état against Pres. Hipólito Yrigoyen by Gen. José Félix Uriburu.

In these early narrative exercises, Borges seems excited and even optimistic about the potential that new mass audiences have brought to the cultural landscape of Buenos Aires and Latin America. His outlook and optimism would soon change, most likely with the advent of Peronism, the most important political force after 1945.

NEW CONTRACTS FOR A NEW PUBLIC

Crítica's reading contract conceived a much more sophisticated public than did the Argentine political press of the late nineteenth century. And the level of engagement and participation it proposed to its audience went above and beyond what had been the norm even for innovative turn-of-the-century magazines like *Caras y Caretas* and *PBT*. The readers of this new mass press were required to navigate the nuances of a short story like Borges's "Monk Eastman, Purveyor of Iniquities." They were also expected to participate in writing, dance contests, and philanthropic raids, as well as to send in articulate opinions about political leaders, report and contribute to the process of information gathering, and become active members of charity campaigns and public fundraising rallies.

These new demands blurred the lines that separated citizens from consumers, as well as political actors from the mass public. By purchasing a newspaper, new readers were not merely entering an imagined community of peers. They were also acquiring a number of social responsibilities vis-à-vis their community. By holding up their end of the contract, as mediators between individual readers and the civil society, as well as charitable and philanthropic institutions and the state, mass newspapers became central players in an emerging mass-mediated democracy.

Argentine evening newspapers started to develop these strategies around

1913, mainly in pursuit of a larger readership. Many of these techniques were reminiscent of a paradigm (independence, fairness, and the pursuit of "objectivity") that the new American journalism had adopted with the ascent of the *New York Times* after 1896, while others were comparable with the techniques adopted by the sensational press (the incorporation of graphic elements such as headlines in large typeface, as well as illustrations and comics), a model that had reigned unchallenged with Hearst and Pulitzer until Alfred Ochs's *New York Times* set a new, coexisting standard (Schudson 1978, 88–120).[12] The fusion of both models in *Crítica* and other Argentine and Latin American broadsheets and tabloids does not speak to the blind adoption of foreign press models in Latin America but, most likely, to how easy it was to amalgamate both commercial strategies into a tradition that had always considered journalism to be an instrument of political and social action, as discussed in previous chapters.

The commercial success of these strategies was such that, soon after the evening newspapers adopted them, the morning newspapers started to apply them as well. With renewed reading contracts, *Crítica*, the leading afternoon newspaper, and its main competitor, *La Prensa*, which came out in the morning, offered an array of services to the public. These services radically changed the functions of journalism in Argentina and Latin America, while enhancing its perceived social and political role. This "social task imposed on journalism" fostered an even more personable type of connection between journalists, editors, and their audiences (Saítta 1998, 138).

By 1924 the leading Argentine newspaper, *La Prensa*—with a circulation of 230,000—had not only opened a public library with more than 25,000 volumes but was also running a free medical clinic, a bureau for free legal assistance, a bureau for chemistry and agro-related consultations, and a public music school. This service model peaked between the mid-1920s and the 1930s after fifteen years in the making. In fact, following a trip to Argentina in 1916, Spanish writer Vicente Blasco Ibáñez described *La Prensa*'s headquarters in awe: "[*La Prensa*'s newsroom is in] a popular building where thousands of people enter every day. [. . .] Few are the citizens of Buenos Aires who haven't visited that royal building of marble skirting boards and luxurious domestic workers, entering it as if it were everyone's home. They popularly call it *the house of the town*. [*La Prensa*] is the widest read newspaper in the republic, because it is favored by different social classes, and it equally accesses the most unreachable mansions and the homes of the working masses" (Blasco Ibáñez 1920, 411, 413; my translation). Circulation numbers and this rapport with their readers gave tabloids, *Crítica* in particular, considerable leverage and clout in the political theater of democracy.

THE POLITICAL STANCE

Although *Crítica* took pride in its independence (when it first came out, its motto was "Illustrated evening newspaper, unbiased and independent" [Saítta 1998, 38–39; my translation]) and promoted its objectivity and impartiality, its style was far removed from the objective stance proclaimed by the American mass press between 1896 and the 1920s.[13]

In a September 15, 1924, article that celebrated *Crítica*'s eleventh anniversary, the editorial position was clear: "Before our time, newspapers here were one of two things: either combat papers, more or less scandalous and militant, or instruments of pure information. *Crítica came to life both as an information and as a combat newspaper*. Before us, every social activity had its paper: political parties, commercial entities, the industry; [but] the people, the modest classes, didn't have one. *Crítica* is the first great Argentine newspaper devoted to the people" (Saítta 1998, 72; my translation and italics). This dual position, as an informer and a mediator between the public and the state, granted by its leading position in the information market, allowed *Crítica* to operate on a political level.

Crítica, however, was not the first mass medium to assume the role of political arbiter. Other newspapers and popular magazines, like *Caras y Caretas* and *PBT*, had already claimed that position decades earlier, with very distinct results. In the early 1900s *Caras y Caretas* had started to successfully implement the information model based on impartiality and objectivity imported from the American press. But after the violent event known as Tragic Week in January 1919, the magazine demanded in its issue of January 18 the resignations of the heads of several ministries and the imprisonment of anarchist immigrants deemed responsible for the incident: "[The] right to petition is fair; but the imposition [of the ideas] that those anarchists are instigating cannot be tolerated. [. . .] Maybe it's everybody's fault, since with our apathy we have held open our doors to the wrongdoers of the entire world. [. . . But] we haven't been shaping our nationality for years to see it destroyed by men to whom we owe nothing, and are neither useful nor memorable" (qtd. in Pignatelli 1997, 304).

Years later, *Caras y Caretas* embraced the 1930 coup d'état against Hipólito Yrigoyen, the first in a long series of coups against popular, democratically elected governments in the history of Argentina: "The revolution of September 6 will enter History as one of the most significant accomplishments that has taken place in the Argentine scene. [. . .] The revolution had the virtue of rousing people's patriotism to unprecedented levels," the magazine proclaimed, one day after Yrigoyen was ousted (qtd. in Pignatelli 1997, 309; my translation).

But the difference between *Crítica* and *Caras y Caretas* and many other publications that strived to become political power brokers in the 1920s was the fact that, for the first time in the history of the Argentine media, a newspaper, *Crítica*, had claimed its place at the top of the political ladder based on the breadth of its readership and its market penetration.

With circulation peaks of eight hundred thousand daily copies for all its editions, an ever-growing following, a direct rapport with its readers, and a popular news agenda, the newspaper founded by Uruguayan journalist Natalio Botana openly campaigned for candidates close to its preferences, political inclinations, and circumstantial needs.

While extraordinary market success granted *Crítica* economic freedom from political power brokers and from both the party system and the government, this success also helped the newspaper reverse the equation between political power and the press, granting the newspaper direct leverage over Argentine politics well into the 1940s. Instead of separating the sphere of information and the sphere of politics, the quick transition from a political press to a market-supported publishing industry meant for *Crítica* both legitimacy and independence, and for its editors, representativity; they, much more so than democratically elected officials, considered themselves "the voice of the people."

Arlt's "Etchings" for *El Mundo* gave a material presence to that voice, while Borges's "Universal History of Infamy" in *Crítica* offered a platform for debate and the exercise of a democratic dialogue. Both types of writing worked throughout the 1930s, in contrast to each other and simultaneously, to further the inclusion of the masses into the public discourse of early twentieth-century Latin America.

PART III

· · ·

BOTTOM-UP JOURNALISM

CHAPTER 6

•　•　•

LATIN AMERICAN NARRATIVE JOURNALISM
AND THE CUBAN REVOLUTION

ON APRIL 16, 1961, the day of the Bay of Pigs invasion, Rodolfo Walsh was where most journalists in the world would have wanted to be.

Following his colleague and friend Jorge Ricardo Masetti, the thirty-three-year-old balding, shortsighted, slim, and jovial Walsh had arrived in Havana in 1959 with his partner, Stella "Poupée" Blanchard. He was there to join a project that was about to gain historical significance.

In 1958, from the depths of the Cuban jungle in Sierra Maestra, Masetti had broadcast the first interview with Fidel Castro and Che Guevara for Argentine Radio El Mundo and had remained in Cuba at the request of Che to create the first Latin American news service, Prensa Latina.

In Walsh's own words, Masetti was an "integral rebel" and a socialist militant of "admirable coherence" (Walsh 1996, 103). After Cuba, which he left in 1964, Masetti fought in Algeria and then went back to Argentina, where he died in the woods of Salta while fighting against the Argentine army that had overthrown the democratically elected government of Juan Domingo Perón (110–12).

In the early years of the 1960s, however, Prensa Latina was still Masetti's main commitment and obsession. Its goal was to counterbalance the "deformation of the news about Cuba spread by the international press" (Walsh 1996, 105; my translation).

On two occasions in 1957, the American wire service United Press International (UPI) had announced—in a story seasoned with details and an array of apocryphal testimonies—the death of Fidel Castro. This report had a tremendously demoralizing effect on the revolutionary forces, and Castro perceived it as a defamation campaign set in motion by UPI and the Associated Press (AP). The wire reports were discredited by the journalist Herbert Matthews in a long feature published, complete with photos of Castro and Che, in the *New York Times* on February 24, 1957. But from that point on, information balance became key for the Cuban revolutionaries, who would form a government in 1959. At the time, there was little doubt in Che's and Castro's minds that the US State Department was behind these rogue stories, although these assumptions could not be substantiated.[1]

"[The news] agencies that monopolize the global news market have initiated an avalanche of information garbage that still continues today, and prepared the field for a chain of aggressions that led to Playa Girón [the Bay of Pigs invasion of 1961]," Walsh (1996) wrote years later (105–6; my translation). Such a challenge demanded a prompt reaction, which was the founding of Prensa Latina.

To create the news service, Masetti put together a superb team of journalists and writers: Plinio Mendoza and Gabriel García Márquez in Colombia, Mario Gil in Mexico, Eleazar Díaz Rangel in Venezuela, Teddy Córdova in Bolivia, Aroldo Wall in Brazil, Rogelio García Lupo in Ecuador and Chile, Juan Carlos Onetti in Uruguay, Edgar Tríveri in the United States, and Angel Boan as a floating correspondent (Walsh 1996, 106).

Prensa Latina soon signed agreements with TASS, ČTK, Tanjug, Hsin Hua, and the Egyptian, Japanese and Indonesian news agencies. In less than three years, it opened ten bureaus across Latin America, as well as offices in New York, Washington, Paris, Geneva, Prague, and London (Walsh 1996, 107). By 1961, the headquarters at the Edificio del Seguro Médico in Havana had also incorporated a state-of-the-art room with eight Teletype machines, all connected to an antenna on the roof that hacked into several frequencies, including the Associated Press, Agence France Press, United Press International, and International News Service. "It was a matter of life or death," García Lupo, who was in Havana in 1961, recalled during a telephone conversation we had on March 12, 2011. Prensa Latina could not pay for those services, but it needed them to keep up with the international news cycle.

By 1961, Prensa Latina was producing information not only for many newspapers in the region but also for *L'Express* in Paris, the *New Statesman* in London, and *The Nation* and the *New Republic* in the United States. The American sociologist Charles Wright Mills, the writer and journalist Waldo Frank, and the French philosopher Jean-Paul Sartre were part of a stellar army of international contributors who added a second and third layer of analysis to the news. Opinions, with emphasis on Cuba and Latin America, had already engaged many other intellectuals, writers, and journalists from all over the region, as well as from Europe and, to a lesser degree, the United States. Some of those conversations initiated at Prensa Latina would contribute to shaping the scope and direction of Latin American journalism, literature, and politics into the next half century.

During a time of high political instability and hemispheric tensions with the potential for global impacts, literary journalism reverted to its political roots. From that newsroom at the Edificio del Seguro Médico, Walsh, García Márquez, and their peers involved themselves directly to influence politics at an unprecedented scale—following through on a promise uniquely ingrained in the Latin American tradition. This "extraordinary undertaking" (in the words of García Lupo) became a springboard, both literally and ideologically, for a movement that remarried politics and journalism in the form of a new genre: *testimonio*. The Cuban Revolution would institutionalize, consolidate, and harness testimonio to further drive the mass public into political action. Aligning in some ways, but contrasting starkly in others, with an emerging "new journalism" in the United States, testimonio would serve first as a tool for analysis, then for action, and finally for justice: the moral of the story became the official record of History.

THE MAN WHO BEAT THE CIA

To give an idea of how deeply Prensa Latina influenced Latin American literature, journalism, politics, and culture, it suffices to offer a brief résumé of three of its staff writers and the feats they would accomplish in the ensuing years.

Gabriel García Márquez was a thirty-four-year-old journalist. He had just published his first novella, *La hojarasca* (*Leaf Storm*), as well as a groundbreaking literary journalistic series for the Colombian newspaper *El Espectador*, "The Story of a Shipwrecked Sailor." (The feuilleton would be turned into a book in 1970.) In 1982, García Márquez would earn the Nobel Prize in Literature, the highest literary honor in the world.

Juan Carlos Onetti, a fifty-one-year-old Uruguayan writer and the author of *El pozo* (1939), *La vida breve* (1950), and *El astillero* (1961), had been chief editor of the Uruguayan weekly *Marcha* between 1939 and 1941. He had worked for Reuters between 1941 and 1955, and in those years he also directed *Vea y Lea* magazine in Buenos Aires. In 1980, Onetti would be awarded the Premio Cervantes, the most important literary prize for Spanish-language works.

Finally, Rodolfo Walsh—not yet the full-fledged revolutionary he would eventually become—was a thirty-four-year-old writer who had gained enormous notoriety after the release of *Variaciones en rojo* (Variations in red) in 1953. This book of short crime fiction was awarded the Municipal Prize of Literature of Buenos Aires, a distinction shared by authors of the caliber of Jorge Luis Borges and Julio Cortázar. Walsh had also published journalism in the weeklies *Vea y Lea* and *Leoplán* and an investigative literary journalism book, *Operación Masacre* (1957), followed a year later by a groundbreaking investigation, *El caso Satanowsky*, appearing in *Mayoría* magazine between June and December 1958. Journalism had granted Walsh the status of a star, with his investigations avidly read throughout the entire region.

In an article published in 1974, Gabriel García Márquez described the excitement he felt during the early days of Prensa Latina and the impact that Walsh's journalism had had on his writing:

> For readers during the '50s, when the world was young and less urgent, Rodolfo Walsh was the author of overwhelmingly good crime novels that I used to read during slow hangover Sundays in a pension for students in Cartagena. Later, he became the author of tremendous, implacable reportages that denounced the nocturnal massacres, the corruption and scandals in the Argentine Armed Forces. In his entire work, even in those parts that seemed to be simply fictional, he always showed a distinct commitment to reality, excelling due to his almost unbelievable analytical talent, his personal courage, and his relentless militancy. For me, aside from that, he was also a joyful friend whose peaceful nature little resembled his warrior-like determination. But, above all, Walsh for me will always be the man who beat the CIA. (García Márquez, 1974; my translation)

It is interesting—and necessary—to quote a second paragraph from this article. In it García Márquez describes how it was that Walsh "beat" the CIA and what his role had been on April 16, 1961. Contrary to what the CIA had suspected back then, it was not a team of Soviet cryptographers but Walsh himself who decoded the encrypted messages between the CIA officials stationed in Guatemala and their headquarters in Washington—a feat that would have a tremendous impact on the outcome of the failed invasion of the Bay of Pigs.

> In truth it was Rodolfo Walsh who discovered, many months earlier, that the United States was training Cuban exiles in Guatemala to invade Cuba in Playa Girón [the Bay of Pigs] in April 1961. Walsh was at the time chief of Special Services for Prensa Latina, in the headquarters in Havana. His compatriot Jorge Ri-

cardo Masetti, who was the founder and director of the agency, had installed a special room for Teletypes to receive and analyze, in our editorial meetings, the information published by rival news agencies. One evening, due to a mechanical accident, Masetti found a Teletype roll in his office with no news but a long message written in intricate code. It was a commercial traffic dispatch from "la Tropical Cable" sent from Guatemala. Rodolfo Walsh, who secretly loathed the crime short stories he had published, was determined to crack the messages, assisted only by a few amateur cryptography manuals he had bought in a used bookstore in Havana. He cracked the code after many sleepless hours, without having done this ever before in his life, and without any training. And what he found was not only an amazing piece of news for a militant journalist but also providential information for the revolutionary government in Cuba. The cable was addressed to Washington by the chief of the CIA in Guatemala, who was attached to the personnel of the American embassy in that country, and it was a detailed report on the preparations for a landing in Cuba, as planned by the American government. It even revealed the place where the training had started, the Retalhuleu hacienda, an old coffee plantation in the North of Guatemala. (García Márquez, 1974; my translation)[2]

This "extraordinary undertaking," which was among the causes of the tremendous defeat suffered by the counterinsurgent Cuban movement, was confirmed by García Lupo in a brief article published in 2000 and during our phone conversation in March 2011. Like the good journalist he was, though, García Lupo also added a few nuances and made a few amendments to García Márquez's story: the Teletype machines worked twenty-four hours a day, and the logs, arranged by source, were stored in eight separate bins. García Lupo, Masetti, and Walsh searched the bins for relevant information almost every hour, to keep up with competing news services and stay on top of the news cycle. "That [encrypted] information came out of one of those bins," Lupo said during our conversation. "But García Márquez was wrong in his account, because Walsh didn't need to use cryptography books to decode it; he had been interested in cryptography for a while, he was a fairly experienced cryptographer himself, and [he] had already used some of those techniques in his literature."

In his notes, written many years after 1961, Walsh would discuss his role as a cryptographer in Cuba. He would also argue that Prensa Latina had sometimes exceeded the limits of conventional journalism, publishing, months before it was known by other news organizations, "the exact location in Guatemala—the Retalhuleu hacienda—where the CIA was preparing the Cuban invasion, and the little island of Swan where the Americans had concentrated their radio propaganda activities in the hands of the [Cuban] exiles" (Walsh 1996, 108; my translation).

These and many other activities related to the wire service and the multiple literary and journalistic institutions created by the Cuban revolutionary government in those years—one of them Casa de las Américas, explored later in this chapter—should be considered part of a broader movement anchored in a long Latin American tradition of literary journalism. This lineage, as discussed in previous sections, combined journalism, politics, and literature almost in equal parts—the heritage for which Rodolfo Walsh and Gabriel García Márquez were, during those early years of the 1960s, the standard-bearers.

AT THE ORIGINS OF *TESTIMONIO* (AN INTERLUDE)

In the 1950s, Rodolfo Walsh and Gabriel García Márquez authored two of the most revolutionary narratives in literary journalism in twentieth-century Latin America. Walsh wrote *Operación Masacre* in 1957 as his first long-form journalistic piece, an investigative work that, using Tom Wolfe's (1972) words, "read like a novel." The book proved with obsessive precision the illegality of the detention and summary execution of a group of dissidents in the aftermath of the Revolución Libertadora, a military coup that ousted the democratically elected president of Argentina, Juan Perón. A few years earlier, in 1955, Gabriel García Márquez had authored a journalistic investigation written in the style of a feuilleton and published by the Colombian newspaper *El Espectador*; it was later published as a book, in 1970. *Relato de un náufrago* (*The Story of a Shipwrecked Sailor*) was also a vivid exposé of a contraband operation, conducted by the Colombian navy, that had cost the lives of seven Colombian sailors.

These two works of literary journalism, both of which appeared in installments, are the roots of what the prestigious cultural institution Casa de las Américas would formally define as "testimonial literature," a genre that crystallized years later in works such as Miguel Barnet's *Cimarrón* (1966). Described by García Márquez as "journalistic reconstructions," Walsh's and Márquez's testimonial stories not only prefigure the topics, techniques, and ideas at the core of testimonio as a narrative genre. These two books are also strong links between the Latin American and the Anglo-American literary journalism traditions.

As participants in the operation of Prensa Latina and the Cuban Revolution in its early years, Walsh and García Márquez had an active role in the discussions that defined testimonio. Perhaps more of a central figure in the consolidation of the genre than Márquez, Walsh was a member of the

Premio Casa de las Américas jury in 1968 for the short-story category, in 1970 for the testimonio category (inaugurated that year), and in 1974, again for the short-story award. Walsh also produced two books, *Quién mató a Rosendo* (Who killed Rosendo?) from 1969, and *El caso Satanowsky* (The Satanowsky case) published in 1973, which helped consolidate both literary journalism and testimonio as Latin America's preeminent narrative genres.

The sections that follow will explore some of the main aspects of *Operación Masacre* and relevant features of *Relato de un náufrago* in their role as models for the tradition of testimonio. The sections will later focus on Miguel Barnet's *Cimarrón*, the quintessential example of the early days of this genre in the Americas.

Testimonio is a broad and intricate socioliterary genre that evolved and spread in influence and range in the years that followed the Cuban Revolution, a genre still vibrant and ever changing. Casa de las Américas awarded its first testimonio prize in 1970 to *La guerrilla tupamara*, a series of reportages compiled by María Esther Giglio. Since then, testimonios have greatly varied in form, style, and content: from series of isolated reportages to first- or third-person narratives; from accounts with a neutral observer's point of view to groundbreaking literary experiments such as Diamela Eltit's 1989 *El padre mío* (Father of mine), which attempted to capture in writing the discourse of a psychotic patient in a Chilean mental institution.

A large international audience has coalesced around testimonio. Many correlates can be seen on other continents, in the context of what the critic Fredric Jameson has described as a common literary dynamic during the decolonization years.[3] But what distinguishes the testimonio in Latin America, it could be argued, is a link to social militancy and political—sometimes armed—action (Nance 2006, 23–47).

By exploring the connections between testimonio and literary journalism, as well as establishing the roots of testimonio via Walsh but also García Márquez, it will become evident that the genre not only exists in a broader historical arc but also bridges developments in the Southern Hemisphere with the lineage of investigative and nonfiction writing blossoming in the North during the post–World War II era.

THE NEW JOURNALISM IN THE REVOLUTIONARY 1960S

Political testimonio, a factual genre consolidated between the late 1950s and the late 1970s—and the key to understanding the evolution of literary journalism in Latin America— did not develop overnight. It was the product of a cultural, social, and political tradition combined with a series of intense changes that took place during those two decades, both in Latin America and the United States.

The 1960s were years of radical change, as much in the Americas as in the United States. Many of the social advances witnessed in the North were simultaneously taking place in the South.

In the early 1960s UNESCO (1961) reported that for every one hundred Latin Americans there were 7.4 copies of daily newspapers, 9.8 radio receivers, 3.5 cinema seats, and 1.5 television sets. By the end of the decade, these figures had tripled.

In the early part of the that decade, left-leaning Latin American governments' theoretical and political interest in "building and improving the mass media" grew exponentially, as these knowledge networks were considered an efficient means to foster literacy and economic development (McNelly 1966, 346–57).

In part as a result of this technological push, but also as the consequence of strong literacy campaigns promoted by Latin American governments, in the years between 1960 and 1970 illiteracy rates in the region's population between fifteen and nineteen years of age dropped from 25 to 16.6 percent, although averages show a homogeneity that does not reflect the reality of many Latin Americans (Rama and Tedesco 1979, 191–203).

College enrollment also grew exponentially. "[Enrollment] has been so large that a crisis developed in the functions traditionally assigned to the university by the social system," pedagogues Germán Rama and Juan Carlos Tedesco (1979, 198) noted with surprise. Between 1960 and 1975, according to UNESCO, higher education enrollment in Argentina grew from 11.3 to 28 percent; in Cuba from 3 to 9 percent; in Colombia from 1.7 to 8.4 percent; and, in Peru, from 3.6 to 22.8 percent (Rama and Tedesco 1979, 207).

The expansion in college enrollment, literacy levels, and media exposure was accompanied by the development of a critical mass of avid new readers who would become the main targets of the Latin American literary boom and other new literary and journalistic forms (Ferro 1999, 129–30).

But these changes were part of a very particular social, political, and cultural context—a context that shaped Latin America's narrative journalism in a very unique way.

An equivalent cultural shift was happening in the United States, although in different categories. The consumerism that had thrived until the early 1960s suddenly fell under severe scrutiny and started to be questioned by American youth and intellectuals, and a strong countercultural movement arose (Cross 2000, viii). The 1960s in the United States were also the suburban years, the civil rights movement years, and the Vietnam years, the years of experimentation, and the age of Aquarius. And inside many newsrooms in the United States, these were also the times of the "new journalism."[4]

As in Latin America, there was a boom in college enrollment. When Daniel Bell first wrote about the "knowledge revolution," there were 3.5 million students in US universities. That figure had doubled by the end of the decade. The number of new books published each year increased by 65 percent between 1950 and 1960, and that figure had doubled again by the mid-1960s (Abrahamson 1996, 11–17). According to a study of emerging consumerism, "in 1950, 9 percent of American homes had a TV, but by 1960, nearly 90 percent of households had the tube and it was watched an average of five hours per day" (Cross 2000, 100). The 1960s in the United States reflected fast changes that had to be tracked at a fast pace.

The growth of radio networks and the boom in commercial television after the unprecedented economic expansion following World War II led to the development of new journalistic forms that were adapted specifically for the electronic revolution during a time when information started to circulate at a much higher speed. Faster, more energetic, and more vivid than newspapers, radio and TV became the media of choice to satisfy the increasing demand for breaking news in an information-driven culture.

The increase in college enrollment, paired with the expansion of the editorial market and the news market, also fostered a new, more knowledgeable public, one eager to gain access to more sophisticated forms of written journalism. This demand soon met its supply amid the magazine boom that since the mid-1940s had started to feature longer pieces written with literary skill, techniques, structures, mechanisms, and topics. Narrative journalism undoubtedly made its way to the core of the magazine boom during the sixties.

Several authors have attempted to define narrative nonfiction or literary journalism, differentiating it from other types of nonfiction, such as memoir, ethnography, history, and essay. These authors present a number of common criteria that could amount to a definition of literary journalism in the context of the United States: a type of referential narrative prose whose protagonists, characters, and situations have documented existence in the real world; its focus is generally a current event, its style is novelesque, and its main purpose is both literary and referential.[5]

In a 1972 article published in *New York* magazine and later reproduced in his 1973 *Anthology of New Journalism*, Tom Wolfe explained some aspects of the narrative boom as seen from the point of view of a journalist: the development of a personal voice and a personal style, as well as the incorporation of several techniques used primarily in fiction writing. These were a reaction to the old-style, formulaic journalism that had dominated American print media between the 1930s and the early 1960s:

> The *Herald Tribune* hired [Jimmy] Breslin to do a "bright" local column to help offset some of the heavy lumber on the editorial page, paralyzing snoremongers like Walter Lippmann and Joseph Alsop. [. . .] At that time, 1963 and 1964, Sunday supplements were close to being the lowest form of periodical. Their status was well below that of the ordinary daily newspaper, and only slightly above that of the morbidity press, sheets like the *National Enquirer* in its "I Left My Babies in the Deep Freeze" period. As a result, Sunday supplements had no traditions, no pretensions, no promises to live up to, not even any rules to speak of. They were brain candy, that was all. Readers felt no guilt whatsoever about laying them aside, throwing them away or not looking at them at all. I never felt the slightest hesitation about trying any device that might conceivably grab the reader a few seconds longer. I tried to yell right in his ear: Stick around! . . . Sunday supplements were no place for diffident souls. That was how I started playing around with the device of point-of-view. (Wolfe 1973, 35, 37–38)

Young reporters like Wolfe, Jimmy Breslin, and Gay Talese were critical not only of the forms but also of the substance of American journalism. The "new journalists" were reacting to the "abuse" of the notion of objectivity and the government management of news (Schudson 1978, 160). They were also much more open than their predecessors to an "adversarial culture" that promoted what was called "interpretive journalism" (160–63).

The development of these new narrative forms in the United States was, additionally, a consequence of some important changes in the reading public. On the one hand, audiences developed a need for narratives more closely attuned to the "altered nature of reality in America than the conventional realistic novel" (Hollowell 1977, 14–15). On the other hand, the blunt journalistic approach to "just the facts," the Cronkite-esque assurance that "that's the way it [is]," was becoming harder and harder to swallow for audiences who, after Vietnam, had become more aware of the multiple points of view involved in a story, the political interests behind the sources, and the inherent limitations of "objectivity." Thus, literary and muckraking journalism, two "submerged traditions," came back in full force during those years (Schudson 1978, 160–61). "In the thirties," Schudson writes, "there had also been a nascent sense that the activity of reporting itself was problematic and that the experience of reporting should be included in the report—James Agee's *Let Us Now Praise Famous Men* is the chief example. But in the sixties this sensibility was more richly elaborated and more widely endorsed. *It responded to, and helped create, the audience of the critical culture*" (187–88;

my italics). In a time of radical changes, when questions were raised about the death of the novel and the decay of journalism, literary journalism and testimonio emerged to give a more vivid, more profound account of new social realities.

CASA DE LAS AMÉRICAS'S PROGRAMMATIC ATTEMPT TO INSTITUTE A SOCIAL LITERATURE

The Cuban Revolution of 1959 was key to the development and institutionalization of an already existing tradition of Latin American literary journalism that—as described in part I of this work—began with Domingo Sarmiento's *Facundo*. Through Casa de las Américas, a cultural organization set up by Che Guevara and Haydée Santamaría in 1959 to foster cultural dialogue between Latin American countries, Europe, and the United States, the new Cuban regime helped formalize and revitalize the interest in literary journalism and other types of documentary narratives, both in the region and worldwide. In fact, only a few months after the ousting of Cuban US-backed dictator Fulgencio Batista, Casa de las Américas had already become a central node of intercommunication between European and Hispanic American intellectuals: "[It did so through] the bimonthly *Revista Casa de las Américas* (1960), congresses, literary prizes, printings of the works of the younger novelists less known internationally and printings of critical collections, valuable continental, ideological coherence and revolutionary literary expectations evolved. Furthermore, this example of cultural openness influenced other magazines (*Marcha* in Montevideo, *Primera Plana* in Buenos Aires, *Siempre* in Mexico, *El Nacional* in Caracas) and publishing houses all over the continent, which adopted the same systems of interrelation and information" (Montero 1977, 6–7).

The forced-march pace of Cuban modernization after 1959 rapidly renovated Cuba's cultural landscape, and the scope and vibrancy of the changes, in turn, generated expectations and hope across the region. Latin American, European, and American intellectuals engaged in a spontaneous conversation not only about the role of the intelligentsia in a revolutionary context but also about the role of the state, science, and literature as agents of social change. Writers, scientists, and scholars from all over the world flew to Cuba to share their thoughts and ideas at conferences and cultural congresses.

In 1960, the Premio Casa de las Américas, the literary prize of the organization, started to reward different artistic expressions, no matter how experimental, as long as they "depicted Latin American problems" (*Diccionario de la literatura cubana* 1984, 1904–5).

In those days of hope and profound political change, many of the more impoverished nations in the region started to see in Cuba a model for cultural and economic development. A country that, in a matter of three years, between 1959 and 1961, had transitioned from a semirural economy into an international cultural hub was also likely to become a beacon for an underdeveloped region striving to enter modernity. Walsh noted this in the introduction to his 1969 compilation, *Crónicas de Cuba*:

> The revolution in Cuba created a printing industry, a public, an exchange with intellectuals from all over the world, scholarships and prizes, the best literary magazine being published in the Castilian language [*Revista Casa de las Américas*]. Certain events, such as the annual prize of Casa de las Américas or the recent Cultural Congress [of 1968], which was attended by intellectuals from seventy countries, received coverage almost comparable to what our newspapers allot to car races and soccer matches. After having to endure history, writers and artists, more than enjoying it, are part of its making (Walsh 1996, 76; my translation).

The role of intellectuals and the repositioning of journalism and literature at the center of culture, politics, and history was a key aspect of the debate opened in those years by the Cuban Revolution—a debate that coalesced in Casa de las Américas and a few other institutions created by the Cuban government. Naturally, the tensions between literature, political action, and modern journalism soon crystallized in the works of numerous young Latin American writers, journalists, and intellectuals. But it was in Rodolfo Walsh's work that all these forces converged with the purest sense of urgency.

As a writer and a journalist, Walsh was deeply rooted in the intellectual tradition of Sarmiento, Martí, Borges, and Arlt, all constantly present in his writings. Thanks to his multilingual and multicultural background—of Irish descent, Walsh had been raised bilingual—his influences also came from beyond Latin America; Stephen Crane, Oliver Wendell Holmes (both father and son), Erskine Caldwell, Ernest Hemingway, William Faulkner, John Steinbeck, and James T. Farrell were all part of his vast library (Romano 2000, 87–88).

Walsh's interest in *Time* magazine and *Esquire* was also influential enough that those periodicals are mentioned time and again throughout his work:

> I am reading in the great *Time Magazine*—began Walsh's tribute to journalist Jean Pasel—the vivid, colorful, almost enthusiastic story about the extermination of the invaders of Haiti. I fancy how great it would be to be able to write like that, with such precise adjectives. Maybe in order to train myself, to assimilate some of that mastery, I'll go back to my days as a translator:

"Last week one of Duvalier's tactical companies crept up on the 30-man invasion force that slipped in from Cuba a fortnight ago."[6]

"Fed up, satiated, choked"—the magazine uses only one word, *gorged*, but I am a bad translator and I need three to convey its integral meaning—"gorged with a feast of barbecued lamb in which they had indulged, most of the invaders died on the field under the striking fire of automatic guns."

Here I stop and wonder whether it is the poverty of the Castilian language, that has no words like *gorged* (which in six letters conveys as many ideas as gluttony, greed, and general satiety) that prevents us from writing as brilliantly as *Time Magazine*. (Walsh 1996, 15–16)

After his Cuban experience, however, Walsh started to revisit these American authors in the context of a humanistic tradition profoundly critical of the way democracy was functioning in the United States. In Walsh's reevaluation of the authors he had deeply admired in his youth, there was a new critique, as he described in a 1956 article for *Leoplán*:

Caldwell's ferociousness, however, is not gratuitous, and does not resort to oratorical techniques. When he talks about the oppressed blacks, the poor people in which he appears to deposit an inexhaustible compassion, when he speaks about those who tire and humiliate them, one could say that he deliberately restrains himself, he punishes his own indignation, he purifies his contempt, and then the narrative flows[,] apparently serene, without grandiloquence, almost photographic, but loaded with something muttered, terrible. Many of Caldwell's stories are real time bombs in a society from which slavery hasn't yet been rooted out. (Romano 2000, 87; my translation)

Unlike many of his colleagues in Prensa Latina, Walsh did feel he was part of the larger tradition of modern North American literary journalism. And that dual allegiance, to both Latin American and Anglo-American culture, added yet another layer of tension between literature, politics, and journalism, which would be manifest in his masterpiece, *Operación Masacre*, in 1957.

CASA DE LAS AMÉRICAS AND THE RISE OF *TESTIMONIO*

From a curatorial point of view, the mission of Casa de las Américas was to promote and give cohesiveness to a series of—what had been until then—uncoordinated efforts to develop a purely Latin American art form: a type of art mainly anchored in reality, an art both popular and accessible. In the realm of literature, this meant promoting cheap editions, as well as incorporating literature into newspapers and magazines and developing narratives referred to, written by, or directly related to the dispossessed and the humble. This programmatic effort, supported in many cases by liberal and progressive movements in the region, was sealed in the definition of testimonial literature produced by the Instituto Cubano de Literatura y Lingüística (the Cuban Institute of Literature and Linguistics):

> Testimonial literature must document some aspect of Latin American or Caribbean reality from a direct source. A direct source is understood as knowledge of the facts by their author and his or her compilation of narratives or evidence obtained from the individuals involved or from qualified witnesses. In both cases reliable documentation, written or graphic, is indispensable. The form is left to the author's discretion. But literary quality is also indispensable. [. . .] In testimonial literature the biography of one or many subjects of research must be placed within a social context, be tightly connected to it, typify a collective phenomenon, a class phenomenon, an epoch, a process (a dynamic), or a non-process (a stagnation, an arrest) of the society as a whole, or of a characteristic group or stratum, inasmuch as this phenomenon is current, actual in the Latin American agenda. (*Diccionario de la literatura cubana* 1984, 1904–5)

In her study *Can Literature Promote Social Justice?*, Kimberly Nance describes testimonio as not only a type of text but also a project of social justice in which the text is merely an instrument. In that sense, the goal of testimonio is not strictly pedagogic (to show the social conditions of Latin America through a story in which the narrators, who are in turn real-life men and women, are also the main characters) but also rhetorical, inasmuch as it tries to persuade its readers to take action (Nance 2006, 19).

Going a little beyond the purely rhetorical aspect of this form, though, it could also be argued that testimonio developed—exactly like the literary journalism that preceded it—as a political instrument. Its goal was not just to motivate actions of different kinds but to motivate strictly political actions aimed against the social and political injustices that had fueled its narratives.

The word *testimonio* in Spanish means to bear truthful witness, as John Beverley (2004, 3) has explained in *Testimonio: On the Politics of Truth*. This would be a tall order for any literary genre, and it also has its limitations in testimonio. Although the unofficial slogan of the form, "to give a voice to the voiceless," is still sometimes used to define it in the United States, this idea of voicelessness is more metaphorical than literal: the narrators or main characters of testimonio are not always illiterates requiring the intervention of a white scribe to put their pleas on paper. Even the decision of choosing who is voiceless is problematic; it usually falls to the narrator. As Beverley has explained, testimonial narratives are geared to "adequately represent" different types of "altern social subjects." But the question of alternativity (who *is* alternative and belongs outside of the norm, versus who *is not* alternative and belongs to the cultural norm) is itself profoundly political. In reality "truthful witness" often equals "Western, white witness," and "Truth" itself often implies the concomitant white point of view, because both legal and scientific systems of proof under which this definition operates are also white and Western.

In the United States, testimonial literature is occasionally considered the Latin American equivalent of "tape-recorded" books, a pejorative moniker imposed on the ethnographic genre by some scholars: "Usually intended to give a voice to the voiceless, [tape-recorded books] have rarely sought a literary level, but the pioneering studies of Oscar Lewis were conceived in self-conscious rivalry with fiction and merit study within the context of literary nonfiction" (Zavarzadeh 1976, 211). Undoubtedly, books like the American ethnographer Oscar Lewis's 1961 *The Children of Sánchez*—an account of the life of a family immersed in poverty in a slum of Mexico City—have some of the technical and artistic qualities that would have qualified it for the Casa de las Américas testimonio category. But even so, Lewis's book is not testimonio. The Latin American genre is the result of an entire institutional effort, appearing at a time when many governments were creating programs to foster scientific and artistic depiction, description, and analysis of their national realities in order to assess the region's potential for development and its challenges. Testimonio was key to these efforts, and its approach undoubtedly brought out the political nature of the literary practice. While Lewis's work aimed at understanding how a "culture of poverty" originated and reproduced, testimonio had, within a similar ethnographic scaffolding, a further political aim: to improve the societal conditions it portrayed—albeit within the paradigm of that particular society.

During those early years of the Cuban Revolution, the list of intellectuals interested in joining the debate was long. Latin American writers, journalists, and thinkers such as Julio Cortázar, Rodolfo Walsh, and Juan Gelman (all of Argentina); Mario Benedetti (Uruguay); Gabriel García Márquez (Colombia); Carlos Fuentes (Mexico); Mario Vargas Llosa (Peru); Alejo Carpentier, Miguel Barnet, and Guillermo Cabrera Infante (all of Cuba), as well as many Europeans, such as Régis Debray, Roger Callois, Jean-Paul Sartre, and Simone de Beauvoir (France); Günter Grass (Germany); and Italo Calvino (Italy), among many others, all shared their opinions about the role of literature, intellectuals, testimonial narratives, and politics through Casa de las Américas (Montaner 1994). And although a large number of them parted ways with the forum sometime in the early seventies, after the radicalization of the Castro regime—in particular after the jailing of poet Heberto Padilla in 1971 (Larsen 1992, 776–77)—the institute and the award remain a beacon for Latin American writers to this day.[7]

After the Premio Casa de las Américas was awarded for the first time in 1960, the relevance of the Cuban institution for Latin American intellectuals became undeniable. "For the young back then, and this is still current nowadays, such distinction operated as a springboard to public and supra-regional life," noted the Chilean author Antonio Skármeta (qtd. in Ramb 2009).

By 1970, the Premio Casa de las Américas had added the category of testimonio. And the genre, which was already Latin America's primary form of literary nonfiction, became institutionalized. That year too, the Guatemalan writer Manuel Galich proposed Rodolfo Walsh serve as head of the nonfiction jury. Walsh, who had been back in Buenos Aires since the fall of 1961, immediately accepted the position and continued to work with Casa de las Américas until his death in 1977. "This is the first legitimation act for an extremely effective means of popular communication," Walsh wrote in his acceptance letter in 1970 (qtd. in Ramb 2009).

The incorporation of testimonio as an award category provided a Latin American answer to the controversial question about the role of intellectuals in politically tense times, a question that had been raised in *Les temps modernes* by Jean-Paul Sartre and Albert Camus almost twenty years earlier (Vargas Llosa, 1981).[8]

LITERARY JOURNALISM AS AN "INSTITUTION" IN THE UNITED STATES

Literary journalism, an extremely popular genre in the United States by the mid-1960s, had been widely ignored by the public, the industry, and the critics until then. Among literary genres, it was the novel that had always conjured up the dreams and hopes of young writers: "At this late date—partly due to the New Journalism itself—it is hard to explain what an American dream the idea of writing a novel was in the 1940s, the 1950s, and right into the early 1960s. The Novel was no mere literary form. It was a psychological phenomenon. It was a cortical fever. It belonged in the glossary to A General Introduction to Psychoanalysis, somewhere between Narcissism and Obsessional Neuroses" (Wolfe 1973, 33).

James Agee's *Let Us Now Praise Famous Men*, the account of the daily lives of three families of white sharecroppers in desperate poverty, was—as noted by Michael Schudson—among the most direct predecessors of the emerging new style of journalism. But a certain lack of interest in more "subjective forms" kept the genre away from the American literary canon until well into the 1960s (Schudson 1978, 187–88). In fact, Agee's book, published in 1941, sold fewer than seven hundred copies until it was reissued twenty years later. Narrated by Agee himself and photographed by Walker Evans, no other journalistic work before it had offered such deep, detailed self-reflection on its own methods and productive processes. In order to find these same levels of self-examination in journalism it would be necessary to wait until Norman Mailer's *The Armies of the Night*, published in 1968.[9]

A major indication of the new momentum of literary journalism appeared in 1962, when the Pulitzer Prize committee at Columbia University established a general nonfiction category for books, although the definition was broad enough to include essays, literary journalistic pieces, and political, scientific, and historical-philosophical narratives. In 1969 the prize went to Mailer's masterpiece. Although the National Book Award, a recognition "by writers of writers" and sponsored by members of the publishing industry, was inaugurated in 1950, it did not have a nonfiction category until 1984.[10] Unlike in Latin America, where testimonio was in a clearly defined category and generally eligible for one prize, literary journalism in the United States began to gain recognition only later, in various award competitions, sponsored by multiple institutions and in broad categories, thus fragmenting the genre and writers' approach to it.

Possibly one of the most significant differences between North American and Latin American nonfiction was, in fact, that in the United States no single entity developed the institutional authority to define the boundaries of narrative nonfiction or had the clout to set general guidelines for the genre. Not even during its peak in popularity in the early 1970s, when Tom Wolfe published his anthology *The New Journalism* (1973), was there any agreement about the main principles, styles, or techniques of this literary form. This lack of "cultural consensus" or "preexisting criteria" about what exactly constituted a "nonfiction novel" (as described by authors like Nick Nuttall, John Hollowell, or John Russell) was a complete contrast to the situation in Latin America, where Casa de las Américas almost univocally dictated the norms that defined testimonio. Aside from a few scholarly attempts to consolidate the genre in the mid-1980s, there still appears to be a lack of consensus about literary journalism in the United States.[11]

This "taxonomical uncertainty" (Nuttall 2007, 131–32) in the Anglo-American tradition, which has led to a substantial number of exegetical efforts to disentangle the nature of the genre, has at the same time nurtured a certain plurality of forms and efforts in the context of this narrative style. In contrast, Latin America's testimonial tradition, especially after the programmatic definition offered by the Cuban Institute of Literature and Linguistics in 1970 and at least until the early 1980s with the return of democracy to the region, has accepted almost unanimously the Casa de las Américas award as its holy grail, arguably not enjoying the same levels of openness and experimental freedom.

THE AUTHORIAL STANCE

In the American "new journalism" of the 1960s, authors, protagonists, narrators, and observers tended to converge in one central figure. And although some preferred the third-person narrative as a way to avoid questions about the factuality of their reportages, these accounts also displayed clear signs of their narrator-author.

Truman Capote, whose *In Cold Blood* was written in the third person, was one of the many new journalists who gave credit to the first-person approach when explaining why he had not used it in his masterpiece: "Ordinarily, the reporter has to use himself as a character, an eye-witness observer to retain credibility. But I felt that it was essential to the seemingly detached tone of that book [*In Cold Blood*] that the author should be absent" (Capote 1980, xv–xvi).

The use of the third person in *In Cold Blood* could also be attributed to the fact that Capote's book was written in the early stages of the "new journalism" boom. In that vein, perhaps as an inflection point before first-person-centered narratives prevailed, was Norman Mailer's "strictly personal approach"—as he defined it—to the 1967 protest march on the Pentagon. *The Armies of the Night*, a tribute to Capote's nonfiction, has a suggestive subtitle: *History as a Novel, the Novel as History*.

In his narrative, Mailer did not directly resort to the first-person voice either, opting instead for a mixed approach. "He used the unusual device of becoming a character in the story but not the 'I' character. Mailer is the protagonist produced by Mailer the omniscient narrator" (Nuttall 2007, 138–39). Through direct observation and personal narrative methods, both Mailer and Capote seemed to fuse, at the highest level, the roles of observer and maker (Weber 1980, 50). The absence of the "I" in their works was, as Ronald Weber (1980, 26) pointed out, "a matter of appearance," since the presence of the writer was distinctly felt in the re-creation of events and in the selection and arrangement of the material.[12]

Although Mailer opted for the third-person narrative voice, he also acknowledged that a novelistic first-person approach was in order when some level of intimacy was required or, as he put it, when the writer needed to *correct* some of the inaccuracies generated by the imperfect tools used to record and write history (Mailer 1968, 284).[13] The focus on the self was not, in that sense, just a way to show Mailer's involvement and participation in the protest against the Vietnam War but also and especially a way to help readers learn about the march through the author's own eyes and feelings and particularly through his own bias. By getting a VIP pass into Mailer's point of view, the readers of his narrative nonfiction gained access to a vantage point that would enable them to feel the real experience of the march. After Mailer, the nonfiction novel systematically shifted its main focus from the objects of the author's perception to the author's perception itself.

An extreme case of subjective reporting is without a doubt Tom Wolfe's 1968 *The Electric Kool-Aid Acid Test*, which trails the activities of the novelist Ken Kesey and a group of followers known as the Merry Pranksters through their psychedelic journey across the United States. Wolfe uses the first-person narrative throughout a substantial part of his book, but he opts for the third-person voice in some instances during the central part of the account, when he did not directly participate in the Pranksters' activities.

One of the most distinctive devices that Wolfe used to convey a sense of reportorial authenticity was "a kind of stream of consciousness that attempts to re-create from within the mental atmosphere of people and events" (Weber 1980, 99). Although at times very effective, this device has made critics question Wolfe's reportorial factuality. The device, intended to expand on and reveal the characters' psyche and emotions, ended up creating a centripetal force around the narrative "I." "It is," as Ronald Weber (1980, 101) notes, "Wolfe's frantic imagination as affected by Kesey and Pranksters that is the book's most attractive feature."[14]

Although some of the best American new journalists followed Capote's lead in using the third-person viewpoint, most tended to shift the focus of the objects of perception to the narrative "I," emphasizing the authorial stance in their account of an actual event.

The use of the first-person narrative made these authors media stars. Through their participant-observatory role, the new journalists also became the spokespersons for the peculiar events they had witnessed and written about (Hollowell 1977, 49–62). The "star reporter" status turned these journalists into the avant-garde, the guides and gurus of a generation "through regions of contemporary hell" (Hollowell 1977, 33).

None of this could have happened to Latin American testimonio authors for at least two reasons: the first, contextual, and the second, ideological.

First, the United States enjoyed a democratic stability throughout the twentieth century that Latin America lacked. At the time of the nonfiction boom, the growth in literacy and college enrollment, the rise of a new public eager to get exposure to more meaningful and sophisticated forms of journalism, and the expansion of the middle classes and consumerism were, at different levels, occurring both north and south of the Rio Grande. But while in the United States democracy was never in question, Latin America went through a series of violent disruptions of its fragile democratic order.

Citing David Scott Palmer, Arturo Valenzuela (2004, 5) has noted that "[b]etween 1930 and 1980, the 37 countries that make up Latin America underwent 277 changes of government, 104 of which (or 37.5 percent) took place via military coup." Under authoritarian rule, most of these countries experienced either severe censorship or a substantial restriction in freedom of speech.[15] If these changes had an impact on the region's fictional narratives (as authors Germán Rama, Beatriz Sarlo, Neil Larsen, and Francine Masiello have noted), they clearly had an even larger impact on documentary and political forms such as testimonio.[16]

Second, after the Cuban Revolution and the consolidation of testimonio as a literary genre, Latin American documentary forms were incorporated into a political program under a progressive teleology. It was an ideological mandate of these genres to focus on the objects of reportage and not on the reporters, in order to contribute to social advancement on different fronts. Authors, and even sometimes the protagonists of these narratives, assumed a secondary role, dependent on class and national interests. The main characters of these Latin American narratives tended to fulfill a symbolic function and their narratives, an allegorical one. In the case of testimonio, the dual nature of its authorial system, which fluctuates between the "subject" of the testimonio and the "lettered scribe" who puts the story in writing, also assumed a completely different dimension.

Kimberly Nance (2006) has described some of the complexities of testimonio through an Aristotelian analysis of its rhetorical strategies. She notes that the three main forms that characterize testimonio as a discourse are (1) the forensic approach, which takes place when a text asks decision-makers to "characterize past actions as just or unjust"; (2) the epideictic, which is a way to engage spectators by asking them "to categorize present actions as noble or shameful"; and (3) the deliberative, which "asks decision-makers to determine whether or not to undertake a future action; it means persuasion and dissuasion" (23). Of these three strategies, the deliberative is the most clearly political and one that is easily recognizable in Rodolfo Walsh's 1957 *Operación Masacre* and Gabriel García Márquez's 1955 *Story of a Shipwrecked Sailor*. Both narratives require intervention from the authorities and are addressed directly to them in more than one way.

A clear example of the sociopolitical role that literary journalism has had since the 1950s in Latin America was García Márquez's publicized decision in 1974 not to write any more fiction so long as Gen. Augusto Pinochet ruled Chile (Martin 1982, 217). Through this promise—which García Márquez did not keep—the author expressed a connection between narrative nonfiction and political commitment that had been a common understanding among Latin American writers for a long time.

In terms of the authorial stance of testimonio, neither García Márquez nor Rodolfo Walsh were characters in their stories—much less the central figures. When they did play a role, their intervention was generally limited to marginal, sometimes paratextual references, incorporated sometimes decades after publication.

Finally, much of Latin American literary journalism during the 1950s, 1960s, and 1970s was written in secret or under serious political duress. At the time of either reporting or publication, Latin American authors were prosecuted, silenced, ostracized, exiled, and even abducted and killed by the military governments in the region.[17] One could reasonably speculate that this looming threat to their lives and activities was a valid reason for the lack of explicit authorial stance in their work.

In fact, most Latin American narrative nonfiction authors during those years pursued different strategies to distance themselves from the subjects of their stories. This buffer (safety?) zone between the narrator and the author on one hand, and between the author and the object of the narration on the other—topped with the paratextual concealment of the authorial figure—was one among many significant structural differences between Latin American and Anglo-American literary journalism in the 1950s and 1960s. Latin American journalists had to be more immersive, participatory, and collaborative, both in process and in tradition—working as part of a collective. Although their perspective could be subjective and individual, they did not have the identity-driven and persona-dependent voice their American counterparts did. Perhaps this is another reason why, while American literary journalists like Mailer and Capote would become media stars upon the release of their books, writers like Walsh and García Márquez would become—over time—something else entirely: historical heroes.

WALSH AND THE POLITICS OF TRUTH

Argentine journalist and writer Rodolfo Jorge Walsh was born on January 9, 1927, in Choele Choel, Río Negro. His parents were Dora Gill and Miguel Esteban Walsh, both of Irish descent and native English speakers.

Miguel Walsh worked as a butler in a hacienda in Río Negro, which meant a rather comfortable middle-class income for the family of seven: his wife, plus Rodolfo, three older sons, and a younger daughter. In 1932, Miguel

Walsh rented a farm in the vicinity of Benito Juárez, a town two hundred and seventy miles south of Buenos Aires, so that his children would eventually have access to a good education in the big city. But his financial situation deteriorated rapidly, and when the family went bankrupt in 1937, Rodolfo was sent to the Instituto Faghi, a boarding school in Moreno run by Irish priests. The institute would have a lifelong impact on Walsh's literature, and it appeared in a series of short stories that were part of Walsh's "Irish saga" (Lafforgue 2000, 285–328).[18]

Rodolfo applied to the Naval Lyceum in 1944 but was rejected due to his poor performance in technical drawing. A year later, when his father was killed in a horse riding accident, Rodolfo had to secure a job and an income, and he found both as a copy editor with Hachette publishers in Buenos Aires. It did not take long before the young writer had an offer to do translation work; Cornell Woolrich's masterpiece *After-Dinner Story* (a novel published under one of Woolrich's pseudonyms, William Irish) was Walsh's first paid translation into Spanish, accomplished at the tender age of twenty-one.

Woolrich opened Walsh's eyes to crime fiction, and the genre soon became his favorite. In those early years Walsh also worked on translations of Victor Canning, Ellery Queen, and other authors that would become part of Hachette's Orange series. As he grew familiar with the genre, Walsh also began to work on his own anthologies, and by 1953 he had put together *Diez cuentos policiales argentinos*, the first collection of Argentine crime fiction. *Diez cuentos policiales argentinos* included short stories by Walsh himself, as well as by Jorge Luis Borges, who would be an ongoing reference for Walsh.

In those years Walsh also took a few literature and philosophy courses in college, but he dropped out and in 1950 married Elina Tejerina. That same year the couple moved to La Plata, the capital city of the eponymous province, thirty-two miles southeast of Buenos Aires. María Victoria and Patricia, his two daughters, were born there in 1950 and 1952, respectively. Those formative years in La Plata are key to understanding Walsh's interest in literary journalism.

A small mimeographed fanzine distributed by hand by a group of literature students at the Universidad de La Plata saw Walsh's first pieces of investigative journalism. These articles encouraged him to enter his work in a writing contest organized by the publishing house Emecé in collaboration with *Vea y Lea* magazine, a biweekly publication whose self-aggrandizing subtitle was "La gran revista de América" (The great American magazine).

Vea y Lea, published since 1946 by Emilio Ramírez, came out with sixty pages in a nine-and-a-half-by-thirteen-inch format, and its main focus was a combination of "high culture" literature, arts, and events (Romano 2000,

80). It also dedicated a six-page section to the life of patrician Argentine families, a subject that was unpopular with the higher echelons of the Peronist government in power at the time, who considered it "oligarchic" (Romano 2000, 73–74).

Vea y Lea's jury for the writing contest, composed of the famous playwright Leónidas Barletta and internationally renowned authors Jorge Luis Borges and Adolfo Bioy Casares, awarded Walsh's fiction piece "Las tres noches de Isaías Bloom" (The three nights of Isaías Bloom) an honorable mention and 250 pesos in cash. The story appeared in *Vea y Lea* in 1950. The magazine only published one short story per issue, and each one was usually introduced in a prologue written by a stellar figure such as Borges or Casares. This was the first of many consecratory steps in Walsh's early literary career (Romano 2000, 80).

In the years that followed, Walsh published more than ten short stories and his first journalistic pieces in *Vea y Lea*, while also starting to collaborate with another weekly, *Leoplán*.

Leoplán was a popular magazine published by Editorial Sopena. It came out in 180 pages on heavy, lower-quality paper and had the inexpensive cover price of 1.5 pesos. *Leoplán* also "helped" its audience to manage their reading experience with paratextual references such as each piece's reading time ("Story to be read in ten minutes"), genre ("crime" or "romantic"), and multiple sections ("sciences" or "current affairs"). In the 1940s *Leoplán* also started publishing an entire short novel within every issue, usually crime or detective fiction by a European or an American author. This was complemented by three or four short stories and some news articles on science, geography, politics, and the arts (Romano 2000, 77). *Leoplán*'s target audience was the urban middle-class male aspiring to broaden his cultural horizons and move up the social ladder (Romano 2000, 77).

As a part of its strategy, the magazine also encouraged its readers to contribute articles and short stories. In early 1951, for instance, it featured a section in which readers were asked to send their "short stories, tales or legends, or real things that happened in the countryside [which was a way to expand its readership to the provinces]. If anything interesting has happened to you, please send us your story, and if it's riveting we will publish it, paying you 15 pesos. Don't worry about molding [your contribution] into literary form or style. Just send us the event—with your name and address—and we will turn it into journalism" (qtd. in Romano 2000, 78).

By 1953 Walsh had already published a series of articles in *Leoplán* about Ambrose Bierce and Arthur Conan Doyle. And, while still working for Hachette, he had gained renown as one of the best crime fiction experts in

Argentina. Some of his English translations, as well as a few from French, were also featured in *Leoplán*, *Vea y Lea*, and *Panorama* magazine (Braceras, Leytour, and Pittella, 2000, 99).

AFTER THE COUP OF 1955

By all accounts, including his own in the prologue to *Operación Masacre*'s third edition, Walsh remained fairly apolitical and rabidly anti-Peronist until the aftermath of the coup that overthrew Pres. Juan Perón in 1955. In those years, and until the mid-1960s, the "New Left" in Argentina—Walsh included—began to review and reassess its relationship with Peronism in the development of Argentina's political culture (Ferro 1999, 140).

This revision began when the de facto government that overthrew Peron, led by a civic-corporate-military group, started to test a series of deregulatory policies known as the Prebisch Plan. Named after the economist Raúl Prebisch, this strategy contemplated the dismantling of labor unions, the entry of Argentina into the International Monetary Fund, and the gradual privatization of services and industries that, until then, had been controlled by institutes and organizations subordinated to the national government. These institutes, which sometimes ran entire economic sectors, such as energy, telecommunications, health, education, and transportation, had been created and put in place during the Perón regimes between 1945 and 1955 (Halperín Donghi, 1994a).

Although partially rejected, the Prebisch Plan set the basis for a long, gradual process of liberalization of the Argentine economy, a process that would peak during the military coup of 1976–1983 (Halperín Donghi, 1994a).

The economic and political changes brought about by the coup caused the Argentine anti-Peronist Left, which had backed the ousting of Perón, to begin questioning its allegiance to the de facto regime of Gen. Eduardo Lonardi and Pedro Eugenio Aramburu (Ferro 1999, 140).

It was not until 1956, however, that Walsh started to change his own opinion about the coup. An article published in December 1955 in *Leoplán*, titled "2-0-12 no vuelve" (2-0-12 [Perón] won't return), shows that until then the journalist was still partial to anti-Peronism. The piece was a "tribute" to the Argentine Naval Air Force, which had taken part in the ousting of Perón on September 16, 1955. In a prior attempt to oust Perón, on June 16, the force had bombed Plaza de Mayo, killing 308 people and wounding some 700 more, mostly civilians and pedestrians caught off guard (Romano 2000, 87). The episode was known as the Masacre de Plaza de Mayo. Walsh was so vehemently opposed to Peron that he seemed unmoved by the atrocity when writing his article, feeling compelled to pay homage "to most of the men who forged the triumph and to some acts of individual heroism that would make proud any armed force in the world" (qtd. in Romano 2000, 87).

In the years that followed the coup, amid continuous restrictions on individual rights and freedoms and persecution of the opposition, the Argentine Left rekindled its contacts with Peronism through a gradual approach to the exiled leader (Ferro 1999, 140). It was also during those years that Walsh translated Erskine Caldwell's *Kneel to the Rising Sun* and when his readings of Ernest Hemingway, William Faulkner, John Steinbeck, and James T. Farrell started to take on a new meaning. Those were also his formative years in journalism, which would prepare him for *Operación Masacre*.

"I WANTED TO WIN THE PULITZER"

When in 1973 the literary critic and professor Aníbal Ford invited Rodolfo Walsh to share his writing experiences in class, the first reaction was a question that came from a female student: "Tell us, Walsh, what ideals prompted you to write *Operación Masacre*?" Ford said that Walsh didn't hesitate: "Ideals? I just wanted to be famous . . . I wanted to win the Pulitzer . . . to make money" (Ford 2000, 11; my translation).

It was true. Until late 1956 Walsh was not involved in militancy or politics; he remained focused on his work as a translator, his readings and writing, and his long evenings playing chess. And that was exactly what he was doing when the counterrevolution led by two generals, Raúl Tanco and Juan José Valle, broke out one fall night in 1956.

The evening of June 9 was a cold one in La Plata. Walsh had walked the few blocks that separated his home from the Capablanca chess club near Plaza San Martín. There, he chose a table by the wall, wrapped his head up in a scarf to stay warm and focused, and, leaning over the board, he lit a cigarette and poured himself a full glass of *ginebra* (Ferro 1999, 144).

Close to midnight the sound of gunfire erupted from the street. It was the attempt by an army faction loyal to ousted President Perón to take back barracks and military headquarters, in strategic points all over the country, from the military that was supporting an illegitimate government. The rebels' goal was to overthrow the de facto regime of Gen. Pedro Eugenio Aramburu and call for open presidential elections in 180 days' time. In La Plata, a few battalions were attacking the Second Division Command and the police department, but the revolt was rapidly overcome by the military and quashed in under twelve hours (Walsh 1988, 66). Walsh would minutely reconstruct the historical sequence in *Operación Masacre*:

Around one hundred thousand bullets were shot, according to official estimates. There were half a dozen deaths and some twenty people wounded. But the rebel forces, whose material superiority is at first sight overwhelming, would not achieve the least ephemeral bit of success.

Ninety-nine out of one hundred citizens ignore what's happening. In the very same city of La Plata, where the fight goes on incessantly throughout the night, many are asleep and only the next morning will they know.

At 23:56, Radio del Estado, the official voice of the Nation, stops playing Stravinsky and airs the marching song that usually ends their transmission. The "speaker's" voice bids good night and at 24:00 the transmission is interrupted. All of this is registered in Radio del Estado's official transcript, on page 51, signed by speaker Gutenberg Pérez.

Not a single word has been uttered about the subversive events. Martial Law has not been mentioned either, not even marginally. Just like any other law, Martial Law has to be passed and publicly announced before it can take effect.

At 24 hours of June 9, 1956, Martial Law does not take effect anywhere in the National territory.

Yet it has been applied. And it will be exerted on men captured before it takes effect, and without the excuse—one of those was used in Avellaneda—that these men were bearing arms. (Walsh 1988, 68–69; my translation)

Dodging bullets and the ubiquitous barricades, it took Walsh hours to walk the few blocks that separated the chess club from his residence. But even when finally in his bedroom, as he recalled in the prologue to the third edition of *Operación Masacre*, the sound of isolated clashes kept him awake all night. At some point, a man yelled outside his window before machine guns mowed him down. Hours later Walsh would learn that the man was a young rebel recruit. But what puzzled him the most was that the soldier did not die swearing love and loyalty to his country but cursing his colleagues for leaving him behind (Walsh 1988, 10–11).

After that night Walsh tried to go back to the "many things [he did] to earn a living," despite the fact that violence had crept into his life and was "splattered all over the walls." The memories of that night and a quote from T. S. Eliot ("A rain of blood has blinded my eyes") led him almost directly into literary journalism (qtd. in Walsh 1988, 11).

Six months later, during the suffocatingly hot night of December 18, 1956, Walsh's longtime friend Enrique Dillon, sitting at a bar and sipping cold beer, would spark Walsh's journalistic curiosity once again with a phrase that resonated throughout the entire investigation leading to *Operación Masacre*: "Hay un fusilado que vive" (One of the dead is still alive).

The night of the upheaval back in June, a group of civilians had been arrested, transported to a nearby field in José León Suárez, thirty-one miles south of Buenos Aires, and summarily shot, execution style. One of those men, Juan Carlos Livraga, had survived the volley of shots and was willing to talk. Walsh met Livraga on December 21, 1956. "I found the man who bit the dog!" he wrote years later (Ferro 1999, 144).

Operación Masacre was the fruit of Walsh's investigation of that episode, as well as the literary-journalistic proof of the corruption and violence of the military government of General Aramburu. The process of identifying and locating the survivors, added to the imminent threat created by an increasingly restrictive and violent sequence of military dictatorships, had a tremendous impact on the completion of Walsh's project. The account was first published between January and June 1957 as a series of articles in the magazine *Revolución Nacional* (according to Walsh, a "trembling bunch of yellow sheets of paper") and later, in full, in *Mayoría* magazine. The project first appeared as a book in 1957, with subsequent editions in 1964 and 1969, until its fourth and final one in 1972.

Operación Masacre soon became the archetypal example of the Latin American "documentary narrative." It was broadly read by journalists and critics all over the region, and, in the words of the renowned Uruguayan critic Ángel Rama, it was "the first political testimonio in Latin America" (qtd. in Foster 1984, 42–43).[19] Each subsequent edition was resisted by the respective government in power at the time of its publication. In that sense, the book's impact was renewed and adapted to every new context, following the tradition of the malleable text as political tool begun with Sarmiento's *Facundo.* Every new prologue actualized the content of the book and reinterpreted its narrative within the contemporary political circumstances—proof of the quintessential insight that testimonio could capture. In spite of its contextual nature, the genre could transcend its immediacy precisely because of its ability to show the emblematic behind the particular.

In order to write and publish *Operación Masacre*, Walsh had to devote himself completely to the book for several years, without receiving advances or compensation of any kind, while he circumvented the tight limits and restrictions imposed by successive military governments. In the prologue to the 1972 edition, the author recalled what his life had been like during the investigation that led to his masterpiece:

> The long night of June 9 comes back to me, for the second time it takes me away from the "supple, tranquil seasons." Now, for almost a year I won't think of anything else, I will abandon my house and my job, I will be called Fran-

cisco Freyre, I will carry a false ID under that name, a friend will lend me a house in Tigre, during two months I will live in a freezing shack in Merlo, I will carry a gun, and at every moment the figures in that drama will come back to me obsessively: Livraga, covered in blood, walking along that unending alley through which he escaped death, and the other guy who saved himself by running across the fields, dodging the bullets, and the others who saved themselves without him knowing, and those who did not make it at all. (Walsh 1972, 11–12)[20]

Revolución Nacional was a small magazine published by the Organo del Instituto de Cultura Obrera (Organ of the Institute of Working Class Culture), which had its headquarters in a basement on Leandro Alem 282. The publication was mostly read by union workers and had a rather small circulation, around three thousand. During the serialized publication of *Operación Masacre*, however, it reached a peak of six thousand. *Revolución Nacional* was nationalistic in tone and deeply militant in its approach to the news (Ferro 1999, 158).

"[The story] comes out unsigned, with a terrible layout, with the titles changed, but it finally comes out," Walsh recalled in the prologue to the 1972 edition (Walsh 1972, 13–14). The lack of a byline in *Revolución Nacional* was mostly due to Walsh's need to remain under the radar of the military regime that was after him. At some point, however, Walsh started to add his initials—R.J.W.—at the bottom of the page. But in the last week of February 1957, Wilfredo Rossi, a contributor to the same weekly, was arrested due to a confusion between his own initials—W.R.—and Walsh's. After the incident, Walsh defiantly started signing subsequent installments with his full name (Ferro 1999, 159–60).

In the 1972 prologue to the book, Walsh paid tribute to the editor—without naming him—at *Revolución Nacional*, Luis Benito Cerrutti Costa (Ferro 1999, 130–31). He was the only person who agreed to publish the piece, and he did it under a suggestive headline: "I Was One of the Executed."[21] About him, Walsh wrote, "I find a man who will dare publish it. Trembling and sweating, because he is no movie hero, but simply a man who dares, and that is much more than a movie hero" (Walsh 1988, 13). In that account Walsh also recalled the passivity and indifference with which the story was received by the mainstream media, as well as the sense of journalistic urgency that, despite all that indifference, made him carry on with the research and publication of the book. "I thought I was running a race against time. That any minute a newspaper was going to send a dozen reporters and photographers [to scoop me] just like in the movies. [. . .] After twelve years you can check out the newspapers of that time and this story did not exist (Walsh 1988, 12–13).

After the investigation was published in full in *Revoluci* Walsh started to work on the book version. He shared some init with Noé Jitrik, a prestigious literary critic, who agreed to circu among opinion leaders and politicians of different parties in ord some funding and support. Walsh and Jitrik estimated that the pub...cation would cost around 45,000 pesos, but when it became clear that the contributions would never materialize, Walsh got in touch with Tulio Jacovella and Bruno Jacovella, publishers of *Mayoría*, a weekly illustrated political magazine with Peronist leanings (Ferro 1999, 163).

On May 22, 1957, Walsh received an advance of 1,000 pesos for the book, the first payment since he had started working on the story in 1956. And between May 27 and July 29, 1957, *Operación Masacre* appeared in *Mayoría*, for the first time under its current title, as a series of nine articles in a literary-journalistic format (Ferro 1999, 130). The book came out in December and was continually modified by Walsh until 1972 (Ferro 1999, 130–31, 140–43).

Talking about *Operación Masacre* that same year, Walsh described it as both an ideological tool and a journalistic investigation, which aligns his work with the long tradition of Latin American literary journalism initiated by Sarmiento's *Facundo*:

> I wrote this book for it to be published, for it to act. [. . .] I investigated and recounted these awful events to bring them to light in the fullest way possible, to provoke fear, to have them never happen again. (Walsh 2013, 155)

> When I wrote this story I was thirty years old. I had already been a journalist for ten. Suddenly, I thought I had understood that all I had done before had nothing to do with what I had learned about journalism, but this last investigation did—the quest, at the risk of losing everything, of the deepest, most hidden, and most painful testimony. This one book did match my idea [of what journalism had to be]. Following those same guidelines I immediately wrote a second story, the *Satanowsky Case*. It gained more notoriety, but the results were the same: the crime was proven, the culprits at large. (Walsh 1969, qtd. in Ferro 1999, 131; my translation)

As David Foster has argued, reporting in repressive societies creates a number of hurdles not only in terms of the investigative process that non-fiction requires but also and especially in terms of the "authorial stance toward one's material" (Foster 1984, 42–43). Walsh's book is a good example of the extent to which a politically repressive environment can condition not the making but also the fabric of narrative nonfiction. Those structural qualities would become some of the criteria on which the Cuban Institute of Literature and Linguistics would base, a few years later, its definition of testimonio as a narrative genre.

OPERACIÓN MASACRE AND THE MORALS OF DEATH

Death, with its imminence and its materiality, was an important aspect of *Operación Masacre*. Immediately after Walsh started working on the book in December 1956, he shared a draft of the preliminary report with Sam Sumerling, a correspondent working with the Associated Press. The American journalist was expected to publish the report in full in the United States in the event that Walsh was apprehended, tortured, or killed (Ferro 1999).

In the prologue to *Operación Masacre's* third edition, Walsh explained that he could not figure out what was so appealing about the story of the massacre until he finally met Livraga. Seeing those marks on Livraga's face, the near-death expression that was indelibly inscribed in his skin, Walsh felt morally obligated to investigate the events of that night in José León Suárez. "I don't know what is so appealing about this story, so diffuse, so foreign to me, so studded with improbabilities," he wrote. "I don't know why I ask to speak to that man, why I am talking to Juan Carlos Livraga. But after talking to him, I know. I look at that face, the hole in his cheek, the larger hole in his throat, his broken lips, and the opaque eyes where the shadow of death still remains, floating. I feel insulted in the same way I felt insulted when I heard that recruit yelling outside my window" (Walsh 1988, 11).

Death, the one Livraga narrowly escaped but that still marked his flesh, and the deaths of those who were killed that night—death in all its arbitrariness and complexity—is one of the recurring themes in Walsh's literary journalism. Death and the narrative of a "dead man talking" are for Walsh not only morally interesting but also newsworthy: "One ends up believing in the crime novels that one has read or written and thinks that newsrooms are going to fight over a story like that, with a *dead man talking*" (Walsh 1988, 11; my italics).

In order to break the imposed narrative, Walsh needs to see for himself, to trace the fissures—the mark on Livraga's cheek—up close. Executed, but still alive to tell of it—the speaking dead—Livraga's second chance is also Walsh's. In a disorienting world, testimonio can summon meaning by confronting myths and rumors with facts and experience.

Death in *Operación Masacre* is, on the one hand, a topic of journalistic interest and political denunciation. But it is also a complex mechanism that provides a catalyst for Walsh's moral system. Through the narrative imposition of a death sentence or the execution of an arbitrary assassination, the two moral sides of Walsh's universe are revealed: the pole of justice and the pole of injustice. In other words, if a "legal death" can be the vehicle for justice and order, an "arbitrary death" or an "unjust death" can have the opposite effect: it can create unrest and chaos. The unjust death also redeems the victim and turns him or her into a martyr or a saint. The death of Mario Brión in *Operación Masacre* is a good example of this mechanism. Brión, an innocent casualty of the executions of June 1956, with no political or militant background, is portrayed as a saint in chapter 27: "The night guard at the morgue was accustomed to seeing dead bodies. When he arrived that afternoon, however, there was something that had quite an intense impact on him. The body of one of the men executed [in José León Suárez] had his arms open to the sides, his face lying on the shoulder. It was an oval face, with blond hair and a growing beard, a melancholic grin and a string of blood coming from the mouth. He had a white jersey on, his name was Mario Brión, and he looked like a Christ" (Walsh 1988, 114).

Religious iconography dominates that visit to the morgue, which Walsh turns into a holy sepulcher with a Christ—Brión—buried in it and glowing inside. In fact, while Brión's strictly journalistic story ends with his life and the legal confirmation of his death, Walsh "resurrects" Brión literarily. In chapter 29, when the man's father visits San Martín's clinic to identify the corpse of his son, the authorities let him see the body for only a few seconds: "All of a sudden they uncovered the corpse and as suddenly as before they covered it back up again" (Walsh 1988, 125). That quick, uncertain glimpse opens a chain reaction of doubt in the mind of Mr. Brión, who a few days later starts receiving telephone calls and messages telling him that his son is still alive (124–26). Mario Brión, the purest, the least political of all victims in Walsh's account, is turned into a ghost, a spirit. He becomes one of the first saints in Walsh's hagiography.

An idea that prevails in many of Walsh's stories in which victims are portrayed as Christ-like, Virgin Mary–like, maybe-resurrected figures, or even as dead men talking, is that death is not an absolute category. Both in his fiction and in his journalistic writings Walsh describes death as an ambiguous zone, a permeable territory, one from which characters—both real and fictional—can be redeemed.

THE VERTICAL DEATH

In Walsh's narratives there is also a graphic, almost conventional way to represent the moral quality of a dying—dead—character. Those characters who die standing on their feet are generally good, positive, brave, and just.

Those who die lying down are bad, mean, cowardly, and unjust. The degree of verticality at the moment of death maps in Walsh's narratives a spatial-moral canon, one in which heroes, villains, and martyrs take the place they morally deserve.

The multiple deaths that had occurred during the summary executions narrated in *Operación Masacre* are represented by Walsh in various forms. Some of the victims die standing, others on their knees, others begging for mercy. Some of them, of course, escape.

The most paradigmatic among these executions and deaths are Brión's and Livraga's. Brión dies standing, in the middle of a garbage dumpster. He is dressed in white and bathed in a white halo of light: "Brión's sweater shines so white it's almost incandescent" (Walsh 1988, 95). As mentioned above, Walsh resorts to this image several times, turning Brión's character into a resurrecting Christ.

Livraga, who was dressed entirely in black the night of the massacre, was one of the victims who escaped the execution. Although Walsh describes him as factually alive in the journalistic account, the author surreptitiously displaces Livraga to an uncharted, intermediate territory between life and death, a place where he remains suspended: "Livraga cautiously starts cutting to the left. Step by step. He is dressed in black. All of a sudden, what seems like a miracle: the lights stop bothering him. He is out of the luminescent field. He is alone and he is almost invisible in the dark. Ten meters ahead there appears to be a ditch. If only he could reach it" (Walsh 1988, 95).

Livraga lies down in the ditch, thus escaping the volley of shots.

Between Livraga and Brión, Walsh builds a symbolic wall that develops into two different moral orders. Livraga, the "dead man talking," one of the survivors, carries the marks of death on his face. He is alive because he can still breathe, but he is also indelibly scarred by a shameful shadow of cow-ardice, which in Walsh's system is another form of death. These signs will stick to Livraga throughout the entire book. Brión, on the other hand, faced his destiny standing on his feet and is narratively turned into a martyr, as Walsh invests in the character all the external qualities of a saint.

On the literal level—in the factual account—Walsh does describe Brión's death at the dumpster: "Brión has few possibilities to run away; his white sweater beams in the night. We don't even know if he tried" (Walsh 1988, 98). But after the massacre, Brión's character rises morally above all the rest. In Walsh's system Brión represents the innocent victim, immolating himself for some greater good, confronting his destiny with eyes wide open. The reward for his heroism merits, in Walsh's spatial-moral system, a type of literary canonization.

In his later work, Walsh applied this mechanism even more directly to two of his most important nonfictional characters: Eva Perón and Vicky Walsh, the writer's own daughter, killed by a paramilitary task force in 1976.

"Esa mujer" ("That Woman") is a 1963 short story in which Walsh—narrator and main character—is looking for the secret burial place of Eva Perón's embalmed corpse.[22] The story is based on the "essentially real" dialogue between a "writer" (Walsh) and a "colonel" (probably Carlos Eugenio de Moori Koenig), who was the custodian of the body of "that woman" (Eva Perón) and had been in charge of protecting it from attempts by the CGT (National Workers Union) to recover it, as well as from military groups who were trying to destroy it.[23] Many of the topics in this story go back to the origins of Latin American literary journalism and the separation between civilization and barbarism installed as a literary leitmotif by Sarmiento's *Facundo*.

Discussing "Esa mujer," Argentine critic Gonzalo Aguilar (2000, 65) argued that Walsh wrote fiction when he could not fully unveil the journalistic truth. When he was able to solve the mystery, however, his narratives immediately became testimonial. "Esa mujer" was, for Aguilar, a good example of this logic: when, in the story, the Colonel decides not to reveal the final destination of Eva Perón's body, Walsh's fiction mechanisms are immediately released to reign free (65–66).

Although Eva Perón's death has already occurred at the time Walsh's narrative begins, her body is still subject to a moral transfiguration, one that has no effect on the living characters in the story—Walsh and the Colonel. This intense process starts at the point when the Colonel describes how shocking it was for him to see the naked corpse in the coffin: "she looked like a virgin" (Walsh 1981, 167).

The story pivots on the Colonel's account of how the body of "that woman" had to be transported to a series of different locations in order to keep it hidden. Along with the multiple changes in destination, the corpse suffers physical modifications, fractures, lacerations, and blows that alter its external, virginal look. But there are also processes that alter the corpse's virginal status on a moral level: at some point, for instance, the Colonel recalls that he found the embalmer "raping" the body. The account of the eventful journey of "that woman's" body ends up reading like a surreal Via Crucis. At the end of its pilgrimage, however, Eva's body has mutated from its original virginal status into a masculinity that suggests the strength of a warrior: "She is standing!—the Colonel shouts. I buried her standing on her feet, just like Facundo, because she was a macho!" (Walsh 1981, 170).

The reference to *Facundo* and the myth of Facundo Quiroga buried standing is not casual. The caudillo from La Rioja was, according to Sarmiento, "buried standing" like a warrior. And the connections between Eva Perón and Quiroga, Sarmiento's quintessential model of barbarism, displayed in all their verticality and masculinity, elevate Eva Perón to the stature of an ambivalent historical hero. Through this narrative device, Eva enters a mythical zone in Walsh's literature, a zone in which the body, detached from its physicality, is also separated from its earthly limitations. After Eva's masculinization, Walsh's short story can finally operate its last transformation on her, canonizing her and turning the character into a saint.

Walsh also used this narrative device, which I will refer to as "literary canonization," in two more of his most memorable nonfiction texts: the two open letters he wrote to the military *juntas* after the assassination of his daughter Vicky.

Throughout the letters, Vicky's character—just like Eva in "Esa mujer"—transitions from her original state of pure, delicate femininity into one of strong, warrior-like masculinity, and finally from mortality to sanctity.

Walsh tells us in "Letter to My Friends," three months after his daughter's death, that after working as a journalist for a short while Vicky had become disenchanted with the profession and had started to volunteer as a teacher and a social worker in the slums of Buenos Aires. "She came out of that experience converted to an impressive asceticism," Walsh states (qtd. in Link 1996, 244). This "ascetic conversion" also had the narrative power to start gradually blurring Vicky's female traits: "Vicky, just like so many other *boys* who suddenly became adults, had to jump from here to there, running away from one home to the next" (245; my italics). The transformation of Walsh's daughter into one of the "boys" is the first step in the process of her narrative canonization. This process also involves Vicky joining the paramilitary organization Montoneros, which was the armed group of the Peronist party resisting the 1976 military coup. Amid a wave of state terrorism and kidnappings, "[the] sin was not to talk, but to turn yourself in [to the dictatorship]" Walsh adds later in the letter (245). Of course, instead of turning herself in, Vicky chose to die. She stayed, therefore, "clear of sin."

A second step in Vicky's transformation lies in the account of her "suicide." In a key passage of his letter, Walsh describes his daughter running out of ammo, standing on her feet, opening her arms in the shape of a cross, and addressing her final words to the military patrol that had ambushed her and some other rebel friends at the door of their hideout. Walsh reconstructs the scene based on the "testimony of a conscript" who mysteriously reached out to him (qtd. in Link 1996, 245):

The combat lasted more than an hour and a half. A man and a girl shot at us from the roof. We noticed the girl because, every time she shot a round at us and we dodged, we heard her laugh.

Suddenly there was silence—the soldier said. The girl dropped her machine gun, stepped up on the parapet, and opened her arms. She was skinny, had short hair, and was wearing a nightgown. She started talking to us loudly but in a very calm voice. I don't remember exactly what she said. But I do remember the last phrase; in fact that phrase keeps me awake at night: "'You are not killing us'—she said—'we choose to die.'" And then she and the man put their guns at their temples and killed themselves in front of us." (245–46; my translation)

Many are the possible references to religious narratives and iconography in this passage, which as a scene works like a pagan Sermon on the Mount. Vicky's nightgown and her thinness, her open arms and the speech to the crowd, and her self-immolation are only a few of the most salient connections between Walsh's account and the iconic scene in the New Testament.[24] In the second to last paragraph of his letter Walsh reinforces the interpretation of Vicky's death as part of a religious sequence: "Her death yes, her death was gloriously hers, and for this pride I commend myself, and it is me *who is reborn from her*" (qtd. in Link 1996, 246; my translation and italics).

Redemption through the death of a martyr—a political one in this case— is one of the directions in which much of Walsh's literary journalism can be read. Like a Christ who willingly submitted to death, Vicky sacrificed herself to save not only her peers but also her father, her mother, and a whole nation oppressed under the yoke of a violent dictatorship. As a character in Walsh's letter, Vicky also glorified herself and her cause in a supreme act of martyrdom. And, exactly like Eva Perón or Mario Brión, she died and was immortalized by Walsh, standing on her feet.

CANON AND DEATH, STORY AND HISTORY

Walsh's narrative device of literary canonization and the efficacious use he made of a series of extremely powerful religious stereotypes in his literary journalism, his fiction, and his letters have had a profound impact on how Argentines and Latin Americans in general have approached journalism, politics, literature, and history after the return of democracy in the early 1980s.

The historical reports of Walsh's own death, for instance, tend to work in parallel with the author's testimonial accounts in *Operación Masacre*, "Esa mujer," and Vicky's death in the open letters discussed above. The multiple stories and the historical truth of Walsh's assassination have been suffused with the myth of divine heroism that Walsh himself crafted in his work. During the Latin American democratic transition in the early eighties, this myth was also instrumental in the incorporation of Walsh's figure into the Argentine and Latin American literary, political, and journalistic canons.

An example of the interpolation of these literary narratives into history (an operation that, from Sarmiento's *Facundo* on, has defined the hybrid nature of literary journalism in Latin America) would be the collective efforts of some of the survivors of the clandestine detention and torture centers at the Navy Mechanics School (ESMA) to reconstruct Walsh's last hours. Not by chance, many of these reconstructions follow Walsh's own narrative topoi and overlap with the spatial-moral canon the author developed in his literary journalistic work.[25]

According to some of those testimonies, a task force at the ESMA was ordered to capture Walsh alive in March 1977, take him to the detention center, and extract from him as much information as possible before killing him. The writer, who had already spent a year hiding from the de facto government, was marked for torture and death. Caught by surprise at the entry to his hideout, located at the corner of San Juan and Entre Ríos, Walsh tried to resist and opened fire with a small-caliber gun, a Walther PPK .22, but was gunned down by the task force (Verbitsky 2000, 25).

In 2006, former ESMA detainee Ricardo Croquet added some relevant details to the narrative. Croquet said that the plan orchestrated by the task force was, in fact, to capture Walsh alive. Several undercover agents waited outside Walsh's hideout, and when he showed up, the infamous torturer, naval captain, and rugby player Alfredo Astiz tried to tackle him to the ground. Walsh—who had also played rugby in high school—dodged the tackle and, still standing, managed to pull the small gun from his pocket. He opened fire, wounding one of the men before being gunned down by them. Croquet, whose account came secondhand from a supposed member of that task force, quoted his source directly: "We took Walsh down. The motherfucker stood behind a tree and he shot back with a .22. We sprayed him good, but he wouldn't drop, the motherfucker" (qtd. in "Jaque a los asesinos" 2006; my translation).

This was the version of Walsh's death that became the most widespread among family, colleagues, friends, and the press.[26] It not only survived many other competing narratives but also became the official story and is today an integral part of judicial testimonies, as well as legal and official records. It is not by chance that it also works in parallel with Walsh's accounts of the deaths of many of his nonfictional characters, including his own daughter. Just like Vicky Walsh, Eva Perón, and Mario Brión, Walsh met his destiny head on. And after dodging the treacherous tackle of an infamous torturer, he faced death standing on his feet. **A**

In another open letter, the one that Argentine writer Julio Cortázar dedicated to Walsh after his death, the author of *Hopscotch* imagined how vehemently Walsh would have opposed any form of posthumous tribute. "Here what counts is that the disappearance, the torture, and the deaths *transmute* into something different at this end of the thread," Cortázar (1994, 316; my translation and italics) wrote. That transmutation, that moral alchemy, was in fact started on paper by Walsh himself but has ended up projecting him into history, legal documents, and testimonies before judges, journalists, and the public. Walsh's literary and historical canonization is a symbolic operation that, beginning in Walsh's own writing, has incorporated his myth into the Latin American canon of literary journalism. This was a transmutation that Walsh had efficiently applied to some of his most important characters, those who appeared in his literary journalism.

LATIN AMERICAN NARRATIVE NONFICTION AND THE CONCEALING NARRATOR

As noted earlier, because Walsh faced persecution and threats, he had to conceal the authorship of some of his journalistic work at the time of publication and for some time thereafter. Also discussed earlier was how this concealment affected his journalistic narratives on a structural level.

When in 1955 Gabriel García Márquez wrote *The Story of a Shipwrecked Sailor*, a testimonio published over fourteen consecutive issues of *El Espectador*, the Colombian writer faced a predicament similar to Walsh's: the military government of Gustavo Rojas Pinilla immediately threatened his life. The threat "would almost cost my life," García Márquez wrote in a prologue added to the story when it was first published as a book in 1970 (García Márquez 1987, 8).

The Story of a Shipwrecked Sailor was written in the first-person narrative voice of a twenty-year-old sailor, Luis Alejandro Velasco. In its original serial form, the story's author was identified as Velasco and its text told how the young man, working for the Colombian navy, survived for ten days while adrift in the Caribbean Sea. The government had originally blamed a tropical storm for the incident that set Velasco adrift and cost the lives of seven of his colleagues, but García Márquez's piece unveiled an official cover-up of the events surrounding the shipwreck, thus putting the government under public scrutiny. The deaths and Velasco's ten days adrift had, in fact, been caused by overweight contraband poorly distributed on and inadequately lashed to the deck, plus a number of other questionable practices customary for the Colombian navy of the day.

As García Márquez wrote in the 1987 prologue to his book, "the dictatorship took heat and orchestrated a series of drastic retaliations which would end a few months later with the closing of the newspaper" (12; my translation)—and, a few months after that, with the author's exile in Paris.

García Márquez's name was first associated with the narrative when *The Story of a Shipwrecked Sailor* was published as a book in 1970. This brings us back to testimonio's "problem of authorship," which in recent years has been justly criticized as a tendency toward appropriation and colonization of the source story and culture. As Gisela Norat (2002, 64) has pointed out, the question of "authorship" in testimonial literatures can be problematic, "since the first stage of bearing witness in a '*testimonio*' generally involves a recording of the subject's story by a professional (often a social scientist, journalist or writer) for later transcription because in many cases the informant lacks the skills to write the personal account." The "informant" is the initial storyteller; but the "professional" (often white, of European descent, and informed by Western values) takes ownership and credit for the story as the "author," through his or her ability to write and disseminate it.

But the "authorship problem" has even more complex roots. It had, in fact, originated as a solution to a specific set of political circumstances due to which, while attempting to share the story, both author and informant could come under threat. The structural conundrum of authorship inherent to testimonio preceded the consolidation of the genre and was already present as a solution to impending death threats—for the multiple political reasons described above—in the works of literary journalism that anticipated the consolidation of the genre, notably Walsh's and García Márquez's.

That "solution"—which I have referred to as the "concealing narrator"— was one of the defining features of the foundational testimonial literatures in Latin America and of many of the factual narrative forms that predate it.

THE QUESTION OF LITERARY AUTONOMY

Although it is clear that both *Operación Masacre* and *The Story of a Shipwrecked Sailor* belong to the realm of long-form prose, in terms of their motivation it would be hard to prove that these narratives were written for intrinsically aesthetic purposes. Both García Márquez's and Walsh's stories have a strong political undertone. Both present a sense of journalistic urgency and humane disgust regarding the aberrations committed by the authoritarian regimes in their countries. In that sense, both pieces express deep concern for the dilemmas rooted in Latin America's political instability, and both display—more or less clearly—a moral vision aimed at the restoration of democracy in the region.

This anti-authoritarian undertone not only gives their stories an ethical imprint but also makes them much more politically motivated than purely aesthetic. "[Evidently], political denunciation translated into the art of [the] novel becomes innocuous. It doesn't bother anyone at all, meaning that it becomes sacralized as art," Walsh said during an interview with Argentine novelist Ricardo Piglia (1998, 399) in January 1973. During that exchange, Walsh argued against the novel—which he defined as an obsolete, bourgeois form—in favor of more politically committed narratives such as testimonio, which he thought were more in tune with Latin American reality.

In Buenos Aires in 1963 Walsh had joined the staff of the innovative publishing house Jorge Alvarez. This move proved central to his understanding of the bigger picture in the Latin American narrative of the 1960s and 1970s. In those years Walsh read and edited some of the books that would fuel the revolutionary boom of magic realism in Latin America. Walsh, Susana "Pirí" Lugones, Julia "Chiquita" Constenla, Rogelio "Pajarito" García Lupo, Joaquín "Quino" Salvador Lavado, and Ricardo Piglia were all part of that stellar team of readers and editors who helped popularize authors such as Mario Vargas Llosa (*Los jefes* was first published in Argentina by Jorge Alvarez in 1963), Manuel Puig, Abelardo Castillo, Juan José Saer, Oscar Masotta, David Viñas, and, surely enough, Walsh himself, whose *Los oficios terrestres* was also published by Alvarez.

"We were all employees and we had huge hits, but we couldn't keep the authors we discovered for ourselves [because] bigger publishers would lure them in with better [publishing] rights," noted Jacobo Capelluto, an accountant for Jorge Alvarez, in an interview. "We lacked the experience to deal with the cost of paper, the lack of credit, and the delays in payments. [. . .] We never harvested what we sowed" ("Los libros" 2005).

In those years Walsh would isolate himself on an island in Tigre to write, translate, and work on a theory for a new Latin American literature, more popular and militant and less influenced by the representational canon of the nineteenth century. Thanks to Jorge Alvarez, his work in short stories and long-narrative literary journalism began to gain exposure and was soon noticed by critics such as the Uruguayan powerhouse Ángel Rama, who praised *Operación Masacre*, noting that what Walsh had "construed as a novel [had] autonomous literary value [but] at the same time [was] great, powerful journalism, some of the best [that had ever been written]" (Lafforgue 2000, 230).

However, literary autonomy was something that Walsh was conflicted about until the day he died. For him, literature, journalism, and political action had to work in parallel. With that in mind, he returned to Cuba for the Congreso Cultural de la Habana of January 1968 and participated in the ninth Premio Casa de las Américas. In 1970, back in Havana, Walsh was finally elected as a juror for the testimonio category that he had helped to establish, awarding the prize for the first time that year. One of the books that Walsh had in mind while establishing the prize for testimonio was Cuban author Miguel Barnet's *Cimarrón*. *Cimarrón* (*The Autobiography of a Runaway Slave*) aimed exactly in the direction that Walsh had envisioned for a new Latin American literature.

Published in 1966 by the Instituto de Etnología y Folklore (Institute of Ethnology and Folklore) in Havana, *Cimarrón* was a documentary text with a clearly political subtext: "the documentation of both the authentic folk culture of Cuba that the revolution sought to recover, and the deplorable human conditions that justify the revolution and its subsequent programs" (Foster 1984, 51). *Cimarrón* is written in the first-person voice of 104-year-old Esteban Montejo, a slave who had hurled a stone at a slave driver in Spanish-controlled Cuba and then fled to the mountains to live in solitude. The narrative tells the story of how Montejo returns from the mountains to Havana, becoming a wage-earning farmhand. Finally, due to a dismal life under capitalism, Montejo joins the uprising. Mainly thanks to Barnet's testimonio, Montejo and *Cimarrón* became symbols of the Cuban Revolution.

Barnet was aware of the impact that Montejo's story would have on the imagery of the Cuban Revolution. In an essay included in the 1987 edition of the book, the writer quoted the previously mentioned American anthropologist behind *The Children of Sánchez*: "I think that I have proven that the lives of those men who belong to what Oscar Lewis called the culture of poverty don't always lack the will of being, or of a historical conscience. And when they are anchored in feelings of marginality, the flames of those lives show us the path to the future" (Barnet 1987, 214–15; my translation). Through the reconstruction of Montejo's troubles and tribulations, Barnet presented what he defined as the portrayal of a whole class and, eventually, of a whole nation, as well as the path for its liberation through the communist revolution.

In the context of the Castro regime, Montejo's narrative became a literary benchmark. After the publication of *Cimarrón* in 1966, Barnet's work entered the literary canon of the Cuban Revolution, and in the years that followed, in part thanks to Walsh, the Cuban writer gained acclaim as a cornerstone for Latin American testimonio. The framing of Montejo's story as an autobiography put in parallel the lives of the slaves in the Spanish colony and the lives of the working classes under capitalism. Also, and by contrast, it projected into the future the qualities and possibilities of life under the new communist regime.[27] The dual political-artistic nature of the work was also noted by English writer Graham Greene in the prologue to the first edition of Barnet's work: "There wasn't a book like this before, and it is quite improbable it will be repeated" (Barnet 1987, 210). What Greene thought he was discovering, however, was the crystallization of an already established literary trend that had started in Latin America almost ten years earlier with political testimonio and the new literary journalism of Walsh and García Márquez.

In order to develop the twofold nature of his nonfiction, Barnet resorted to a particular strategy: he positioned himself as a mere scribe for Montejo, giving "voice to the voiceless" slave. The absence (concealment?) of Barnet as a narrator in the first editions of Cimarrón also creates a rather seamless interplay between autobiographical documentary and social narrative, adding a new dimension to an already problematic authorial category. "Montejo's symbolic status as a rebel against the institution of slavery, his participation in the struggle for Cuban independence, his membership in the Cuban Socialist Party, and, above all else, his representations of the solidarity first of the black slave society and subsequently of the black ethnic minority all attest to values promoted by the official mythopoesis of the Castro government" (Foster 1984, 51–52).

Like Walsh and García Márquez, Barnet chose his subject not only for its particularities but mainly for its emblematic qualities. Cimarrón aimed at describing a common Cuban experience; in Barnet's own words, it aimed at becoming a "sounding board for the collective memory of my country" (Barnet 1987, 214; my translation). Many Latin American literary journalists were already intent on describing those communal experiences, delineating and projecting through allegorical resonances the historical-dialectical development of the Latin American state. This narrative direction, in part a by-product of the intellectual debate conducted through Casa de las Américas and heavily influenced by Georg Lukács's Theory of the Novel, greatly differed from the "atypicality" of the characters and stories presented in American narrative journalism, which in the end assumed neither a shared reality nor a self-evident, sui generis existence within a shared reality.

The political environment in the region also created a common setting for Latin American literary nonfiction. Testimonio in postcolonial Latin America emerged precisely as the means to re-create a political memory that had been challenged, silenced, annulled, and often deleted from official records by a long series of authoritarian, antidemocratic governments. By hijacking democracy and the market, an action both political and economic, by restraining the freedom of speech and the potential for realization in ange of ideas—and products—the military governments in the

.irectly caused the division of intellectual labor to revert to con-

.hat would exist in a premodern state. This political context was the

.op for a collective experience that had to be rebuilt, restored, and re-

.porated into the official records. Journalists had to become, once again, pedagogues, record keepers, and statesmen all in one.

The task of re-creating a political memory—one that Walsh, García Márquez, and Barnet, among many others undertook—could not possibly remain separate from politics, one of the main reasons for which literature, journalism, and political action, following the tradition of Sarmiento and Martí, regained their profound interconnectedness in those years of turmoil.

However strong, this connection between literature, journalism, and politics still had its limits. As Barnet wrote in a 1987 afterword to *Cimarrón*, testimonial narratives could not generally offer much more than a synthesis of some of the aspects of the Latin American problem. "Social solutions," he added, "are the mandatory duty of politicians" (Barnet 1987, 214).

THE MATRIX OF PROXIMITY

As discussed earlier, during the 1960s and 1970s American literary journalists showed their authority and command over their subjects through their direct access to topics. This proximity was represented in text by the use of the first-person narrative voice. But this was not a new device. Stephen Crane had resorted to personal experience as the main source of his nonfiction. Mark Twain, particularly during his time as a traveling correspondent for the *San Francisco Alta California*, had used the first-person voice to reveal the true nature of the places he visited and the people he met. "Like Whitman," Shelley Fisher Fishkin writes, "Twain was disturbed by people's willingness, as Whitman had put it, 'to take things at second or third hand,' 'to look through the eyes of the dead . . . [and] feed on the spectres in books" (Fishkin 1988, 66–67).

The figure of the narrator-protagonist is designed to reduce the distance between the implied reader and the text. The physical, temporal, and emotional proximity between the author and the events narrated—between the author, the author's subjects, and their stories—also creates a *metonymic* narrative axis.[28] By proximity, Anglo-American authors of narrative journalism show authority, knowledge, and command over topics and subjects. Any one of them can say, *I see this, I am here, I know this*. In that same direction, the Anglo-American literary nonfiction tradition has become a subjective, experiential record of a time as seen, suffered, and enjoyed by its direct witnesses.

In the Latin American tradition of literary journalism, though some components remain the same, the narrative matrix is substantially different. As marginalized counterbalances against an official, monolithic narrative, these texts strive to show themselves to be as free from subjectivity as possible. The clearest example, once again, is Walsh's *Operación Masacre*, in which the impersonal register of the narrator creates a channel for the different points of view to be expressed, allowing them to converge in the reader's mind as one conclusion: the government has committed a crime against its citizens. The dominant metaphoric aspect of these narratives allows them to stay open through relevant iterations and historical change.

In this type of Latin American narrative nonfiction, authors operate under the premise of distancing themselves from the events they write about. Even when some of these stories resort to the first-person narrative voice, they still usually revolve around a *metaphorical* axis, using factuality on an allegorical level. It is as if they were saying, *This story happened in the past, and this is how it can be used in the present.* Latin American literary journalism works as an allegorical account of the present, through the narration of past events, which can either be fully loaded with political undertones or plainly interpreted as a novelized historical record. This is what we learned from the literary evolution as it progressed from Sarmiento to Walsh.[29]

THE OFFICIAL STORY?

As discussed in the past few sections of this work, many of the structural features of Latin American literary journalism can be traced back to a political-historical-communicational origin, but they also need to be connected to a literary tradition. Both Latin American and Anglo-American nonfiction resort to similar techniques, of which scenic construction and full dialogue transcription are the most evident. However, there is a general contextual and ideological substrate—a central part of that tradition—that enhances the structural disparities.

These disparities, which receded between the 1910s and the 1930s, grew stronger in the years that followed due to the politically oppressive climate in Latin America, first as a direct consequence of the Cuban Revolution and later because of the programmatic approach to literature fostered by Casa de las Américas. These events ended up confirming that in Latin America the sphere of culture and the sphere of politics did not (could not?) function with total autonomy.

Institutionalized and legitimized by Casa de las Américas, testimonial literature was conceived and fostered—following literary journalism—with a political finality and could not be analyzed in merely artistic terms. It could also be argued that, historically, most Latin American documentary narratives were also born in contexts of a strong push toward modernization (from Sarmiento to Walsh, the desire for progress, modernization, and democracy has been a constant preoccupation). Since its inception, Latin American literary journalism has increasingly been subordinated to politics. As authoritarianism spread across the subcontinent, the efforts to develop this form of nonfiction were usually hindered, banished, persecuted, and silenced. And it was, as indicated above, certainly due to the advent of authoritarianism that testimonial narratives turned in an even more metaphorical direction.

Unlike, for instance, the acts of violence in *In Cold Blood*, which most critics—and Capote himself—have considered inexplicable, the ones Walsh describes in *Operación Masacre* have a direct explanation in Argentine contemporary politics (Foster 1984). The political backdrop and the violence of the authoritarian regime work as context and, ultimately, as the final explanation for the crimes described in these narratives.

Latin American narrative journalism, therefore, oscillates between the "official story," which is a false account produced by the government, a masking of the violence that emanates from the authoritarian state, and the "fictionalized account" of the real story, which contradicts the official statements and unveils the truth. As long as they remain marginal, Latin American narrative nonfiction accounts are tolerated by the authoritarian power. When these stories gain popularity and their power to negate the official narrative increases, the stories and their authors start suffering persecution, banishment, and censorship.

In part due to this politicization, the role of the author-protagonist in Latin American nonfiction has become much more problematic and intricate than it is in the Anglo-American tradition.

Latin American nonfiction, which was equally prepared to record and track social changes during the 1960s and 1970s, had from its inception a much more political nature. Its proactive inclination made the genre prone to an external political finality. In that sense, testimonial literature, an offspring of literary journalism, remained for the most part outside the realm of pure art and was continually judged, evaluated, and characterized through a moral-political lens. Both literary journalism and testimonio, though, have been from their inception moral-political and literary forms inscribed within a limited teleology: just like the contraband that caused the wreckage in García Márquez's story, the central goal of these narrative types in Latin America, these journalistic "contraband truths," in the words of David William Foster, was to contribute to the wreckage of the authoritarian state in the subcontinent—a goal that would not be realized until the first years of the 1980s.

CONCLUSION

● ● ●

THERE'S AN INHERENT CHALLENGE, if not an outright contradiction, in assigning a fixed value to cultural, historical, or even political contexts when reading the pathbreaking works of Latin American literary journalism. The writers and readers were not merely part of a new world inventing itself from scratch—dismissing roots or reference points from the past and rejecting them, actively and violently, in favor of the freedom to choose a new, as yet unknown identity. They were also writing and reading in a setting where languages and media were in permanent flux.

From those writers who, like Sarmiento, Martí, and Soiza Reilly, were simply too busy absorbing and redefining what it meant to be Latin American, to those who, like Arlt and Borges, were questioning and scrutinizing the very processes that made them and their readers Latin Americans, to the ones who, like Walsh and García Márquez, sought to challenge the boundaries and constructs of that identity by employing testimonial techniques that questioned the conditions of statehood deemed unjust or corrupt under undemocratic regimes—all of them had one thing in common: they were profoundly willing and extraordinarily capable of collaborating with their time, their audiences, their media, and their traditions. Indeed, they were such agile and subtle participants and interactors that they became, to an extent, signs of their time.

If journalism in the Western world has developed concomitantly with democracy and the markets—an idea that has proven its productivity in American journalism studies for years—it could also follow that journalism adopts its own particular identity, and perhaps even a different set of core values, when it emerges in predemocratic societies; when it consolidates during a time when democracy and the markets have not yet become fully integrated; or when that integration is being questioned, fractured, or simply arrested. Some of these ideas have been examined in this book.

But there is also an intrinsic problem at the core of that materialistic argument, one that can be fully appreciated only after the multiple observations made throughout these pages. This work has shown that despite the interruptions and transitions in the democratic-market continuum in Latin America—a region riddled with political instability—literary journalism has maintained a core of guiding principles. Although journalistic forms, practices, and genres have changed, developed, and matured as political and economic shifts occurred in the region while democracies were being hijacked by dictatorial powers or markets seized by the public sector or by corporative monopolies, literary journalism—or at least a significant part of it—still kept alive its allegiance to certain constants: democratic values, freedom of expression, the public good, justice, and truth. As a genre, it stayed attuned to its foundational values, which aimed for the establishment and consolidation of republican and democratic institutions in the former colonies.

It has been argued here that social and political circumstances could shape the tone and the fabric of literary journalistic narratives. Thus, for many of the authors discussed in this work, producing literary journalism under oppressive political regimes required a strategic combination of both enunciative distance between themselves and the events they wrote about, as well as research proximity to the subjects of their investigation. Curiously, however, even when resorting to the first-person narrative voice—matching author and narrator—in times of relative freedom and social stability, these same journalists produced accounts that tended to revolve around a metaphorical axis, presenting factual stories under a heavy allegorical imprint. This is where the materialistic approach should perhaps give way to a more complex conceptualization of the development of literary journalism and other narrative forms in the region.

Literary journalism congealed as a tradition in Latin America during the late nineteenth century and since then has operated under what might be called a shifting or oblique referentiality. It can be argued that referentiality depends in great measure on how a text is read, as opposed to how it is written. But due to the instrumental nature of literary journalism in the region—

these stories sometimes served a political, sometimes a pedagogic function, and sometimes both—the authors set up these mechanisms at the time of writing. Unlike journalistic traditions that allow for the metaphorical reading of a piece in reception, this ingrained oblique referentiality embedded in the text from inception facilitated the use of these texts in shifting political conditions. It made them historically flexible, adaptable, and ultimately apt to circulate, as well as be read and understood, beyond the potential restrictions of any particular era, beyond the political uncertainty and the collapse of legal frameworks.

For that same reason, upon close textual analysis, these narratives also reveal strong built-in moral systems and teleologies. When legalities vanish and the institutional structures shake and implode, it is morality that becomes an anchoring point for factuality and truth in journalism. This is the place to which journalism retreats. The moral narrative, a constant in Latin American literary journalism, has become more common today across the world, during a time of "alternative facts" and "fake news."

This book does not claim to have even scratched the surface of what it took to create Latin America's literary journalism, as it can barely touch upon the most influential and well-read writers of their respective eras (predominantly male and white, two of the main traits of the modernity we have described).[1] However, it can claim to have noticed a few lines connecting authors and periods. Literary journalism as a genre in the subcontinent has followed a distinct path of development, one certainly connected to the historical reality of the region. Due to institutional instability, on the one hand, but also to literary tradition and literary history, on the other, it has evolved as an allegorical account of the present—a narrative form that could either be read as richly riddled with political undercurrents or interpreted plainly as a novelized historical record.

This tension between tradition and the present, but also between the story (what is *told*) and History (what the narrative actually *means*), has been at the center of this genre since its earliest iterations. Despite many changes, a commitment to republican and democratic values has also remained at its core. Justice, truth, freedom, and the public good have been, as suggested in this study, some of the forces behind literary journalism in Latin America, either floating on the narrative surface of its texts or palpitating beneath the heavy waves of rhetoric and a—more or less—oblique approach to facts.

These observations also confirm one of the main premises upon which this book was based: the fact that democracy and market capitalism are central elements in the consolidation of a strong modern journalism. But this revised view of how literary journalism as a genre has evolved throughout different historical periods in Latin America, under governments that were at times open and democratic and at other times severely repressive, speaks to a less restrictive, perhaps even liberating idea of how the process of communication is shaped in our societies, as well as to the relative independence that certain genres develop at maturity, in order to remain immune to the material, political, and economic historical environment.

The interconnectedness of the world today is confronting us directly with different, new, and vibrant journalistic models. It is clear, for instance, that the late twentieth and early twenty-first centuries have brought nonbinary and female narratives to the forefront. Elena Poniatowska in Mexico, Pedro Lemebel in Chile, Leila Guerriero in Argentina, and Gabriela Wiener in Peru are exemplars of this new trend and deserve an entire study. Some communications scholars, however, have taken the unfortunate position of rejecting these and other traditions, styles, and genres that, although not resembling the ones they have grown accustomed to in the West, have long been considered to be journalism in their societies of origin—narratives that are read as journalism by those who live under different political and social regimes.

This form of intellectual chauvinism is a shortcoming that twenty-first-century communications scholarship cannot afford to indulge any longer. In their own particular way, many of these narratives do respond to what we in the West consider journalism, a discursive form that is geared toward creating the conditions of justice by finding the truth—a truth that is sometimes called "objective" and other times is called "the voice of the people"—a quest that committed men and women have made their own despite challenges and risks, all in pursuit of the greater good of their societies.

Journalism is not an abstraction. It is a practice that takes place in societies, within a historical context, under an array of different political settings. Like any other human pursuit, journalism is not a self-defined and self-contained entelechy that moves across space and time without changes or contradictions. It is an activity of men and women deeply connected with their historical circumstances. It is an activity permeated by political, social, and technological processes that, like tectonic plates, are in constant shift and movement. This state of perpetual change makes journalism rich and dynamic, full of inconsistencies, tension, and chaos. Journalism is a human undertaking in ceaseless redefinition, crossed by personal and collective interests, an activity through which we express not only our ideas about the present but also our deepest fears and our most visionary dreams. As such, journalism has also the potential to define who we are as a people and to have a profound impact on the societies we create.

NOTES

• • •

INTRODUCTION

1. The Latin root of the word *inform* refers to the process of imposing form, giving shape to something. For more detailed discussions about genres, see the work of Liddle (2009) and Seriot (2007) and the classic studies of Bakhtin (1984) and Todorov (1970). For a historical approach to the journalistic genres, see the work of Gomis (2008).

2. For an exploration of the notion of print capitalism, see Benedict Anderson's *Imagined Communities* (1983). For a succinct but convincing analysis of how a "democratic market society" was at the core of the development of the penny press, the first historical link in the chain of modern journalism, see Schudson's *Discovering the News* (1978), especially the introduction and chapter 1, "The Age of Egalitarianism: The Penny Press."

3. In the words of the Russian literary critic Mikhail Bakhtin, genres are a way to access multiplicity through the unique. So in their uniqueness, concreteness, and singularity, each one of the manifestations of literary journalism can also become a typical representation of the genre. The structuralist linguist Tzvetan Todorov (1970, 10–11) defined literary genres as sets of internal rules that functioned similarly across different texts or as rigorous systems of rules that corresponded to series of probabilities and expectations. Modern cognitive science follows, in part, these preliminary observations with scientific evidence that transcends structuralist case observations.

4. To explore the notion of bureaucratic authoritarianism, see Rouquié's *The Military and the State in Latin America* (1982).

5. For a more detailed definition, see chapter 6 of this book.

6. See "The Ideal of Objectivity" in the work of Schudson (1978), as well as works by Tucher (1994) and Mindich (1998).

CHAPTER 1. The Trial of Francisco Bilbao and Its Role in the Foundation of Latin American Journalism

1. Closely overseen by the Spanish Crown, Mexico acquired its first press in 1540, Lima in 1584, Santo Domingo in 1600, Paraguay in 1715, and Buenos Aires in 1780 (Campbell 1962, 545).

2. Chapter 2 discusses *caudillismo* and the role of these strongmen in the development of nation-states in postcolonial Latin America.

3. The newspaper bore the name of the Philadelphia *Aurora*, founded by Benjamin Franklin's grandson, Benjamin Bache.

4. After ascending to the throne in March 1808 in the course of the Napoleonic invasion of the Iberian Peninsula, Spain's King Fernando VII was captured by the French and confined in the Château de Valençay for six years. During his captivity, a local junta was formed in Seville to run the state and fight the invaders. The Junta de Sevilla, as it was called, also named viceroys to administer the king's business in the colonies. But the creole elites in the Americas banished these delegates, arguing that in the absence of the king the locals were entitled "by divine right" to form their own provisional governments. These patriotic governments usually comprised prominent members of the colonial society, especially members of the clergy, military officers, lawyers, and other white local elites who had lived or studied in Spain.

5. For information about the trial of Francisco Bilbao, see works by F. Bilbao (1897), M. Bilbao (1866), Eyzaguirre (1948), Lastarria (1885), Lipp (1975), and Quinet (1897).

6. For general historical and social data about Chile and its press in the postcolonial years, see works by Halperín Donghi (1993), Bushnell and Macaulay (1994), Ibarra Cifuentes (2014), Yeager (1991), and Rojas (2009).

7. As Diego Barros Arana (1913, 461) mentions, news publishers usually received discretionary support from the government through the purchase of yearly subscriptions for government agencies. He gives the example of Manuel Rivadeneyra's *El Mercurio de Valparaíso*, which had "twenty subscriptions counting particulars and four for the Ministry of Public Instruction."

8. The government, however, was still channeling 16,468 pesos of its 3 million peso budget to support newspapers, journals, and magazines. The importance of this number becomes clear when it is compared to the allocation for the Univer-

sidad de Chile, which in 1843 was 14,000 pesos. Between 1853 and 1858, funds destined for the press remained steady at 16,000 pesos, increasing substantially in 1859 to 40,000 pesos, only to be reduced again to 20,000 pesos between 1861 and 1863 and cut to 10,000 between 1863 and 1876. By 1876, the dwindling contributions had finally disappeared from the national budget altogether (Jaksić 1994, 40–41, 58). Juan Bautista Alberdi, an Argentine politician, lawyer, and the main author of the Argentine constitution of 1853, noted the originality of the Chilean press legislation during his exile in Chile. "The government (and in these matters Chile's is the only one in the world), aside from protecting the inviolability of press circulation, fosters and supports it through *strong stimuli*," he wrote in his 1846 study of the Chilean press. Although it proved harder to implement with the sustained expansion of the press during the second half of the nineteenth century, Alberdi wrote that government subscriptions to newspapers still counted as a significant portion of the Chilean budget until 1846. "On November 23, 1825, 'willing the government [these are the words of the decree] to stimulate the distribution of writings in the Republic and to protect as much as the treasury permits both journalists and printers . . . the government subscribes to two hundred copies of *every paper* to be published [in Chile]," Alberdi copied from a presidential decree. Due to the large number of new publications appearing after the 1840s, the government was forced to cancel its subscription to several periodicals, but it continued "favoring those papers that due to their enlightened principles contained and promoted useful ideas, and which deserved to be communicated to the people" (Alberdi 1846, 57–58; my italics and translation from Spanish).

9. Gilliss's observations may, however, have been colored by the fact that as, an avid reader himself, the Georgetown-born official had grown accustomed to a different type of literature, journalism, and press. In 1833, Gilliss entered the University of Virginia, but he lasted less than a year. According to one account, "Excessive study impaired his health, and a severe inflammation of the eyes confined him for many weeks to a dark room. Upon his partial recovery he made a fourth cruise, ending in October, 1835, after which he resumed his studies in Paris, and pursued them there for about six months, before returning to his professional duties" in the US Navy (Gould 1877).

10. The Argentine writer, journalist, pedagogue, and politician Domingo Sarmiento was certainly in Lastarria's mind when he called for the formation of the Sociedad Literaria, as discussed in the next chapter.

11. It should be noted, however, that in Chile, as in the rest of Latin America, public opinion was different from the commonly accepted views in the Habermasian literature on the topic. The forms of publicity in postcolonial Latin America differed substantially from the practices observed in Europe and the United States. In fact, in Chile in those years, less than 17 percent of the population was literate

(Jaksić 1994, 41). For an excellent contextualization of the idea of publicity in post-colonial Latin America, see the work of Garavaglia (2007).

12. Lastarria writes that *El Crepúsculo* had been issued regularly, once a month, since June 1, 1843. It was printed at a press owned by Juan N. Espejo and Juan José Cárdenas and later bought by a business owner named Cristóbal Valdés. The articles were written by some of the "most enthusiastic young members of the Sociedad Literaria" (Lastarria 1885, 276). (All translations of Lastarria's *Recuerdos literarios* texts are mine.)

13. All translations of Manuel Bilbao's work are mine.

14. For more details about the press law, see the works of Alberdi (1846) and Jaksić (1994).

15. Yeager (1991) offers a thorough analysis of the Instituto Nacional's impact on Chile's attempt to form an educated elite.

16. The incident is described in detail by Lastarria (1885, 285–86), who also transcribed the Supreme Court's decision, putting special emphasis on the curious fact that, according to the resolution, Bilbao's article had to be burned by a *verdugo* (an executioner). The reasoning was anchored in an ancient law of the Spanish East India Company. Lastarria also gives the names of the judges who signed the resolution. In a footnote, Jaksić (1994, 57) offers a brief but interesting interpretation of the event.

17. The complete transcript of the trial was published by Francisco's brother, Manuel, in *Obras completas de Francisco Bilbao* (1866).

18. Aside from Francisco Bilbao's own verbal portraits, I base my description of the young writer on an article that Madame Quinet, wife of the French philosopher Edgar Quinet, Bilbao's professor at the Collège de France, published in the Argentine newspaper *La República* at the time of Bilbao's death (Quinet 1897, 1–8).

19. The exact amount of the fine is a subject of debate. Some sources state that it amounted to only 600 pesos. In any case, the same sources agree that the fine was exorbitant for the time. See discussions in Lastarria (1885), Jaksić (1994), and M. Bilbao (1866).

20. For a detailed analysis of the Chilean press acts of the nineteenth century, see works by Ibarra Cifuentes (2014) and Santa Cruz (1988).

21. Years later Arcos again became a traveling companion, this time of Domingo Sarmiento on a trip to the United States.

CHAPTER 2. Domingo Sarmiento, *Facundo*, and the Birth of Latin American Nonfiction in the Hands of a Political Exile

1. This anecdote is recounted by Sarmiento in his autobiographical *Recollections of a Provincial Past*, originally published in 1850. In order to complete the picture, I consulted Sarmiento's correspondence with Manuel Montt (Vergara

Quiroz 1999), with Félix Frías, and finally with his family. Also consulted was Altamirano and Sarlo's (1994) essay and Molloy's "The Unquiet Self: Mnemonic Strategies in Sarmiento's Autobiographies" (1994), in which the author elegantly argues that *Recollections of a Provincial Past* is *the* founding text of the Spanish American autobiographical genre. Also consulted were works by Illanes (2003) and Sagayo (1874).

2. In 1823, young Sarmiento lost his first opportunity to receive a government scholarship to study at the prestigious School of Moral Science in Buenos Aires. After leaving for San Luis in 1825 to undertake a regimented education under his uncle, the Federalist priest José de Oro, in 1827 Sarmiento received the good news that San Juan's liberal governor had finally agreed to grant him a scholarship to study in Buenos Aires. But a short time after that, on the very same day Sarmiento returned to his hometown, the caudillo Facundo Quiroga overthrew the provincial government and revoked the scholarship.

3. "On the night of November 17, at two o'clock in the morning, a group on horseback came to a stop in front of the prison, shouting: 'Death to the Unitarian savages!' So unmotivated was this manifestation, so cold and composed was that cry that issued from the mouths of those who pronounced it, that it was clear it was a calculated, concerted, and passionless act" (Sarmiento 2005, 181). Sarmiento's escape from the mob, which inspired one of the most powerful literary pieces of the period, Esteban Echeverría's "El Matadero," can also be found at the end of chapter 16 of Sarmiento's *Recollections of a Provincial Past* (2005).

4. For Sarmiento's articles about the government and incendiary newspapers, see, for instance, "Un jurado de imprenta," *El Mercurio*, March 16, 1841, "Cosas de estudiantes," *El Mercurio*, April 3, 1841 (Sarmiento 1948–1956, 1:17–19), and "Libertad de Imprenta," *El Mercurio*, March 8, 1841 (Sarmiento 1948–1956, 9:55–59).

5. In April 1845, Juan Manuel de Rosas sent a diplomat, Baldomero García, to Santiago in order to persuade the government of Manuel Bulnes to control Argentine agitation against the Argentine government in the Chilean press. Andrés Bello, who was an official in the Chilean Ministry of Foreign Relations, indicated in *El Araucano* that the government had no authority to control the press (Jaksić 1994, 47).

6. The English translation of the book title was *Civilization and Barbarism: Life of Juan Facundo Quiroga and Physical Aspect, Customs and Habits of the Argentine Republic.*

7. In their thorough study of this anecdote, Altamirano and Sarlo speculate that Sarmiento tailored the narration to fit the mythical structure of the "change of fortune." In this episode, Sarmiento dresses as a miner in part because of his extravagant taste for costume and in part for comfort's sake. A visitor, in fact, takes him for a miner. In a turn of the conversation, Sarmiento shows a level of educa-

tion and language higher than his (apparent) social condition: "In order to delay and consequently increase the satisfaction of the eventual recognition, [Sarmiento] does not intervene in a conversation that had already covered several topics" (Altamirano and Sarlo 1994, 166).

8. All translations of *Ambas Américas* are mine.

9. In the 1840s, less than 17 percent of the population in Chile was literate (Jaksić 1994, 41). In Argentina, after the student census of 1884, which was prepared right before the parliamentary debate on the Ley de Educación Común (Law for Common Education), there was a population of 497,947 school-age children, of whom only 145,660, or 29 percent, attended classes. The illiteracy rate just after 1884 was 40 percent (Bustamante 1989, 212).

10. For this section of my analysis, I use Kathleen Ross's translation of *Facundo* (Sarmiento 2003).

11. Sarmiento (2003, 43–44) wrote, "I have omitted the introduction as useless, and the last two chapters as superfluous today, recalling something you indicated in Montevideo in 1846, when you insinuated to me that the book was finished with the death of Quiroga."

12. For a quick look at the dialectical method, see the work of Georg W. F. Hegel (1988).

13. See works by Chalaby (1996) and Tucher (2006).

14. "Specifically, journalism insists on language's utilitarian aspect—particularly its subordination to the laws of the market, to money—and on language's transitivity, its transparency as a medium through which information is conveyed as objectively as possible" (A. González 1993, 5).

15. The translation is mine.

16. I cite the Oxford University Press edition of 2005, with translations by Elizabeth Garrels and Asa Zatz.

17. For an introduction to the idea of objectivity, factuality, and the changes introduced by the penny press, see works by Tucher (1994, 2006), Chalaby (1996), and Robertson (1997).

18. Pointing out the fact that the entertainment model described was becoming dominant is not meant as an argument against historians' and journalism scholars' valid views about the role of information and newspapers in the formation of communities.

19. On why the expansion of urban centers triggered a higher demand for entertainment, several concurrent reasons are explored by Gitlin (2002) and Schudson (1978).

20. "Within months of the war's end, three of the original Bohemians had rushed into print with thick memoirs of their wartime experiences" (Tucher 2006, 139). In these books "intended for a mass audience [for the first time, journalists]

recorded what they thought about the work they did. They pictured themselves as a special kind of person, doing a special job. [. . .] In fact, journalists were seeking a double distinction, differentiating themselves not just from ordinary people but also from the many other kinds of authors—novelists, playwrights, poets—who were also struggling to define themselves as skilled professionals. [. . .] Taken together, their insouciance about money, their devotion to their art, their unconventionality, and of course their talent made them feel radically, irremediably *not like* other people even as they were like each other, a community apart, exclusive and close-knit and special" (Tucher 2006, 132, 137–38). Fiction writers also tried to separate themselves from journalists. In his novel *A Modern Instance* (1882), William Dean Howells features a newspaper reporter as the central character—a weak, morally obtuse man whose writings function as a countertext to the novel. The reporter's articles, as described by Howells, cover the same events narrated in his book but develop an exploitative, condescending view of the subjects. The articles are marked, in Howells's words, by an "essential cheapness" (Robertson 1997, 1–9). Henry James's portrayal of daily reporters in *The Bostonians* was also negative. The novelist showed them as base, lowly, and disreputable characters. Journalists' bad public image, Robertson claims, only started to change after the Civil War, thanks to skillful writers like Stephen Crane and Theodore Dreiser, who had begun their careers as journalists. The early ambivalence toward reporters could also be read as part of the complex relationship between high and low culture in the United States during the late nineteenth and early twentieth centuries (Robertson 1997, 1–74).

21. Between a few attempts at the foundation of a republic and a series of upheavals, internal coups, and the restoration of the Bourbons to the throne, Spain's story of the late 1800s and early 1900s is too rich and complex to be presented even synoptically in a few paragraphs here.

22. Robertson (1997, 2–3) writes that, "early in the nineteenth century, journalism posed little threat to literature. The typical daily newspaper of the era was a four-page journal, sold only by subscription and aimed at a relatively small and almost exclusively male audience interested in business and politics. Newspapers existed to give financial and mercantile information and to promote the viewpoint of a political party or faction."

CHAPTER 3. José Martí and the Chronicles That Built Modern Latin America

1. For details about the arrival of the envoys from South America, see "Greeting the Delegates," *New York Times*, September 25, 1889.

2. For details about the conference, see the work of Cúneo (1955). For details about Blaine's plan, see Crapol (2000).

3. *Caudillismo*, or caudillism, was one of the last refuges for some sections of

the Americas' indigenous and mestizo populations, which would eventually be "Westernized" or eliminated as part of the modernizing push. Guillermo Bonfil Batalla (1996, 62–63) argues that "[the Westernization] of the Indian, nevertheless, turned out to be contradictory, given the stubborn necessity of maintaining a clear distinction between the colonizers and the colonized. If the Indians had stopped being Indians in order to be fully incorporated into Western civilization, the ideological justification for colonial domination would have ended. Segregation and difference are essential for any colonial society."

4. Since the time of the 1889 republic—during which the national motto Ordem e Progresso was coined—Brazilian politicians from the influential state of Río Grande do Sul had been particularly influenced by French philosopher Auguste Comte. Some of them were known as the Brazilian positivists. They rose to power between 1900 and 1930, and the most emblematic among them was Getúlio Vargas, a dictator in Brazil between 1930 and 1945. Some of his political ideas were adapted from Auguste Comte's *Course of Positive Philosophy* (see Freyre 1986, xiii–xxvii). The French philosopher's view is that

> it cannot be necessary to prove to anybody who reads this work that Ideas govern the world, or throw it into chaos; in other words, that all social mechanism rests upon opinions. The great political and moral crisis that societies are now undergoing is shown by a rigid analysis to arise out of *intellectual anarchy*. While stability in fundamental maxims is the first condition of genuine *social order*, we are suffering under an utter disagreement which may be called universal. *Till a certain number of general ideas can be acknowledged as a rallying-point of social doctrine, the nations will remain in a revolutionary state*, whatever palliatives may be devised; and their institutions can be only provisional. But whenever the necessary agreement on first principles can be obtained, appropriate institutions will arise without shock or resistance; for the causes of disorder will have been arrested by the mere fact of the agreement. It is in this direction that those must look who desire a natural and regular, a normal state of society. (Comte 2000, 40; my italics)

5. From that experience came Martí's first important political text, "El presidio político en Cuba" (Political prison in Cuba). The text shows to what extent the independence wars in Latin America shaped even the earliest manifestations of literary journalism in the region. Written in 1871, the article was produced with the intention of shaking up public opinion in Spain, while shedding some light on the atrocities that the colonial government was perpetrating in Cuba. This article on Cuba as political prison was Martí's account of the story of Lino Figueredo, a twelve-year-old sentenced to forced labor by Spain's colonial government on the island. The piece was written at the beginning of Martí's exile in Spain.

6. See works by Molloy (1997) and Dupont (2004).

7. In fact, Martí wrote an obituary for Karl Marx: "Karl Marx was not only a titanic mover of the anger of the European workers, but a profound seer in the reasons for human misery, and in the destinies of men. He was a man eaten with the desire to do good" (qtd. in Gray 1963, 254).

8. Aldrey wrote to Martí that "[the] public is complaining about your latest reviews of Darwin, Emerson, etc., because readers in this country want political news and anecdotes and the least literature possible. In this regard I am relegating the *Sección Constante* [to a secondary position in the newspaper] because people are grumbling about it, complaining that it talks too much about books and poets. Furthermore, the paragraphs are too long. This Section, which I would like to continue, must have short paragraphs" (qtd. in Rotker 2000, 37).

9. In one of his articles Martí criticized the mayor of Brooklyn as "soft wax in the hands of the real 'boss,' the organizer of the political associations in the city" (qtd. in Kirk 1977, 280).

10. In early 1889, after Cleveland had been defeated by Benjamin Harrison and Blaine became secretary of state, Martí was called upon to write a portrait of Blaine. He never did. Instead, in a letter to a friend he expressed how deeply the election's outcome had affected him: "I'm not myself anymore. What I have all along feared and said would happen is upon us—the United States' policy of conquest. A man can take more than he thinks before he dies; because I have been dead a long time, yet I am still alive. If one thing could have killed me, it would have been this. Oh, to console myself with my usual medicine, the only cure for pain, imagined or real, that leaves me with my respect and dignity intact: work" (qtd. in Karras 1974, 83).

11. In fact, Martí's articles soon became so popular that they were broadly reproduced without authorization throughout the region.

12. According to the *New York Times* article "Blaine and Cuba," published on June 17, 1884, "The Cubans residing in Florida and pursuing the vocations either of cigar-makers or of political refugees, are, upon this authority, enthusiastic for BLAINE. They believe that if he were President Cuba would be acquired by purchase. Mr. WICKER, the ex-Collector in question, tells how Mr. BLAINE told him that the island would be worth $500,000,000 to the United States. The Cubans are to carry Florida for BLAINE and BLAINE is to buy Cuba for the Cubans. [. . .] It is none the less characteristic that any man with a wild-cat scheme of this kind on his hands or in his mind should desire the election of BLAINE as the first step toward the realization of his scheme. The favor with which his nomination is received by these people will naturally have the effect of setting still more strongly against him the sober and settled part of the community, who expect to get their living by working and not by flying kites."

13. As discussed by Mindich (1998), the prevailing racist views in the popular press were expressed as criticisms of the allegedly deviant or uncivilized nature and unmanliness of both blacks and Latinos.

14. I have revised and improved parts of the translation in this fragment, comparing it with its Spanish version. "The Cutting Case," mentioned in Grover Cleveland's State of the Union message in 1886, was a diplomatic incident between the United States and Mexico that almost escalated to armed conflict. It was triggered by the imprisonment in Mexico of A. K. Cutting, an American newspaper editor, who had been charged with libel in Texas (Sarracino 2003).

15. It is necessary to note that Roberto González Echevarría has rejected the notion of a Hispanic American modernism, due to the fact that Latin American nations were founded at the outset of modernity and therefore had not seen a different past, as was the case in Europe.

16. The fragment was part of "Class War in Chicago: A Terrible Drama," a chronicle Martí wrote on November 13, 1887. It was published in *La Nación* of Buenos Aires on January 1, 1888.

17. Susana Rotker (1999, 25) identifies three distinct periods of Martí's writing in the United States: the first one, between 1881 and 1884, when his texts show admiration for the American culture and its accomplishments; the second period, between 1884 and 1892, when Martí becomes more critical of the United States— possibly because of his disillusionment due to the Pan-American Conference and American expansionism; and the third period, between 1892 and his death in 1895, when Martí interrupts his collaboration with the press and becomes a full-time revolutionary.

18. See, for instance, the separation that Martí (2002, 93) traces between Americans and Latin Americans in his chronicle of Coney Island: "These people eat quantity; we, class."

19. Following an increase in US tariffs for tobacco imports in the 1860s and the Ten Years' War in 1870, many cigar and cigarette factories formerly on the island of Cuba relocated to Florida with their workers. These immigrants were the main target of Martí's speeches, political platforms, and manifestos (Rodríguez-Luis 1999, xx).

20. Martí and Gómez later reached an agreement that led to the *Manifiesto de Montecristi* in 1895.

CHAPTER 4. Modernity, Markets, and Urban Bohemia

1. Sometimes considered the Argentine analog of Georges-Eugene Haussmann, the famous French urban planner, Marcelo Torcuato de Alvear undertook a series of reforms during his tenure as mayor of Buenos Aires from May 10, 1883, to May 10, 1887. Strongly supported by then-president Julio Roca, the reforms

included the construction of a series of boulevards running east to west, cobblestone paving, and the installation of a sewer system and an electric grid. These improvements were not fully realized until a few years after Alvear's death in 1887 (H. Torres 1975; Sargent 1972).

2. That is why, as Horacio Torres (1975) suggests, most of the census data in Argentina were published bilingually, in Spanish and English—to entice both foreign investment and immigration.

3. Torres estimates that, on average, these plots of land could be paid in full within twelve years by saving the equivalent of two-day's pay a month, assuming that the monthly salary of a skilled worker between 1904 and 1912 was about 2.5 gold pesos and that the plots would cost between 200 and 500 gold pesos. Among immigrants, Italians had the most access to these plots. In 1904, barely 35 percent of them owned real estate, but only five years later, in 1909, more than 43 percent had bought either land or a house (H. Torres 1975, 289–90).

4. For sometimes contradictory and problematic biographical information on Juan José de Soiza Reilly, I have cross-referenced the works of Mirelman (1975), Ludmer (1999), Mizraje (2006), Escales (2008), and Cilento (2009).

5. One of the most prestigious neighborhood newspapers in Flores was *La Idea*. Every Wednesday evening the newspaper hosted a gathering organized by neighborhood poet Félix V. Visillac. Soon-to-become nationally renowned poets, journalists, and writers like Conrado Nalé Roxlo and Roberto Arlt attended these meetings (Saítta 2000a, 19).

6. See Botana (1985, 17) and documents compiled by Gallo and Botana (2007, esp. 599–634).

7. The government was actively involved in these processes. In 1906, the Láinez Law directed 10 million pesos toward the creation of seven hundred new schools. Despite the high dropout rates (sometimes estimated to have been above 75 percent), by 1910 most of the school-age population in Argentina could read and write (Eujanian 1999, 21).

8. Howard M. Fraser (1987, 9) argues that "*Caras y Caretas* might itself be called an exposition of Argentina during the turn of the century."

9. Botana, an émigré, is credited with introducing to news writing in Argentina the techniques of serial novels, which added a dramatic effect similar to what we now call yellow journalism. *Crítica*, located in one of the first art deco buildings in Buenos Aires on Avenida de Mayo 1333, incorporated well-established writers into its newsroom to improve the quality of its journalism. And when, in 1933, twenty years after its founding, it started publishing the *Revista Multicolor de los Sábados* (Multicolor Saturday magazine), Botana hired as coeditors a young writer named Jorge Luis Borges and his friend, a poet named Ulyses Petit de Murat. Between 1933 and 1934, Borges would publish in that magazine a series of fact-based short

stories that in 1935 became his first narrative book, *A Universal History of Infamy* (Saítta 1999).

10. It could be misleading to compare the price of a newspaper with the average wage of a Mexican worker during the Porfiriato, especially because Mexico was a rural economy, and compensation often occurred via trade in goods. That said, during the strikes of textile workers in Río Blanco, which anticipated the Mexican Revolution, the protesters demanded a minimum monthly wage of five pesos and an eight-hour workday. In that context, newspapers would have been priced out of reach for a majority of Mexicans. See the work of Katz (1980).

11. For more information about the social history of tramways in Buenos Aires, see the works by García Heras (1992) and H. Torres (1975). See also González Podestá (n.d.).

12. An example of the cosmopolitanism of Buenos Aires is an editorial that appeared in *Crítica* on September 1, 1927, celebrating the inauguration of its new printing facilities in Avenida de Mayo 1333. The piece, published in Spanish, English, French, and the "languages of all the collectivities in Buenos Aires," saluted the readers and celebrated the acquisition of a new building, the new machines, and announced *Crítica*'s new format: "An organ of Buenos Aires, and interpreter of the cosmopolitan city, *Crítica*, which has a trained ear for foreign accents, has many times noticed, among the rumors of this new Babel, those who are the humblest, those suffering anonymous pain, those whose complaint and protest nobody hears" (qtd. in Saítta 1996, 88; my translation).

13. The crónicas were "El filósofo de los perros," no. 343, 29–34; "En las regiones de la pobreza," no. 345, 13–15; "El invierno de los pobres," no. 348, 3–6; and "Un pueblo misterioso," no. 370, 4–11, an article discussed later. The philosophical short story was "El alma de los perros," no. 378.

14. The dates of publication for this article differ according to two sources. In Soiza's (2006) *La ciudad de los locos*, edited by María Gabriela Mizraje, the article is dated in *Fray Mocho* as Year 1, May 17, 1912. In Nuñez and Idez (2007), the date is June 7, 1912.

15. Soiza's use of *lunfardo*, an argot originating in Buenos Aires and Montevideo at the end of the nineteenth century, prefigures the style that the journalist, writer, and novelist Roberto Arlt, a confessed admirer of Soiza Reilly, would adopt and turn into his trademark during the 1930s and 1940s.

16. Soiza would insist on his stance against anti-Semitism throughout his life. In a column he wrote for his radio show on January 25, 1938, he noted that "there are no laws that persecute [the Jews] . . . I know! But we can't deny that there's a concealed persecution, sly, constant, secret, that insists in denying the Jews their right to eat . . . Why? [. . .] To wish for Argentines to persecute the Jews like some European countries do is not only an attitude that sickens our Argentinity, it is also

dangerous and counterproductive" (qtd. in Ludmer 1999, 455–56; my translation).

17. As Gabriela Mizraje (2004, 174) points out, Soiza Reilly's concern goes beyond the immediacy of the story, to the underlying social conditions that gave rise to it.

18. According to Néstor Aparicio's *Los prisioneros del Chaco y la evasión de Tierra del Fuego* published in 1932, José Félix Uriburu, the head of the military coup that ousted democratically elected Hipólito Yrigoyen, was the owner of an oil field. Col. Emilio Kinkelín, also a member of the de facto government, was the owner of another oil field and concession, and many of their associates were in direct contact, or sometimes on the payroll of, companies such as Astra, Petrolera Andina, and Standard Oil (Escales 2008, 17).

CHAPTER 5. The Mass Press

1. The *Crítica* headline read, "Crítica: me voy a suicidar; vivo en Uruguay 694" (Crítica: I am going to commit suicide. I live in Uruguay 694).

2. "We don't like to follow the rhythm of politics too closely," stated an article in *El Mundo* on January 10, 1929.

3. For a broader take on the relationship between Arlt and Roxlo, see also María Esther Vázquez, "Los cien años de Conrado Nalé Roxlo," *La Nación*, April 1, 1998.

4. Roberto Arlt's "Epístola a los genios porteños" originally appeared in *Don Goyo* magazine on February 23, 1926.

5. This "Etching" was titled "Contestando a los lectores" and appeared in *El Mundo* on October 26, 1930.

6. Arlt also traveled to Brazil, Spain, and Africa, submitting some of his columns from abroad. Generally written to provoke estrangement in the readers by presenting before them foreign images, names, and characters, these pieces exceed the scope of the present work.

7. An earlier version of these ideas appeared in my article for the *Australian Journalism Review* (Calvi 2015b).

8. These announcements were likely supervised by both Borges and Petit de Murat.

9. I will refer to the newspaper series as "Universal History of Infamy" and the edited volume as *Universal History of Infamy* or *UHI*.

10. I render below both introductory paragraphs. Martí's, on Jesse James, first, is my translation of the original in Spanish. Notice the use of dense, metaphorical description and the oxymoronic scaffolding in both texts:

> These days in which New York has been a party, have been of great confusion in Missouri, where there was a bandit of high forehead, beautiful face, and a hand made to kill, who didn't steal bags but banks, not houses but towns, and

wouldn't jump balconies but trains. He was a hero of the jungle. His fierceness was so exceptional that the people of his land esteemed it above his crimes. He was not born of mean father, but of clergyman, didn't look like a villain, but like a knight, neither did he marry a bad woman, but a schoolteacher. And some say he was a political leader in one of his hideouts, or that he lived under false name and came as elected official to the most recent Democratic convention to vote for president. There are the lands of Missouri and those of Kansas, covered in woods and deep forests. Jesse James and his men knew the recesses of those jungles, the hiding places by the roads, the fords in the marshes, and the hollow trees. His house was armory, and another armory was his belt, because around his waistband he carried two cartridge belts loaded with handguns. He came to life during a war, and tore the life away of many long-bearded men when he still had no beard himself. In times of Alba, he would have been [a] captain in Flanders. In times of Pizarro, his lieutenant. In these times, he was a soldier, and was then a bandit. He wasn't one of those magnificent soldiers of Sheridan, who fought for this land to be one, and for the slave to be free, and raised the flag of the North over tenacious Confederate forts. Neither was he one of those other patient soldiers of silent Grant, who rounded up the rebels in terror, like the serene hunter to the hungry boar. He was among the guerrillas of the South, for whom the flag was plundering booty. His hand was an instrument of killing. He'd leave the dead on the ground, and laden with booty go to dole out generously with his fellows in crime, smaller cubs that licked the paws of that great tiger. (Martí 1991, 13:239–41; my translation)

An image of the desert wilds of Arizona, first and foremost, an image of the desert wilds of Arizona and New Mexico—a country famous for its silver and gold camps, a country of breathtaking open spaces, a country of monumental mesas and soft colours, a country of bleached skeletons picked clean by buzzards. Over this whole country, another image—that of Billy the Kid, the hard firm on his horse, the young man with the relentless six-shooters, sending out invisible bullets which (like magic) kill at a distance.

The desert veined with precious metals, arid and blinding-bright. The near child who on dying at the age of twenty-one owed to the justice of grown men twenty-one deaths—"not counting Mexicans." (Borges 1975, 61)

11. See the work of Botana (1985, 17), as well as a number of documents compiled by Botana and Gallo (2007, esp. 599–634).

12. Discussing the journalism of Mark Twain, Shelley Fisher Fishkin has argued that, perhaps due to the West Coast's natural delay in adopting journalistic techniques developed in the East Coast, Twain in the 1860s simultaneously tapped

into the opposing trends of journalism that defined his career: "the push toward greater accuracy and the push toward greater extravagance and fabrication" (Fishkin 1988, 56). Almost seventy years later, the different pace of Latin America's access to modernity and the modern press most likely coalesced in *Crítica* in a similar way, except for the fact that both "accuracy" and "extravagance" were combined and blended—due to a radically different journalistic tradition—with an interest in large social issues and a quest for political influence.

13. For the debate around the origins of objective journalism, see works by Mindich (1998), Tucher (1994), Schiller (1981), and Schudson (1978), among others.

CHAPTER 6. Latin American Narrative Journalism and the Cuban Revolution

1. In a phone interview I conducted on March 12, 2011, with Rogelio García Lupo, an Argentine journalist who was a friend of Walsh and former editor at Prensa Latina, he confirmed that Che Guevara's main focus in creating Prensa Latina was to counterbalance the United Press International (UPI). The announcement of Fidel Castro's supposed death seriously demoralized the revolutionary forces. At the time—García Lupo added—there was little doubt in Che's and Castro's minds that the US State Department was behind the UPI. That assumption, García Lupo said, was never substantiated. García Lupo died in Buenos Aires on August 19, 2016.

2. In an article published in 2000 by the *Washington Post*, journalist Vernon Loeb argued that the CIA still had no certainty as to how the Cubans had learned with such detail about the American plans and the day of the landing. "How the leak occurred is still a mystery," he wrote. There was, however, a strong suspicion of Soviet intervention, a team that might have intercepted American communications. The "mechanical accident" that García Márquez describes as the cause for this mysterious Teletype roll to have been found by Masetti could be linked to that communications interception. However, Loeb's version does not invalidate the role that Walsh played in the decryption of the coded message, a version that is supported not only by García Márquez but also by Rogelio García Lupo and other colleagues of Walsh at Prensa Latina. Loeb's article appeared in the *Washington Post* on Saturday, April 29, 2000, A04. See also Lupo's (2000, 23) account and García Márquez's (1974) full account.

3. An interesting study in this direction is Jameson's (1996) "Literary Import-Substitution in the Third World: The Case of the Testimonio," which considers the process of decolonization as one—among other relevant—conditions for the development of testimonio as a genre.

4. "As I saw it," Tom Wolfe (1973, 22–23) wrote in his manifesto for *New York* magazine, "if a new literary style could originate in journalism, then it stood to

journalism could aspire to more than mere emulation of those aging novelists. [. . .] In any case, a . . . New Journalism . . . was in the air. 'In as I say it; it was not something that anyone took note of in print at the so far as I can remember."

Preliminarily I will use this "working definition" to approach testimonio. Some of the authors are Tom Wolfe in "The Birth of New Journalism" (1972), Mas'ud Zavarzadeh in *The Mythopoetic Reality* (1976), John Hollowell in *Fact and Fiction* (1977), Ronald Weber in *The Literature of Fact* (1980), Norman Sims in *The Literary Journalists* (1984) and *True Stories: A Century of Literary Journalism* (2007), and John Hartsock in *A History of American Literary Journalism* (2001).

6. Walsh is quoting in Spanish an article, "Haiti: Beset President," that appeared in *Time* on Monday, August 31, 1959. I here use the original in English, but Walsh's observations, in Spanish in the original, are my translation.

7. The similarities between testimonial literature and the reportage tradition of the international proletarian writers movement are striking, and it could be speculated that, at some point during the Cold War, this European style and testimonial Latin American literature may have cross-pollinated (Hartsock 2009). However, although the possibilities are suggestive, this aspect remains beyond the scope of this investigation.

8. The Cultural Congress in 1968, which took place one year after the death of Che Guevara, "would devote many sessions to the role of the intellectual, stressing the need to heal the breach between the cultural avant-garde and the revolutionary vanguard" (Franco 1978, 83).

9. Agee's breakthrough in the field of American literary journalism is comparable only with the renovation in the French novel that happened after the publication of Marcel Proust's *À la recherche du temps perdu*. Auto-referentiality—a key mechanism in both Agee's and Proust's works—has been defined as one of the central features of postmodernism (Jameson 1991, chap. 1).

10. For information, see the National Book Award website, http://www.national book.org/about-us/mission-history/.

11. According to Nuttall (2007, 132), "When Truman Capote first considered eliding these genres by writing a non-fiction novel, there was no 'cultural consensus' he could call on and, therefore, no pre-existing criteria to guide him in relation to form, style or subject matter. To that extent, as noted by Tom Wolfe, Capote was a pioneer." Hollowell (1977, 36–37) states that "although Wolfe dates the beginnings of the new journalism in the sixties, fictional techniques are apparent in the magazine articles of the forties and fifties."

12. The absence of an "I" created what Weber (1980, 66, 73) defined as the "recording angel" effect.

13. "More than one historian has found a way through chains of false fact. No,

the difficulty is that the history is interior—no documents can give sufficient intimation: the novel must replace history at precisely that point where experience is sufficiently emotional, spiritual, psychical, moral, existential, or supernatural to expose the fact that the historian in pursuing the experience would be obliged to quit the clearly demarcated limits of historic inquiry" (Mailer 1968, 284).

14. Others, such as Dwight Macdonald, see stream of consciousness as a tendentious and juvenile feature. Wolfe (1972) explained the accuracy of his own stream of consciousness in an article for *New York* magazine: "Writing about Phil Spector ('The First Tycoon of Teen'), I began the article not only inside his mind but with a virtual stream of consciousness. One of the news magazines apparently regarded my Spector story as an improbable feat, because they interviewed him and asked him if he didn't think this passage was merely a fiction that appropriated his name. Spector said that, in fact, he found it quite accurate. This should have come as no surprise, since every detail in the passage was taken from a long interview with Spector about exactly how he had felt at the time."

15. Although there are not definite numbers about the books that were censored during that period in Latin America, there are some striking hints of how censorship operated in different countries in the region. Francine Masiello reports that, in Argentina alone there were at least 242 rock songs that were banned from the airwaves. "In consequence," Masiello (1987, 16) notes, "musicians had to exert a tight control over the metaphoric shiftings in their lyrics."

16. "Therefore, an important portion of the Argentine literature (written and published in the country or in exile) can be read as a *critique of the present*, even when its primary reference may be in the past. Confronted with a reality that was difficult to grasp, because many of its meanings remained hidden, there was an oblique attempt (and not only because of censorship) of the literary field to place itself in a meaningful connection with the present, and to start trying to make sense of a chaotic mass of experiences separated from their collective meaning" (Sarlo 1987, 34; my translation).

17. It is not by chance that the text that inaugurates this book's discussion of Latin American literary journalism, *Facundo*, was also written in exile and under duress.

18. Although there is currently no official biography of Rodolfo Walsh, most of the material contained herein has been obtained either from the works of Lafforgue (2000), Walsh (1964, 1981, 1988), Vinelli (2000), Link (1996), Domínguez (1999), Arrosagaray (2006), and Bocchino, García, and Mercère (2004).

19. "Published almost ten years before Truman Capote's much touted 'nonfictional novel' *In Cold Blood, Operación Masacre* anticipates the techniques credited to Capote" (Foster 1984, 42–43).

20. This and all subsequent translations from *Operación Masacre* are mine.

21. The original headline was "Yo también fui fusilado" (my translation).

22. Many de facto regimes after the ousting of Perón had banned the naming of both Perón and his deceased wife, Eva. "That woman" becomes, in that sense, a direct reference to Eva Perón, not only within the context of the short story but also on a historical plane.

23. The body of Eva Perón was, in fact, embalmed and is still preserved in that state. And the political disputes around the body are essentially accurate, as are the movements to which the corpse was subjected between the fall of Perón and the return of democracy to Argentina.

24. The Sermon on the Mount is in the New Testament, Matthew 5:1–2 to 7:7–29.

25. These testimonies and many others were compiled in *Nunca más* (Never again), a book published by the Argentine CONADEP (National Commission on the Disappearance of People), which collected almost five hundred direct accounts by survivors of abductions and torture between 1976 and 1983.

26. In 2010, a different version of Walsh's death was offered by a witness, Miguel Angel Lauretta. This version challenges the exchange of gunfire between Walsh and the task force and is available at http://www.diasdehistoria.com.ar/content/veo-que-le-tira-un-cuerpo-en-la-vereda (last accessed August 14, 2018).

27. The book was first published as *Biografía de un cimarrón* (*Biography of a Runaway Slave*) in 1966. Its title later changed to *Autobiografía de un cimarrón* (Autobiography of a Runaway Slave), and finally *Cimarrón*. These mutations speak in part to the evolution in the perception of testimonial narratives in Cuba and Latin America and were the consequence of the broader debate about the documental possibilities open to nonfiction.

28. A metonymy, just like a metaphor, is a displacement of meaning. But it is a very particular one. In a metonymy the object receives its attributes from the referent by contiguity, by proximity. In the phrase "the lands belong to the crown" the *crown* is a metonymy of *the king*, who is usually in physical contact with his crown. The *crown* is also a metaphor for power, or ownership, but its metaphoric (purely symbolic) nature is arbitrary. There is nothing in the crown itself that intrinsically gives any right of ownership to its possessor, unless that possessor is, in fact, the king. A metaphor does not require any type of physical proximity between the object and its referent, and it associates them arbitrarily or, in other words, by convention. For a detailed explanation of the different semiotic displacements involved in a metaphor and a metonymy, see the work of Verón (1988). In his book, Verón compares with succinct clarity Saussure's, Peirce's, and Frege's theories of sign, as well as their notions of metaphorical and metonymic constructions.

29. Of course, the fact that the construction of narrative journalism in the

Anglo-American tradition revolves around a metonymic axis does not prevent metaphorical occurrences at the narrative level. This is also clear from Mark Twain to Gay Talese. And the same is valid for Latin American literary journalism narratives, which, though tending to gravitate around a metaphorical axis, can still resort to metonymy—why not?—on the narrative level.

CONCLUSION

1. Mahieux (2011) has recently incorporated female authors and nonbinary approaches into the list of *cronistas*. Alfonsina Storni and Salvador Novo are indeed two interesting voices who, by their sheer existence, expand the scope of the period, though they certainly do not challenge its most dominant aspects as a whole.

BIBLIOGRAPHY

• • •

Abrahamson, David. 1996. *Magazine-Made America: The Cultural Transformation of the Post War Periodical.* Cresskill, NJ: Hampton Press.

Agee, James, and Walker Evans. 1960. *Let Us Now Praise Famous Men.* New York: Ballantine Books.

Aguilar, Gonzalo. 2000. "Rodolfo Walsh, escritura y Estado." In *Textos de y sobre Rodolfo Walsh*, edited by Jorge Lafforgue. Buenos Aires: Alianza.

Alazraki, Jaime. 1971. "Oxymoronic Structure in Borges' Essays." *Books Abroad* 45 (Summer): 421–27.

Alberdi, Juan Bautista. 1846. *Lejislación de la prensa en Chile: Manual del escritor, del impresor y del jurado.* Valparaíso: Imprenta del Mercurio.

Alonso, Amado. 1935. "Borges narrador." *Sur* (Buenos Aires) 14:105–15.

Altamirano, Carlos, and Beatriz Sarlo. 1994. "The Autodidact and the Learning Machine." In *Sarmiento, Author of a Nation*, edited by Tulio Halperín Donghi, Iván Jaksić, Gwen Kirkpatrick, and Francine Masiello, 156–68. Berkeley: University of California Press.

Althusser, Louis. 2014. *On the Reproduction of Capitalism: Ideology and Ideological State Apparatuses.* New York: Verso.

Álvarez, Luis, Matilde Varela, and Carlos Palacio. 2007. *Martí Biógrafo.* Santiago de Cuba: Editorial Oriente.

Amar Sánchez, Ana María. 1994. "La propuesta de una escritura." In *Rodolfo Walsh, Vivo*, edited by Roberto Baschetti. Buenos Aires: La Flor.

Anderson, Benedict. 1983. *Imagined Communities*. New York: Verso.

Anderson Imbert, Enrique. 1953. "Comienzos del modernismo en la novela." In "Homenaje a Amado Alonso: Tomo Segundo." Special issue, *Nueva Revista de Filología Hispánica* 7 (3–4): 515–25.

Aparicio, Raúl. 1969. "Retratos en el despacho." *El Caimán Barbudo*, no. 27 (January). Reprinted in no. 64 (January 1973): 16–20.

Arlt, Roberto. 1940. "Vidas paralelas de Ponson du Terrail y Edgard Wallace." *El Mundo*, August 20, 1940.

Arlt, Roberto. 1960. *Nuevas aguafuertes porteñas*. Buenos Aires: Hachette.

Arlt, Roberto. 1981a. *Obras completas*. 3 vols. Buenos Aires: Planeta, Carlos Lohle, Biblioteca del Sur.

Arlt, Roberto. 1981b. *Las aguafuertes porteñas de Roberto Arlt*. Edited by Daniel C. Scroggins. Buenos Aires: Ediciones Culturales Argentinas.

Arlt, Roberto. 1992a. *Aguafuertes porteñas: Cultura y política*. Buenos Aires: Losada.

Arlt, Roberto. 1992b. *Nuevas aguafuertes*. Buenos Aires: Losada.

Arlt, Roberto. 1993. *Aguafuertes porteñas: Buenos Aires, vida cotidiana*. Edited by Sylvia Saítta. Buenos Aires: Alianza.

Arlt, Roberto. 1996. *Aguafuertes uruguayas y otras páginas*. Edited by Omar Borré. Montevideo: Ediciones de la Banda Oriental.

Arlt, Roberto. 1997. *Nuevas aguafuertes*. Buenos Aires: Losada.

Arlt, Roberto. 1998. *Obras II: Aguafuertes*. Buenos Aires: Losada.

Arrosagaray, Enrique. 2006. *Rodolfo Walsh, de dramaturgo a guerrillero*. Buenos Aires: Catálogos.

Bakhtin, Mikhail. 1984. *Esthétique de la création verbale*. Paris: Gallimard.

Balderston, Daniel. 1993. *Out of Context: Historical Reference and the Representation of Reality in Borges*. Durham: Duke University Press.

Balderston, Daniel. 2003. "Borges and the Gangs of New York." *Variaciones Borges*, no. 16:27–33.

Barnet, Miguel. 1987. *Cimarrón*. Buenos Aires: Ediciones del Sol.

Barnet, Miguel. 1987. "La novela testimonio: Alquimia de la memoria." In *Cimarrón*, by Miguel Barnet, 212–15. Buenos Aires: Ediciones del Sol.

Barros Arana, Diego. 1913. *Un decenio de la historia de Chile 1841–1851*. Volume 15, book 2 of *Obras completas de Diego Barros Arana*. Santiago: Imprenta Litografía Encuadernación Barcelona.

Barthes, Roland. 1975. "An Introduction to the Structural Analysis of Narrative." *New Literary History* 6 (2): 237–72.

Beverley, John. 1991. "'Through All Things Modern': Second Thoughts on Testimonio." *Boundary 2* 18 (2): 1–21.

Beverley, John. 2004. *Testimonio: On the Politics of Truth*. Minneapolis: University of Minnesota Press.

Biagni, Hugo, and Arturo Roig. 2004. *El pensamiento alternativo en la Argentina del siglo XX*. Volume 1. Buenos Aires: Biblos.

Bilbao, Francisco. 1844. "Sociabilidad chilena." In *El Crepúsculo: Periódico Literario y Científico* 2 (2): 56–90.

Bilbao, Francisco. 1897. "Sociabilidad chilena." In *Obras completas: Francisco Bilbao*, 9–50. Santiago de Chile: Imprenta de "El Correo."

Bilbao, Manuel. 1866. "Vida de Francisco Bilbao." In *Obras completas de Francisco Bilbao*. Volume 1. Buenos Aires: Imprenta de Buenos Aires.

Blasco Ibáñez, Vicente. 1920. *Argentina y sus grandezas*. Madrid: Editorial Española Americana.

Bocchino, Adriana, Romina García, and Emiliana Mercère. 2004. *Rodolfo Walsh del policial al testimonio*. Mar del Plata: Estanislao Balder.

Bonfil Batalla, Guillermo. 1972. "El concepto de indio en América: una categoría de la situación colonial." *Anales de Antropología*, no. 9: 105–24. http://www.revistas.unam.mx/index.php/antropologia/article/view/23077

Bonfil Batalla, Guillermo. 1996. *México Profundo: Reclaiming a Civilization*. Austin: University of Texas Press.

Borges, Jorge Luis. 1972. "La violencia: Miradas opuestas" (interview with Gudiño Kieffer). *La Nación*, August 6, 1972, sec. 3, 2.

Borges, Jorge Luis. 1974. "Ensayo autobiográfico." *La Opinión*, September 17, 1974, 16.

Borges, Jorge. 1975. *A Universal History of Infamy*. New York: Penguin.

Borges, Jorge. 1995. *Feuilletons du samedi*. Paris: Anatolia.

Borges, Jorge Luis. 1999. *Collected Fictions*. New York: Penguin Press.

Botana, Natalio. 1985. "El marco histórico institucional: Leyes electorales, alternancia y competencia entre partidos." In *La Argentina electoral*. Buenos Aires: Sudamericana.

Botana, Natalio, and Ezequiel Gallo. 2007. *De la república posible a la república verdadera: 1880–1910*. Buenos Aires: Emecé.

Braceras, Elena, Cristina Leytour, and Susana Pittella. 2000. "Walsh y el género policial." In *Textos de y sobre Rodolfo Walsh*, edited by Jorge Lafforgue. Buenos Aires: Alianza.

Brushwood, John S. 1985. "Reality and Imagination in the Novels of Garcia Marquez." In "Gabriel García Márquez." Special issue, *Latin American Literary Review* 13 (25): 9–14.

Brushwood, John S. 1987. "Two Views of the Boom: North and South." In "The Boom in Retrospect: A Reconsideration." Special issue, *Latin American Literary Review* 15 (29): 13–31.

Burgin, Richard. 1970. *Conversations with Jorge Luis Borges*. New York: Avon Books.

Bushnell, David, and Neil Macaulay. 1994. *The Emergence of Latin America in the Nineteenth Century*. Oxford: Oxford University Press.

Bustamante, Francisco. 1989. "Hacer a los argentinos: La Ley de Educación Común como utopía modernista." In *El Reformismo en Contrapunto: Los procesos de modernización en el Río de la Plata, 1890–1930*. Montevideo: Centro Latinoamericano de Economía Humana.

Calvi, Pablo. 2010. "Latin America's Own 'New Journalism.'" *Literary Journalism Studies* 2 (2).

Calvi, Pablo. 2012. "José Martí and the Chronicles That Created Modern Latin America." In *Global Literary Journalism: Exploring the Journalistic Imagination*, volume 1, edited by Richard Lance Keeble and John Tulloch, 299–316. New York: Peter Lang.

Calvi, Pablo. 2015a. "Juan José de Soiza Reilly: The Profile as a Social Equaliser and Political Act." In *The Profiling Handbook*, edited by Sue Joseph and Richard Lance Keeble. Bury St. Edmunds, UK: Abramis.

Calvi, Pablo. 2015b. "From Literature to Journalism: Borges, *Crítica* and the *Universal History of Infamy* as an Experiment in Democratic Dialogue." *Australian Journalism Review* 37 (2): 109–21.

Calvi, Pablo. 2016. "The Trial of Francisco Bilbao and Its Role in the Foundation of Latin American Journalism." *Information & Culture: A Journal of History* 51 (4).

Campbell, Margaret. 1962. "The Chilean Press: 1832–1842." *Journal of Inter-American Studies* 4 (4): 545–55.

Capote, Truman. 1965. *In Cold Blood: A True Account of a Multiple Murder and Its Consequences*. New York: Vintage Books.

Capote, Truman. 1980. *Music for Chameleons*. New York: Random House.

Carrizo, Antonio. 1982. *Borges el memorioso*. Buenos Aires: Fondo de Cultura Económica.

Chalaby, Jean K. 1996. "Journalism as an Anglo-American Invention: A Comparison of the Development of French and Anglo-American Journalism, 1830s–1920s." *European Journal of Communication* 11 (3): 303–26.

Cilento, Laura. 2009. "Diálogo y ficción en la oferta periodística del primer centenario." *Hologramática* año VI, 3 (11): 67–86.

Comte, Auguste. 2000. *The Positive Philosophy of Auguste Comte*. Kitchener, ON: Batoche Books.

CONADEP. 1984. *Nunca más*. Buenos Aires.

Concha, Jaime. 1994. "On the Threshold of Facundo." In *Sarmiento, Author of a Nation*, edited by Tulio Halperín Donghi, Iván Jaksić, Gwen Kirkpatrick, and Francine Masiello, 145–55. Berkeley: University of California Press.

Cortázar, Julio. 1994. "La voz que no se apaga." In *Rodolfo Walsh, Vivo*, edited by Roberto Baschetti. Buenos Aires: La Flor.

Cortés Conde, Roberto. 1994. "Sarmiento and Economic Progress: From *Facundo* to the Presidency." In *Sarmiento, Author of a Nation*, edited by Tulio Halperín

Donghi, Iván Jaksić, Gwen Kirkpatrick, and Francine Masiello, 114–23. Berkeley: University of California Press.

Crapol, Edward. 2000. *James G. Blaine: Architect of Empire*. Wilmington, DE: Scholarly Resources.

Cross, Gary. 2000. "A New Consumerism, 1960–1980." In *An All-Consuming Century: Why Commercialism Won in Modern America*, 145–91. New York: Columbia University Press.

Cúneo, Dardo. 1955. *José Martí, Argentina y la Primera Conferencia Panamericana*. Buenos Aires: Ediciones Transición.

De Diego, J. L., et al. 2006. *Editoriales y políticas editoriales en Argentina, 1880–2000*. Buenos Aires: Fondo de la Cultura Económica.

Diccionario de la literatura cubana. 1984. Havana: Editorial Letras Cubanas.

Domínguez, Fabián. 1999. "El caso Rodolfo Walsh: Un clandestino." In *El periodismo argentino y su aporte a la identidad nacional*. Buenos Aires: Federación Argentina de la Industria Gráfica y Afines.

Dupont, Denise. 2004. "'Bizcochos de chocolate': José Martí's Reading of 'Bouvard and Pécuchet.'" *Revista Hispánica Moderna* 57 (1–2): 37–51.

Escales, Vanina. 2008. "Bohemia, modernidad y olvido." In *Crónicas del centenario*, by Juan José de Soiza Reilly, 9–23. Buenos Aires: Biblioteca Nacional.

Ettema, James, and Ted Glasser. 1988. "Narrative Form and Moral Force: The Realization of Innocence and Guilt through Investigative Journalism." *Journal of Communication* 38:8–26.

Eujanian, Alejandro. 1999. *Historia de revistas argentinas 1900–1950: La conquista del público*. Buenos Aires: Asociación Argentina de Editores de Revistas.

Eyzaguirre, Jaime. 1948. *Fisonomía histórica de Chile*. Santiago: Editorial del Pacífico.

Fernández, Juan Rómulo. 1943. *Historia del periodismo argentino*. Buenos Aires: Librería Perlado.

Ferreira, Leonardo. 2006. *Centuries of Silence: The Story of Latin American Journalism*. Westport, CT: Praeger.

Ferro, Roberto. 1999. "La literatura en el banquillo: Walsh y la fuerza del testimonio." In *Historia crítica de la literatura argentina*, edited by Noé Jitrik and Susana Cella, 125–45. Buenos Aires: Emecé.

Fishkin, Shelley Fisher. 1988. *From Fact to Fiction: Journalism and Imaginative Writing in America*. New York: Oxford University Press.

Ford, Aníbal. 2000. "Ese hombre." In *Textos de y sobre Rodolfo Walsh*, edited by Jorge Lafforgue. Buenos Aires: Alianza.

Foster, David William. 1984. "Latin American Documentary Narrative." *PMLA* 99 (1): 41–55.

Foucault, Michel. 1968. "Sur l'archéologie des sciences: Réponse au Cercle d'épistémologie." *Cahiers pour l'analyse, no. 9: Généalogie des sciences* (Summer):9–40.

Fountain, Anne. 2003. *José Martí and U.S. Writers*. Gainesville: University Press of Florida.

Franco, Jean. 1978. "From Modernization to Resistance: Latin American Literature 1959–1976." In "Culture in the Age of Mass Media." Special issue, *Latin American Perspectives* 5 (1): 77–97.

Fraser, Howard M. 1987. *Magazines & Masks: "Caras y Caretas" as a Reflection of Buenos Aires, 1898–1908*. Tempe: Center for Latin American Studies, Arizona State University.

Freyre, Gilberto. 1986. *Order and Progress: Brazil from Monarchy to Republic*. Berkeley: University of California Press.

Furtado, Celso. 1970. *Economic Development of Latin America: Historical Background and Contemporary Problems*. Cambridge: Cambridge University Press.

Garavaglia, Juan Carlos. 2007. *Construir el estado, inventar la nación*. Buenos Aires: Prometeo.

García, Eustasio. 1965. *Desarrollo de la industria editorial argentina*. Buenos Aires: Fundación Interamericana de Bibliotecología Franklin.

García Heras, Raúl. 1992. "Capitales extranjeros, poder político y transporte urbano de pasajeros: La Compañía de Tranvías Anglo Argentina Ltda de Buenos Aires, Argentina, 1930-1943." *Desarrollo Económico* 32 (125): 35–56.

García Lupo, Rogelio. 2000. "El lugar de Walsh." In *Textos de y sobre Rodolfo Walsh*, edited by Jorge Lafforgue. Buenos Aires: Alianza.

García Márquez, Gabriel. 1974. "Rodolfo Walsh, el hombre que se adelantó a la CIA." *Revista Alternativa* (Bogotá), no. 124.

García Márquez, Gabriel. 1987. *Relato de un náufrago*. Buenos Aires: Sudamericana.

Garrels, Elizabeth. 1988. "El Facundo como folletín." *Revista Iberoamericana* 143 (April–June).

Garrels, Elizabeth. 2005. "Sarmiento's Past and Present." Introductory note to *Recollections of a Provincial Past*, by Domingo Faustino Sarmiento, xvii–lxxxiii. Oxford: Oxford University Press.

Gayol, Sandra. 2004. "Sociabilidades violentas, o el imposible amor popular." In *El pensamiento alternativo en la Argentina del siglo XX, Vol. 1*, edited by Hugo Biagni and Arturo Roig, 219–32. Buenos Aires: Biblos.

Gicovate, Bernardo. 1964. "El modernismo y su historia." *Hispanic Review* 32 (3): 217–26.

Gitlin, Todd. 2002. *Media Unlimited: How the Torrent of Images and Sounds Overwhelms Our Lives*. New York: Henry Holt.

Goldman, Noemí, and Alejandra Pasino. 2008. "Opinión pública." In *Lenguaje y revolución: Conceptos políticos clave en el Río de la Plata, 1780–1850*, edited by Noemí Goldman. Buenos Aires: Prometeo Libros.

Goloboff, Mario. 2002. "Roberto Arlt: La máquina literaria." *Revista de Literatura Moderna* 32: 107–15.

Gomariz, José. 2007. "The Myth of José Martí: Conflicting Nationalisms in Early Twentieth-Century Cuba." *Cuban Studies* 38:187–90.

Gomis, Lorenzo. 2008. *Teoría de los géneros periodísticos.* Barcelona: UOC.

González, Aníbal. 1993. *Journalism and the Development of Spanish American Narrative.* Cambridge: Cambridge University Press.

González, Joaquín V. 1936. "El periodismo y la literatura." In *Obras Completas.* Volume 18. La Plata: Universidad Nacional de La Plata.

González Echevarría, Roberto. 1980. "The Dictatorship of Rhetoric/the Rhetoric of Dictatorship: Carpentier, García Márquez, and Roa Bastos." *Latin American Research Review* 15 (3): 205–28.

González Echevarría, Roberto. 2003. "*Facundo:* An Introduction." In *Facundo: Civilization and Barbarism,* by Domingo Sarmiento, 1–15. Berkeley: University of California Press.

González Podestá, Aquilino. N.d. "Apuntes sobre la historia del tranvía en Buenos Aires." Asociación Amigos del Tranvía y Biblioteca Popular Federico Lacroze, http://www.barriada.com.ar/varios/ApuntesHistoriaTranvia_Podesta.aspx.

Gould, Benjamin Apthoep. 1877. "Memoir of James Melville Gilliss, 1811–1865: Read before the National Academy, Jan. 26, 1866." In *National Academy of Sciences Biographical Memoirs.* Volume 1, 135–80. Washington, DC: Home Secretary, National Academy of Sciences. Google Books.

Gray, Richard. 1963. "José Martí and Social Revolution in Cuba." *Journal of Inter-American Studies* 5 (2): 249–56.

Green, Raquel Atena. 2010. *Borges y "Revista Multicolor de los Sábados": Confabulados en una escritura de la infamia.* New York: Peter Lang.

Guerriero, Leila. 2013. "Roberto Arlt. La vida breve." In *Plano Americano,* 299–377. Santiago, Chile: Ediciones Universidad Diego Portales.

Halperín Donghi, Tulio. 1969. *Historia contemporánea de América Latina.* Buenos Aires: Alianza.

Halperín Donghi, Tulio. 1980. *Proyecto y construcción de una nación, 1846–1880.* Caracas: Biblioteca Ayacucho.

Halperín Donghi, Tulio. 1993. *The Contemporary History of Latin America.* Durham: Duke University Press.

Halperín Donghi, Tulio. 1994a. *La larga agonía de la Argentina peronista.* Buenos Aires: Ariel.

Halperín Donghi, Tulio. 1994b. "Sarmiento's Place in Postrevolutionary Argentina." In *Sarmiento, Author of a Nation,* edited by Tulio Halperín Donghi, Iván Jaksić, Gwen Kirkpatrick, and Francine Masiello, 19–30. Berkeley: University of California Press.

Hartsock, John C. 2001. *A History of American Literary Journalism*. Amherst: University of Massachusetts Press.

Hartsock, John C. 2009. "Literary Reportage: The 'Other' Literary Journalism." *Genre: Forms of Culture and Discourse* 42 (Spring–Summer): 113–34.

Hegel, G. W. F. 1988. *Introduction to the Philosophy of History*. Indianapolis: Hackett.

Henríquez Ureña, Pedro. 1949. *Las corrientes literarias en la América Hispánica*. Translated by Joaquín Diez Canedo. Mexico City: Fondo de Cultura Económica.

Hollowell, John. 1977. *Fact and Fiction: The New Journalism and the Nonfiction Novel*. Chapel Hill: University of North Carolina Press.

Ibarra Cifuentes, Patricio. 2014. "Liberalismo y prensa: Leyes de imprenta en el Chile decimonónico (1812–1872)." In *Revista de Estudios Histórico-Jurídicos* 36:293–313.

Illanes, M. Angélica. 2003. *Chile Des-centrado: Formación socio-cultural republicana y transición capitalista 1810–1910*. Santiago: LOM.

Instituto de Literatura y Lingüística de la Academia de Ciencias de Cuba. 1984. "Testimonio." In *Diccionario de la literatura cubana*, volume 2. Havana: Editorial Letras Cubanas.

Iriarte, Luis Ignacio. 2003. "Martí y 'la política del acometimiento.'" In *Decirlo es Verlo: Literatura y Periodismo en José Martí*, edited by Mónica Scarano. Mar del Plata, Argentina: Estanislao Balder.

Jaksić, Iván. 1994. "Sarmiento and the Chilean Press, 1841–1851." In *Sarmiento, Author of a Nation*, edited by Tulio Halperín Donghi, Iván Jaksić, Gwen Kirkpatrick, and Francine Masiello, 31–60. Berkeley: University of California Press.

Jameson, Fredric. 1991. *Postmodernism: Or, The Cultural Logic of Late Capitalism*. Durham: Duke University Press.

Jameson, Fredric. 1996. "Literary Import-Substitution in the Third World: The Case of the Testimonio." In *The Real Thing: Testimonial Discourse and Latin America*, edited by Georg M. Gugelberger, 172–91. Durham: Duke University Press.

"Jaque a los asesinos de Walsh." 2006. *Página/12* (Buenos Aires), July 21, 2006.

Jitrik, Noé. 1993. "La gran riqueza de la pobreza." In *Facundo: O civilización y barbarie*, by Domingo Sarmiento. Caracas: Fundación Biblioteca Ayacucho.

Jrade, Cathy L. 1991. "Martí Confronts Modernity." In *Re-Reading José Martí (1853–1895): One Hundred Years Later*, edited by Julio Rodríguez-Luis, 1–16. Albany: State University of New York Press.

Kanellos, Nicolás. 2005. "Hispanic American Intellectuals Publishing in the Nineteenth-Century United States: From Political Tracts in Support of Independence to Commercial Publishing Ventures." *Hispania* 88 (4): 687–92.

Kanellos, Nicolás, and Helvetia Martell. 2000. *Hispanic Periodicals in the U.S.: A Brief History and Comprehensive Bibliography*. Houston: Arte Público Press.

Karras, Bill J. 1974. "José Martí and the Pan American Conference, 1889–1891." *Revista de Historia de América*, no. 77/78 (January–December): 77–99.

Katra, William H. 1996. *The Argentine Generation of 1837: Echeverría, Alberdi, Sarmiento, Mitre*. Madison, NJ: Fairleigh Dickinson University Press.

Katz, Friedrich. 1980. *La servidumbre agraria en México en la época porfiriana*. Mexico City: Ediciones Era.

Keeble, Richard. 2007. *The Journalistic Imagination: Literary Journalists from Defoe to Capote and Carter*. London: Routledge.

Keeble, Richard Lance, and John Tulloch, eds. 2012. *Global Literary Journalism: Exploring the Journalistic Imagination*. Volume 1. New York: Peter Lang.

Kirk, John M. 1977. "José Martí and the United States: A Further Interpretation." *Journal of Latin American Studies* 9 (2): 275–90.

Kirk, John M. 1980. "'Inadaptado Sublime' to 'Lider Revolucionario': Some Further Thoughts on the Presentation of José Martí." *Latin American Research Review* 15 (3): 127–47.

Kirkpatrick, Gwen, and Francine Masiello. 1994. "Introduction: Sarmiento between History and Fiction." In *Sarmiento, Author of a Nation*, edited by Tulio Halperín Donghi, Iván Jaksić, Gwen Kirkpatrick, and Francine Masiello, 1–16. Berkeley: University of California Press.

Laclau, Ernesto. 2014. *The Rhetorical Foundations of Society*. New York: Verso.

Lafforgue, Jorge, ed. 2000. *Textos de y sobre Rodolfo Walsh*. Buenos Aires: Alianza.

Larsen, Neil. 1992. "The 'Boom' Novel and the Cold War in Latin America." *Modern Fiction Studies* 38 (3): 771–83.

Lastarria, José V. 1885. *Recuerdos literarios*. Santiago de Chile: Librería de M. Servat.

Lewis, Annick. 1998. "Instrucciones para buscar a Borges en la *Revista Multicolor*." *Variaciones Borges* 5:246–64.

Liddle, Dallas. 2009. *The Dynamics of Genre: Journalism and the Practice of Literature in Mid-Victorian Britain*. Charlottesville: University of Virginia Press.

Link, Daniel. 1994. *La chancha con cadenas: Doce ensayos de literatura argentina*. Buenos Aires: Ediciones del Eclipse.

Link, Daniel, ed. 1996. *Rodolfo Walsh: Ese hombre y otros papeles personales*. Buenos Aires: Seix Barral.

Lipp, Solomon. 1975. *Three Chilean Thinkers*. Waterloo, ON: Wilfrid Laurier University Press.

Losada, Alejandro. 1983. *La literatura en la sociedad de América Latina*. Frankfurt: Vervuert.

"Los libros del editor Jorge Alvarez, codiciados por los coleccionistas." 2005. *Clarín*, April 2005.

Ludmer, Josefina. 1999. *El cuerpo del delito: Un manual*. Buenos Aires: Perfil Libros.

Mahieux, Viviane. 2011. *Urban Chroniclers in Modern Latin America: The Shared Intimacy of Everyday Life*. Austin: University of Texas Press.

Mailer, Norman. 1968. *The Armies of the Night: History as a Novel, the Novel as History*. New York: Signet Books.

Mañach, Jorge. 1950. *Martí: Apostle of Freedom*. New York: Devin-Adair.

Mann, Mary. 1868. "Biographical Sketch." In *Life in the Argentine Republic in the Days of the Tyrants*, by Domingo Sarmiento. New York: Hurd and Houghton.

Martí, José. 1911. *Amistad funesta*. Berlin: Gonzalo de Quesada.

Martí, José. 1964. *Obras completas*. Volume 1. Santiago: Ed. Nacional de Cuba.

Martí, José. 1991. *Obras completas*. 26 vols. Havana: Editorial de Ciencias Sociales.

Martí, José. 2002. *Selected Writings*. London: Penguin Classics.

Martin, Gerald. 1982. "On Dictatorship and Rhetoric in Latin American Writing: A Counter-Proposal." *Latin American Research Review* 17 (3): 207–27.

Marx, Karl. 1998. *The German Ideology*. New York: Prometheus Books

Marx, Karl. 2000. *The Marx-Engels Reader*. New York: Norton.

Masiello, Francine. 1987. "La Argentina durante el Proceso: Las múltiples resistencias de la cultura." In *Ficción y política: La narrativa argentina durante el proceso militar*, 11–29. Buenos Aires: Alianza.

Masotta, Oscar. 1982. *Sexo y traición en Roberto Arlt*. Buenos Aires: Capítulo.

McNelly, John. 1966. "Mass Communication and the Climate for Modernization in Latin America." *Journal of Inter-American Studies* 8 (3): 345–57.

Mignolo, Walter. 2007. *La idea de América Latina: La idea colonial y la opción decolonial*. Barcelona: Gedisa.

Mindich, David. 1998. *Just the Facts: How "Objectivity" Came to Define American Journalism*. New York: New York University Press.

Mirelman, Victor. 1975. "The Semana Trágica of 1919 and the Jews in Argentina." *Jewish Social Studies* 37 (1): 61–73.

Mizraje, María. 2004. "Juan José de Soiza Reilly (1879–1959)." In *Latin American Mystery Writers: An A–Z Guide*, edited by Darrell B. Lockhart, 173–78. Westport, CT: Greenwood.

Mizraje, María. 2006. "Perdularios, perdidos y emprendedores (los irrecuperables de Soiza Reilly)." In *La ciudad de los locos*, edited by María Gabriela Mizraje. Buenos Aires: Adriana Hidalgo.

Molloy, Sylvia. 1994. "The Unquiet Self: Mnemonic Strategies in Sarmiento's Autobiographies." In *Sarmiento, Author of a Nation*, edited by Tulio Halperín Donghi, Iván Jaksić, Gwen Kirkpatrick, and Francine Masiello, 193–212. Berkeley: University of California Press.

Molloy, Sylvia. 1997. "His America, Our America: José Martí Reads Whitman." In *From Romanticism to "Modernismo" in Latin America*, edited by David William Foster and Daniel Altamiranda, 257–67. New York: Garland.

Montaldo, Graciela. 1994. "El terror letrado (sobre el modernismo latinoamericano)." *Revista de Crítica Literaria Latinoamericana* 20 (40): 281–91.

Montaldo, Graciela. 2006. *La sensibilidad amenazada: Fin de siglo y modernismo.* Rosario: Beatriz Viterbo.

Montaner, Carlos. 1994. "The Cuban Revolution and Its Acolytes." *Society* 31 (5): 73–79.

Montero, Janina. 1977. "Observations on the Hispanic American Novel and Its Public." *Latin American Literary Review* 6 (11): 1–12.

Moreno, María. 2000. "Poner la hija." *Boletín de la Biblioteca del Congreso de la Nación, Identidad Cultural,* no. 120: 97–114.

Nalé Roxlo, Conrado. 1978. *Borrador de memorias.* Buenos Aires: Plus Ultra.

Nance, Kimberly. 2006. *Can Literature Promote Social Justice?* Nashville: Vanderbilt University Press.

Negretto, Gabriel, and José Antonio Aguilar Rivera. 2000. "Rethinking the Legacy of the Liberal State in Latin America: The Cases of Argentina (1853–1916) and Mexico (1857–1910)." *Journal of Latin American Studies* 32 (2): 361–97.

Norat, Gisela. 2002. *Marginalities: Diamela Eltit and the Subversion of Mainstream Literature in Chile.* Newark: University of Delaware Press; London: Associated University Press.

Núñez, Javier. 2005. "Signed with an X: Methodology and Data Sources for Analyzing the Evolution of Literacy in Latin America and the Caribbean, 1900–1950." *Latin American Research Review* 40 (2): 117–35.

Nuñez, Sergio, and Ariel Idez. 2007. "La banda de los travestis ladrones." *Página 12, Radar,* July 1.

Nuttall, Nick. 2007. "Cold-Blooded Journalism." In *The Journalistic Imagination: Literary Journalists from Defoe to Capote and Carter,* edited by Richard Keeble and Sharon Wheeler, 131–43. London: Routledge.

Orgambide, Pedro. 1960. "Roberto Arlt, cronista de 1930." In *Nuevas aguafuertes porteñas,* by Roberto Arlt. Buenos Aires: Hachette.

Ortiz Marín, Ángel, and María del Rocío Duarte Ramírez. 2010. "El periodismo a principios del siglo XX (1900–1910)." *Revista Pilquen* 12 (12): 1–9.

Padula Perkins, Jorge. 1990. "El periodista José Hernández." Primer Premio, rubro ensayo in Certamen de las Artes, las Ciencias y el Pensamiento 1990. Subsecretaría de Cultura de la Provincia de Buenos Aires.

Peláez y Tapia, José. 1927. *Historia de "El Mercurio": Un siglo de periodismo chileno.* Santiago, Chile: Talleres de "El Mercurio."

Piglia, Ricardo. 1993. "Sarmiento the Writer." In *Sarmiento, Author of a Nation,* edited by Tulio Halperín Donghi, Iván Jaksić, Gwen Kirkpatrick, and Francine Masiello, 127–44. Berkeley: University of California Press.

Piglia, Ricardo. 1994. "Hoy es imposible en la Argentina hacer literatura desvinculada de la política." In *Rodolfo Walsh, Vivo*, edited by Roberto Baschetti. Buenos Aires: La Flor.

Piglia, Ricardo. 1998. "Rodolfo Walsh." In *Grandes entrevistas de la historia argentina*, edited by Sylvia Saítta and Luis Alberto Romero, 392–405. Buenos Aires: Punto de Lectura.

Pignatelli, A. 1997. *"Caras y Caretas."* In *Historia de las revistas argentinas*, volume 2. Buenos Aires: Asociación Argentina de Editores de Revistas.

Prieto, Adolfo. 1994. "Sarmiento: Casting the Reader, 1839–1845." In *Sarmiento, Author of a Nation*, edited by Tulio Halperín Donghi, Iván Jaksić, Gwen Kirkpatrick, and Francine Masiello, 259–73. Berkeley: University of California Press.

Puiggrós, A. 1992. "La educación argentina desde la Reforma Saavedra Lamas hasta el fin de la década infame: Hipótesis para la discusión." In *Historia de la educación argentina*, volume 3. Edited by Adriana Puiggrós. Buenos Aires: Editorial Galerna.

Pym, Anthony. 1992. "Strategies of the Frontier in Spanish-American Modernismo." *Comparative Literature* 44 (2): 161–73.

Quesada, Ernesto. 1883. "El periodismo argentino." *Nueva revista de Buenos Aires* 9.

Quinet Madame de. 1868. "Un grand patriote américan." In *Mémoires d'exil (Bruxelles-Oberland)*, 285–92. Paris: Libraire International, 1868.

Quinet, Madame de. 1897. "Un gran patriota americano." In Bilbao *Obras completas: Francisco Bilbao*, volume 1, 1–8. Santiago de Chile: Imprenta de "El Correo."

Ragendorfer, Ricardo. 1997. "La verdadera historia del Rufián Melancólico." *Pistas*, June 6, 1997.

Rama, Ángel. 1981. "El boom en perspectiva." In *Más allá del boom: Literatura y mercado*, edited by David Viñas. Mexico City: Marcha Editores.

Rama, Ángel. 1983. "José Martí en el eje de la modernización poética." *Nueva Revista de Filología Hispánica* 32 (1): 96–135.

Rama, Ángel. 1994. "Las novelas policiales del pobre." In *Rodolfo Walsh, Vivo*, edited by Roberto Baschetti. Buenos Aires: La Flor.

Rama, Germán. 1978. "Educación y democracia." *Desarrollo y educación en América Latina y el Caribe*, no. 3. Buenos Aires: UNESCO/CEPAL/PNUD.

Rama, Germán, and Juan Carlos Tedesco. 1979. "Education and Development in Latin America (1950–1975)." *International Review of Education*, Jubilee number, 25 (2–3): 187–211.

Ramb, Ana. 2009. "Premio Casa de las Américas, 50 años de Luz." *Eco Alternativo*, accessed December 17, 2009. http://www.redeco.com.ar/nv/index.php?option=com_content&task=view&id=2608&Itemid=143

Ramos, Julio. 2000. *Divergent Modernities: Culture and Politics in Nineteenth-Century Latin America*. Durham: Duke University Press.

Reggini, Horacio. 1996. *Sarmiento y las telecomunicaciones: La obsesión del hilo*. Buenos Aires: Ediciones Galápago.

Rivera, Jorge. 1976. "Los juegos de un tímido: Borges en el suplemento de *Crítica*." *Crisis*, no. 38 (May–June).

Rivera, Jorge. 1985. "El escritor y la industria cultural." In *Capítulo 3: Cuadernos de Literatura Argentina*. Buenos Aires: CEAL.

Robertson, Michael. 1997. *Stephen Crane, Journalism, and the Making of Modern American Literature*. New York: Columbia University Press.

Rockland, Michael Aaron. 1970. Introduction to *Sarmiento's Travels in the United States in 1847*. Princeton: Princeton University Press.

Rodríguez-Luis, Julio, ed. 1999. *Re-Reading José Martí (1853–1895): One Hundred Years Later*. Albany: State University of New York Press.

Rojas, Rafael. 2009. *Las repúblicas de aire: Utopía y desencanto en la revolución de Hispanoamérica*. Mexico City: Taurus.

Romano, Eduardo. 2000. "Modelos, géneros y medios en la iniciación literaria de Rodolfo J. Walsh." In *Textos de y sobre Rodolfo Walsh*, edited by Jorge Lafforgue. Buenos Aires: Alianza.

Romero, José Luis. 1976. *Latinoamérica: Las ciudades y las ideas*. Mexico City: Siglo XXI.

Rotker, Susana. 1992a. *Fundación de una escritura: Las crónicas de José Martí*. Havana: Casa de las Américas.

Rotker, Susana. 1992b. *La invención de la crónica*. Buenos Aires: Letra Buena.

Rotker, Susana. 1999. "José Martí and the United States: On the Margins of the Gaze." In *Re-Reading José Martí (1853–1895): One Hundred Years Later*, edited by Julio Rodríguez-Luis, 17–34. Albany: State University of New York Press.

Rotker, Susana. 2000. *The American Chronicles of José Martí*. Hanover, NH: University Press of New England.

Rouquié, Alain. 1982. *The Military and the State in Latin America*. Berkeley: University of California Press.

Russell, John. 2000. *Reciprocities in the Nonfiction Novel*. Athens: University of Georgia Press.

Sagayo, C. M. 1874. *Historia de Copiapó*. Copiapó, Chile: Imprenta del Atacama.

Saítta, Sylvia. 1998. *Regueros de tinta: El diario "Crítica" en la década de 1920*. Buenos Aires: Sudamericana.

Saítta, Sylvia. 2000a. *El escritor en el bosque de ladrillos: una biografía de Roberto Arlt*. Buenos Aires: Sudamericana.

Saítta, Sylvia. 2000b. "De este lado de la verja: Jorge Luis Borges y los usos del periodismo moderno." *Variaciones Borges* 9:74–83.

Saldías, Adolfo. 1973. *Historia de la Confederación Argentina*. 2nd ed. Buenos Aires: Eudeba.

Santa Cruz, Eduardo A. 1988. *Análisis histórico del periodismo chileno*. Santiago, Chile: Nuestra América Ediciones.

Santí, Enrico Mario. 1999. "Thinking through Martí." In *Re-Reading José Martí (1853–1895): One Hundred Years Later*, edited by Julio Rodríguez-Luis, 67–84. Albany: State University of New York Press.

Sargent, Charles S., Jr. 1972. "Towards a Dynamic Model of Urban Morphology." *Economic Geography* 48 (4): 357–74.

Sarlo, Beatriz. 1987. "Política, ideología y figuración literaria." In *Ficción y política: La narrativa argentina durante el proceso militar*, by Daniel Balderston et al. Buenos Aires: Alianza.

Sarlo, Beatriz. 1992. *La imaginación técnica: Sueños modernos de la cultura argentina*. Buenos Aires: Nueva Visión.

Sarmiento, Domingo. 1866. *North and South America: Discourse delivered before the Rhode-Island Historical Society, December 27, 1865*. Providence: Knowles, Anthony & Co. Printers.

Sarmiento, Domingo. 1867. *Ambas Américas: Revista de educación, bibliografía i agricultura, bajo los auspicios de Domingo F. Sarmiento*. Four issues bound in one volume. New York: Mallet & Breen.

Sarmiento, Domingo. 1948–1956. *Obras completas*. 52 vols. Buenos Aires: Editorial Luz del Dia.

Sarmiento, Domingo. 1962. *Páginas escogidas*. Buenos Aires: Ediciones Culturales Argentinas.

Sarmiento, Domingo. 1970. *Sarmiento's Travels in the United States in 1847*. Introduction by Michael Aaron Rockland. Princeton: Princeton University Press.

Sarmiento, Domingo. 1993. *Facundo o civilización y barbarie*. Caracas, Venezuela: Biblioteca Ayacucho.

Sarmiento, Domingo. 1997. *Correspondencia de Sarmiento: Enero/mayo 1862*. Buenos Aires: Asociación de Amigos del Museo Histórico Sarmiento.

Sarmiento, Domingo. 2001. *Epistolario de Domingo Faustino Sarmiento: Cartas familiares*. Buenos Aires: Asociación de Amigos del Museo Histórico Sarmiento.

Sarmiento, Domingo. 2003. *Facundo: Civilization and Barbarism*. Translated by Kathleen Ross. Berkeley: University of California Press.

Sarmiento, Domingo. 2005. *Recollections of a Provincial Past*. Translated by Elizabeth Garrels and Asa Zatz. Oxford: Oxford University Press.

Sarmiento, Domingo, and Félix Frías. 1997. *Epistolario inédito*. Edited by Ana María Barrenechea. Buenos Aires: Facultad de Filosofía y Letras.

Sarracino, Rodolfo. 2003. *José Martí y el caso Cutting: ¿Extraterritorialidad o anexionismo?* Havana: Centro de Estudios Martianos; Guadalajara: Universidad de Guadalajara

Scarano, Mónica. 2003. *Decirlo es verlo: Literatura y periodismo en José Martí*. Mar del Plata, Argentina: Estanislao Balder.

Schiller, Daniel. 1981. *Objectivity and the News: The Public and the Rise of Commercial Journalism*. Philadelphia: University of Pennsylvania Press.

Schiller, Herbert. 1978. "Decolonization of Information: Efforts toward a New International Order." In "Culture in the Age of Mass Media." Special issue, *Latin American Perspectives* 5 (1): 35–48.

Schudson, Michael. 1978. *Discovering the News: A Social History of American Newspapers*. New York: Basic Books.

Schulman, Iván A. 1958. "Los supuestos 'precursores' del modernismo hispanoamericano." *Nueva Revista de Filología Hispánica* 12 (1): 61–64.

Schulman, Iván A. 1960. *Símbolo y color en la obra de José Martí*. Madrid: Gredos.

Schwartz, Kessel. 1973. "José Martí, 'The New York Herald' and President Garfield's Assassin." *Hispania* 56 (April): 335–42.

Seriot, Patrik. 2007. "Généraliser l'unique: Genres, types et sphères chez Bakhtine." *Texto!* 12 (3).

Sidicaro, Ricardo. 1993. *La política mirada desde arriba: Las ideas del diario "La Nación," 1909–1989*. Buenos Aires: Sudamericana.

Sims, Norman. 1984. *The Literary Journalists*. New York: Ballantine.

Sims, Norman. 2007. *True Stories: A Century of Literary Journalism*. Evanston, IL: Northwestern University Press.

Siskind, Mariano. 2014. *Cosmopolitan Desires: Global Modernity and World Literature in Latin America*. Evanston, IL: Northwestern University Press.

Smart, Robert. 1985. *The Nonfiction Novel*. Lanham, MD: University Press of America.

Soiza Reilly, Juan José de. 1914. "Cómo se divierten los ingleses." *Fray Mocho* (Buenos Aires), no. 135, November 27, 1914. http://sugieroleer.blogspot.com/2012/06/como-se-divierten-los-ingleses.html

Soiza Reilly, Juan José de. 1915. "La estrategia de los ratones." *Fray Mocho* (Buenos Aires), no. 156, April 23, 1915. http://laestrategiadelosratones.blogspot.com/

Soiza Reilly, Juan José de. 2006. *La ciudad de los locos*. Edited by María Gabriela Mizraje. Buenos Aires: Adriana Hidalgo.

Soiza Reilly, Juan José de. 2008. *Crónicas del centenario*. Edited by Vanina Escales. Buenos Aires: Biblioteca Nacional.

Sommer, Doris. 1991. *Foundational Fictions: The National Romances of Latin America*. Berkeley: University of California Press.

Talice, Roberto. 1989. *100.000 ejemplares por hora: Memorias de un redactor de Crítica, el diario de Botana*. Buenos Aires: Ediciones del Corregidor.

Terranova, Juan. 2006. "El escritor perdido." *El Interpretador–Literatura, arte y pensa-*

miento, no. 28. https://revistaelinterpretador.wordpress.com/2016/12/01/el-escritor
-perdido-sobre-juan-jose-de-soiza-reilly/

Todorov, Tzvetan. 1970. *Introduction a la littérature fantastique*. Paris: Éditions du
Seuil.

Torres, Horacio. 1975. "Evolución de los procesos de estructuración espacial urbana:
El caso de Buenos Aires." *Desarrollo Económico* 15 (58): 281–306.

Torres, Jose Luis. 1945. *La década infame*. Buenos Aires: Editorial de formación "Patria."

Torres Rioseco, Arturo. 1922. "Estudios Literarios: José Martí; I. El Hombre." *Hispania* 5 (5): 282–85.

Tucher, Andie. 1994. *Froth and Scum: Truth, Beauty, Goodness, and the Ax Murder in America's First Mass Medium*. Chapel Hill: University of North Carolina
Press.

Tucher, Andie. 2006. "Reporting for Duty: The Bohemian Brigade, the Civil War,
and the Social Construction of the Reporter." *Book History* 9:131–57.

UNESCO. 1961. *Mass Media in the Developing Countries*. Paris: UNESCO.

United States Census Bureau. 1901. *Statistical Abstract of the United States: 1900*. No.
23, Bureau of the Census Library. Washington, DC: Government Printing Office.
http://www.census.gov/prod/www/abs/statab1878–1900.htm

Valenzuela, Arturo. 2004. "Latin American Presidencies Interrupted." *Journal of Democracy* 15 (4): 5–18.

Varela, Mirta. 1994. *Los hombres ilustres del Billiken: Héroes en los medios y en la
escuela*. Buenos Aires: Colihue.

Vargas, Margarita. 2003. "Dilemas del 'progreso': Las crónicas neoyorquinas de José
Martí." In *Decirlo es verlo: Literatura y periodismo en José Martí*, edited by Mónica Scarano. Mar del Plata, Argentina: Estanislao Balder.

Vargas Llosa, Mario. 1981. *Entre Sartre y Camus*. Río Piedras, Puerto Rico: Ediciones
Huracán.

Vasquez, Marlene. 2004. "Martí y América: Permanencia del diálogo." *Abrapalabra*
(Santa Clara, Cuba, DR), no. 36. http://biblio3.url.edu.gt/Libros/2011/marti_amer
.pdf

Verbitsky, Horacio. 2000. "De la vida y la muerte." In *Textos de y sobre Rodolfo Walsh*,
edited by Jorge Lafforgue. Buenos Aires: Alianza.

Verdevoye, Paul. 1963. *Domingo Faustino Sarmiento: Educateur et publiciste (entre
1839 et 1852)*. Paris: Institut de Hautes Études de l'Amérique Latine.

Vergara Quiroz, Sergio, ed. *Manuel Montt y Domingo F. Sarmiento: Epistolario 1833–
1888*. 1999. Santiago de Chile: LOM Ediciones.

Verón, Eliseo. 1988. *La sémiosis sociale: Fragments d'une théorie de la discursivité*.
Paris: Presses universitaires de Vincennes.

Viñas, David. *Literatura argentina y política II: De Lugones a Walsh*. Buenos Aires: Sudamericana.

Vinelli, Natalia. 2000. *ANCLA: Una experiencia de comunicación clandestina orientada por Rodolfo Walsh*. Buenos Aires: La Rosa Blindada.

Walsh, Rodolfo. 1964. *Operación Masacre*. 2nd ed. Buenos Aires: Continental Service.

Walsh, Rodolfo. 1967. *Un kilo de oro*. Buenos Aires: Jorge Álvarez.

Walsh, Rodolfo. 1969. *Operación Masacre*. 3rd ed. Buenos Aires: Jorge Álvarez.

Walsh, Rodolfo. 1981. *Obra literaria completa*. Mexico City: Siglo XXI.

Walsh, Rodolfo. 1986. *Los oficios terrestres*. Buenos Aires: Ediciones de La Flor.

Walsh, Rodolfo. 1988. *Operación Masacre*. 17th ed. Buenos Aires: Ediciones de La Flor.

Walsh, Rodolfo. 1996. *Ese hombre y otros papeles*. Edited by Daniel Link. Buenos Aires: Seix Barral.

Walsh, Rodolfo. 2013. *Operation Massacre*. Translated by Daniella Gitlin. New York: Seven Stories Press.

Ward, Thomas. 2007. "Martí y Blaine: Entre la colonialidad tenebrosa y la emancipación inalcanzable." *Cuban Studies* 38:100–24.

Weber, Ronald. 1980. *The Literature of Fact: Literary Nonfiction in American Writing*. Athens: Ohio University Press.

Wells, Sarah Ann. 2011. "Late Modernism, Pulp History: Jorge Luis Borges' A Universal History of Infamy (1935)." *MODERNISM / modernity* 18 (2): 425–41.

White, Hayden. 1980. "The Value of Narrativity in the Representation of Reality." In "On Narrative." Special issue, *Critical Inquiry* 7 (1): 5–27.

White, Hayden. 1981. "The Narrativization of Real Events." *Critical Inquiry* 7 (4): 793–98.

White, Hayden. 1984. "The Question of Narrative in Contemporary Historical Theory." *History and Theory* 23 (1): 1–33.

Williams, Raymond. 1985. "An Introduction to the Early Journalism of Garcia Marquez: 1948–1958." *Latin American Literary Review* 13 (25): 117–32.

Wilson, James Harrison. 1907. *The Life of Charles A. Dana*. New York: Harper & Brothers.

Wolfe, Tom. 1968. *The Electric Kool-Aid Acid Test*. New York: Picador.

Wolfe, Tom. 1972. "The Birth of 'The New Journalism': Eyewitness Report by Tom Wolfe." *New York Magazine*, February 14, 1972. http://nymag.com/news/media/47353/index8.html

Wolfe, Tom. 1973. *The New Journalism, with an Anthology Edited by Tom Wolfe and E. W. Johnson*. New York: Harper & Row.

Yeager, Gertrude M. 1991. "Elite Education in Nineteenth-Century Chile." *Hispanic American Historical Review* 71 (1): 73–105.

Yúdice, George. 1991. "Testimonio and Postmodernism." In "Voices of the Voiceless in Testimonial Literature, Part I." Special issue, *Latin American Perspectives* 18 (3): 15–31.

Zavarzadeh, Mas'ud. 1976. *The Mythopoetic Reality: The Postwar Nonfiction American Novel.* Urbana: University of Illinois Press.

INDEX

• • •

accuracy pact, 5, 11, 47, 56, 245n12, 247n14
Acosta, Cecilio, 78
Agee, James, 190, 196–97, 246n9
Aguafuertes ("Etchings," Arlt), 149–50, 153–58, 177
Aguilar, Gonzalo, 213
Alberdi, Juan Bautista, 9, 38–39, 232n8
Aldrey, Fausto Teodoro de, 77–79, 239n8
allegory, in literary journalism, 14–15, 50, 52, 59, 200, 221, 223, 227, 228
Alonso, Amado, 164
Alsina, Valentín, 53–54
Altamirano, Carlos, 46–47
Álvarez, José S. (Fray Mocho), 119
Alvear, Marcelo Torcuato de, 240n1
Álzaga, Alberto de, 159, 165, 170, 171
Ambas Américas (magazine), 48, 49, 66
Anderson, Benedict, 6, 113
Anderson Imbert, Enrique, 98
Anglo-America, literary journalism in, 5, 186, 193, 197, 201, 222–24, 249. *See also* United States
anti-authoritarianism, 14–15, 218–19
anti Semitism, in Argentina, 138, 242n16
Aramburu, Pedro Eugenio, 204–5, 207
Arcos, Santiago, 32, 51–52, 234n21
Argentina, 70, 113, 117, 162, 241n16; caudillos in, 35, 48–49; Chile and, 51, 235n5; counterrevolution in, 205–8; coups in, 143, 174, 176–77, 181, 186; Década Infame in, 167; democracy in, 122, 215; education in, 112, 241n7; exiles in Chile, 34–35, 39; government of, 36, 38, 215–17, 232nn7,8; immigrants to, 71, 241nn2,3; literacy rate in, 49, 72–73; national identity of, 57, 123; newspapers in, 73, 232nn7,8; politics in, 114, 168, 204–5; repression in, 24–25, 248n25; Sarmiento's roles in, 52, 61, 66; US and, 86, 143. *See also* Buenos Aires
Argentine Communist Party, 152, 154
Argentine republic, 112
Arguedas, Alcides, 91
Arlt, Roberto: cross-pollination between journalism and literature, 155–56; influences on, 149–54; investigations by, 157–58; novels by, 145, 148; popularity of, 146, 155; Soiza as mentor of, 150–52, 242n15; volume of writing by, 152–54; writing by, 123, 147, 149; writing for *Crítica*, 145–46, 148; writing style of, 123, 149, 155
The Armies of the Night (Mailer), 197–99
Asbury, Herbert, 167, 171
Associated Press (AP), 61–62, 182
Astiz, Alfredo, 216
Asunción Silva, José, 92
audience, 116, 124; avant-garde authors on, 130–31; of Borges, 147, 166–68; of critical culture, 190–91; for *Crítica Magazine,* 162; *Crítica's,* 153, 158–60, 163, 169, 171; *El Mundo's,* 154, 158; *Leoplán's,* 203; magazines' relationship with, 119, 122, 130, 158–59;

174, 203; newspapers' relationship with, 146, 153, 169; participation of, 158–60, 165, 173–74; Soiza's, 128, 130, 132, 134, 142, 144; for testimonios, 187. *See also* reading public
authenticity, Martí subordinating, 74
authorial stance, 15, 199, 201, 209
avant-garde, 130–31, 137, 147, 164; *Crítica* and, 161–62; in literary school of Buenos Aires, 149–50
Avellaneda, Nicolás, 67

Balderston, Daniel, 167–68
Bandera Roja (organ of Communist Party), 152, 154
Barnet, Miguel, 186–87, 220–22
Barra, Miguel de la, 41
Bases y Estatutos secretos del Partido Revolucionario Cubano (Martí), 105
Batista, Fulgencio, 191
Battle of Caseros, Rosas deposed by, 54, 61
Battle of Pilar, Sarmiento's house arrest after, 45
Bay of Pigs invasion, 181–82, 184–86, 245n2
Beach, Moses Yale, 61
Bello, Andrés, 23, 39, 41, 235n5
Benavídez, Nazario, 37
Bernárdez, Francisco Luis, 148
Beverley, John, 194–95
Biblioteca Crítica, 115
A Bibliography of Literary Journalism in America (Ford), 11
Bilbao, Francisco, 3, 9, 234n18; charges against, 20, 27; ideas of, 6, 23, 25–26; at Instituto Nacional, 27–28; punishment of, 31, 234n16, 234n19; as scapegoat, 29–31; supporters of, 20, 27; trial of, 19–20, 30, 32
Bilbao, Manuel, 25, 28–29, 33
Bilbao, Rafael, 33
Blaine, James Gillespie, 70, 239n12; expansionism of, 87–89, 100–101; Martí's attacks on, 81, 87, 107, 239n10; Pan-American Conference and, 69, 82–83
Blanchard, Stella "Poupée," 181
Blasco Ibáñez, Vicente, 131, 175
blasphemy, Bilbao indicted for, 27
Bolivia, 71
books, 64; periodicals *vs.,* 3, 5–7
Borges, Jorge Luis, 6, 81, 202; compared to Martí, 169–70, 243n10; compared to Sarmiento, 147, 169–70, 172; crime stories by, 165, 167–68; fictional narratives by, 165–66; innovative genre of, 166–67; Martí and, 99, 243n10; removing context to make stories universal, 167–68, 173–74; *Martín Fierro,* 161; *Revista Multicolor de los Sábados* and, 162, 164, 172, 241n9; Soiza criticized by, 130–31; writing style of, 147, 164, 169–70, 172. *See also Historia Universal de la Infamia* (Universal History of Infamy)
"Borges narrador" (Alonso), 164
Botana, Natalio, 117, 159–60, 173, 241n9; *Crítica,* 153, 163–64, 177; political influence of, 163, 177
Brazil, 71–72, 238n4